Living Pictures on
the New York Stage

Theater and Dramatic Studies, No. 13

Bernard Beckerman, Series Editor

Brander Matthews Professor of Dramatic Literature
Columbia University in the City of New York

Other Titles in This Series

No. 5 *Shakespeare Refashioned: Elizabethan Plays on Edwardian Stages*	Cary M. Mazer
No. 6 *The Public and Performance: Essays in the History of French and German Theater, 1871-1900*	Michael Hays
No. 7 *Richard Boleslavsky: His Life and Work in the Theatre*	J.W. Roberts
No. 8 *Andrea Palladio's* Teatro Olimpico	J. Thomas Oosting
No. 9 *Georges Feydeau and the Aesthetics of Farce*	Stuart Eddy Baker
No. 10 *The Theatre Director Otto Brahm*	Horst Claus
No. 11 *Javanese Shadow Theatre: Movement and Characterization in Ngayogyakarta Wayang Kulit*	Roger Long
No. 12 *The Emergence of the Irish Peasant Play at the Abbey Theatre*	Brenna Katz Clarke
No. 15 *The Art of the Actor-Manager: Wilson Barrett and the Victorian Theatre*	James Thomas

Living Pictures on the New York Stage

by
Jack W. McCullough

UMI RESEARCH PRESS
Ann Arbor, Michigan

Copyright © 1981, 1983
Jack Wheelock McCullough
All rights reserved

Produced and distributed by
UMI Research Press
an imprint of
University Microfilms International
Ann Arbor, Michigan 48106

Library of Congress Cataloging in Publication Data

McCullough, Jack W. (Jack Wheelock)
  Living pictures on the New York stage.

  (Theater and dramatic studies ; no. 13)
  Revision of thesis (Ph.D.)–City University of New
York, 1981.
  Bibliography: p.
  Includes index.
  1. Tableaux–History. 2. Theater–New York (N.Y.)–
History–19th century. I. Title. II. Series.

PN3211.N4M35 1983   792'.09747'1   83-16754
ISBN 0-8357-1479-9

Contents

1 Origins   *1*

2 The Beginning in New York, 1832-1847   *11*

3 Model Artists vs. the Law, 1848   *19*

4 Sensation vs. Artistry, 1850s   *37*

5 Decline in the Face of Competition, 1860-1875   *63*

6 The Fight Begins Again, 1875-1893   *71*

7 Edward Kilanyi: Master Tableau Artist   *101*

8 The Final Blaze of Glory, 1894-1899   *115*

9 Morality Debate in the 1890s   *133*

10 Retrospect   *143*

Appendix   *153*

Notes   *159*

Bibliography of Works Cited   *191*

Index   *197*

List of Illustrations

1. *Venice* (1893), study for a mural, by Kenyon Cox   *2*

2. Tableau vivant of *Venice*   *3*

3. *The Concord Minuteman of 1776* (1899), statue in bronze, by Daniel Chester French   *4*

4. Tableau vivant of *The Concord Minuteman of 1776*   *5*

5. Tableau vivant of *Boreas und Orinthyia* (Berlin, 1802)   *9*

6. "The Three Graces" as they might have been presented by Dr. Collyer at the Apollo Rooms, 1847   *21*

7. Handbill advertising Mme. Pauline's tableaux vivants   *39*

8. Side one of a playbill for the Walhalla, London, listing Madame Warton's tableaux   *43*

9. Side two of the Walhalla playbill   *44*

10. Playbill for the Franklin Museum, dated in pencil 18 August 1858   *47*

11. *Washington Crossing the Delaware* (1851), oil on canvas, by Emanuel Leutze   *54*

12. Tableau vivant of *Washington Crossing the Delaware*   *55*

13. Matt Morgan with a tableau artist in "proper cosutme" to depict "Phryne"   *79*

14. Mary Anderson as the statue, "Galatea" (1)   *94*

viii   List of Illustrations

15. Mary Anderson as the statue, "Galatea" (2)   *94*

16. Mary Anderson as the statue, "Galatea" (3)   *95*

17. Mary Anderson as the statue, "Galatea" (4)   *95*

18. Sandow, the strong man, posed as "The Dying Gladiator"   *97*

19. "The Daughter of the Sheik," one of Kilanyi's living pictures presented in *1492* at the Garden Theatre   *105*

20. Newspaper illustration of one of the tableaux from Kilanyi's Glyptorama   *109*

21. The popular Sandow, revealing his "superb muscular endowment" for photographer Napoleon Sarony   *127*

22. Leonardo da Vinci's *The Last Supper* is prepared by the Pageant Director   *147*

23. Tableau vivant of *The Last Supper* in Santa Maria delle Grazie, Milan, Italy   *148*

24. Modern tableau vivant at the 1983 Pageant of the Masters, Laguna Beach, California, which represents *Orpheus*   *149*

25. *At the Inn* (1886), oil on canvas, by Francis Davis Millet   *150*

26. Tableau vivant of *At the Inn*   *151*

Acknowledgments

I am grateful to my family for their support and assistance during the preparation of this study. My original interest in popular entertainments generally and in tableaux vivants specifically was kindled by Professor A.H. Saxon, whose inspiration guided my work through the early stages. Many professionals in various libraries and archives have made my research not only possible but very enjoyable. I am especially grateful to Mr. Paul Myers and the entire staff of the Theatre Collection, New York Public Library of the Performing Arts, Lincoln Center; to Dr. Mary Henderson, Curator, and Ms. Wendy Warnken, Assistant Curator, of the Theatre Collection at the Museum of the City of New York; Miss D'Aquilar, Municipal Archives and Records Retention Center, New York City; Ms. Martha Mahard, Theatre Collection, Harvard College Library; the staff of the Theatre Collection, the Philadelphia Free Library; the staff of the Microforms Division, Firestone Library, Princeton University; Mr. Harold Thompson, Director of the Trenton, NJ, Free Public Library; and the staff of Roscoe West Library, Trenton State College. I am greatly indebted to Mr. Scott Mahler who edited the manuscrpt for UMI Research Press. Portions of Chapter Three and Chapter Seven appeared previously in the *Journal of Popular Culture* and in *Theatre Survey,* respectively, and I am grateful to those journals for permission to reprint those materials in this volume. Finally, I am deeply grateful to Professors Stanley A. Waren and Daniel C. Gerould, and to Professor Vera M. Roberts. Their expert advice, enthusiasm, and encouragement have made the completion of this study the enjoyable and rewarding accomplishment that scholarly research should be.

1
Origins

Viewed from the present, that entertainment known as tableaux vivants, or living pictures, seems a quaint curiosity, a precious exercise from the past, lacking modern significance. However, perhaps the living pictures are not as distant as we might expect. The "artistic" posing of many a striptease queen; the fanciful scenes on the elaborate Rose Parade floats; the closing scene of the recently popular musical comedy, *1776;* even the "freeze-frame" and "stop-action" techniques of film and television—all of these provide present-day versions of tableaux vivants.

During the nineteenth and early twentieth centuries, tableaux vivants were an important form of popular entertainment. In America, they were featured attractions at major New York variety theatres, and they met with success on road tours of prominent cities throughout the country.

The premise of the tableau was simple: live models represented a static scene from painting, sculpture, or some other source. Often with the aid of elaborate scenery, costumes, properties, and lighting, the representation was made to appear as much like the original work of art as possible. The total effect was a startling display in living color and three dimensions. (Figures 1-4 illustrate two modern tableaux vivants which attempted to capture the spirit of such nineteenth-century productions.[1])

The purpose of this study is to trace the history of tableaux vivants as they appeared in the nineteenth-century New York theatre. First, however, it may help to take a brief look at the roots of this genre.

The idea of using live models to pose in static pictures is an old concept, possibly finding its ancestry in the telling gesture and facial expression of the Doric mimes. It was certainly apparent in the late medieval and early renaissance periods. Bamber Gascoigne describes its use in connection with the *Quem Quaeritis* trope and other liturgical presentations of the eleventh and twelfth centuries.[2] He also describes "the street theatres and tableaux vivants which, from the early fourteenth century in France and a little later in England and the Low Countries, became a familiar feature of a king's entry into a city," often providing "political hints to the ruler."[3] Such presentations were often highly fanciful and extremely elaborate. In 1582, for instance, when Francis,

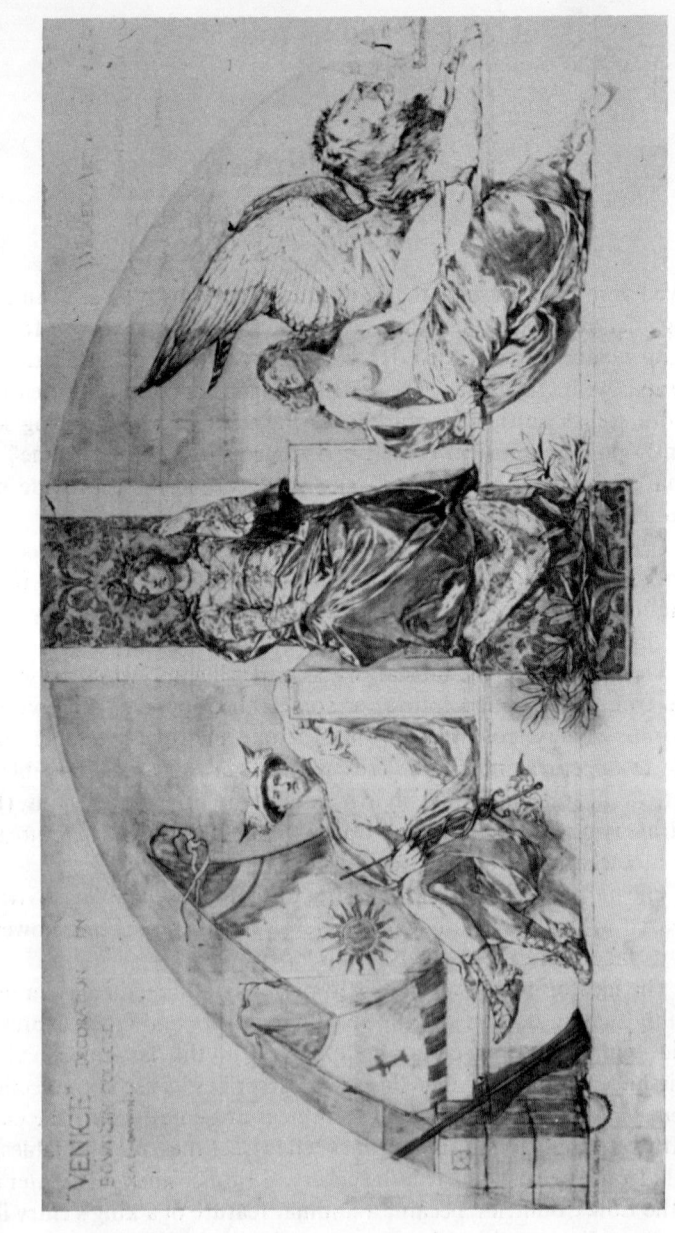

Figure 1. *Venice* (1893), study for a mural, by Kenyon Cox. (Courtesy of Bowdoin College Museum of Art.)

Figure 2. Tableau vivant of *Venice*, presented at the Brooklyn Museum, 20-21 October 1979. The tableau was accompanied by Nevin's "Alba" from *Un Giorno in Venezia* (1913).

Figure 3. *The Concord Minuteman of 1776* (1899), statue in bronze, by Daniel Chester French. (United States Navy Department.)

Figure 4. Tableau vivant of *The Concord Minuteman of 1776*, presented at the Brooklyn Museum, 20-21 October 1979. The tableau was accompanied by Stephen Foster's song, "I'm Nothing but a Plain Old Soldier" (1863).

the brother of the king of France, entered Antwerp on the occasion of that city's celebration of its freedom from Spain and its new allegiance to France, a three-part tableau was presented for the royal visitor:

> The left hand scene shows Samuel tearing off a piece of Saul's clothing to signify that the kingdom shall be taken from his family because of his disobedience; the central scene shows the young David being chosen as his successor; and, in case Francis should be in any doubt as to what was expected of him, on the right he could see David killing Goliath and some verses reminding him that he must "protect his own from the inhuman tyrant."[4]

Gascoigne's description of Marie de Medici's visit to Amsterdam in 1638 indicates the elaborate manner in which tableaux were integrated into the water pageantry for that occasion:

> The queen then saw two *tableaux vivants* in the theatre, which was itself on a floating island constructed for the occasion. One of the *tableaux* was about her own great family and the other about Amsterdam, after which she sailed round to the other side of the island where there was another proscenium with five more *tableaux* on the history of France.[5]

Such events as these suggest the early heritage of tableaux. Strictly speaking, however, they were not so much entertainments as they were ceremonial events, and they did not represent any specific works of art— paintings or sculpture—as later tableaux vivants usually did.

The earliest theatrical tableau on record, which represented the appearance of a painting, appears to have been presented in Paris in 1761 during the Comédie Italienne production of *Les Noces d'Arlequin*.[6] According to Kirsten Gram Holmström, "the *pièce de resistance* occurred in the middle of the second act, when the curtain was raised and the audience saw an exact copy of Greuze's painting, *L'Accordée de Village.*"[7] The painting had recently been on exhibit at the Louvre and had been a popular favorite. This production was enthusiastically received and continued in the repertoire for eighteen years, until November 1779. However, the technique was not repeated in another play until 1780, when a tableau parody of David's *The Sabine Women* was presented at the Opera Comique.[8]

Not all early tableaux were theatre presentations, however. Holmström quotes letters from Goethe, written in 1787, which describe another early method of presenting tableaux:

> On 27 May, Goethe writes from Naples of a second visit to Sir William Hamilton [in Naples], when Miss Emma Hart entertained the guests in the evening with her talents. He tells how on this occasion Sir William took him, together with the landscape painter Hackert, down to a secret art gallery. There they were shown an open-fronted box lined with black cloth and having a gold frame big enough to take a person standing upright. They were told that Sir William had at one time been in the habit of having his mistress pose in brightly coloured costumes within the frame in simulation of antique paintings from Pompeii and various modern masterpieces.[9]

In fact, Sir William's mistress (who later became his wife) did much to popularize a form of tableaux vivants during the late eighteenth century. In what came to be called her "attitudes," she posed to represent familiar figures from antiquity—Agrippina, Sophonisba, Iphigenia, Niobe, and various nymphs, bacchantes, and others. While these performances were private entertainments, presented at home for a fairly close circle of friends and admirers, the presentations did employ such theatrical elements as representational properties and costumes, special lighting, and a designated "stage" space. Emma made no attempt to reproduce specific paintings or sculpture; however, the recognition of her characters by the audience depended mainly on their familiarity with the classical art works.[10]

What Goethe saw on his visit to Hamilton's "secret art gallery" may well have inspired an event in his novel, *Elective Affinities (Die Wahlverwandtshaften)*. In the novel, the character, Luciana, engages in tableaux vivants as a means to show off her rather shallow charm. Van Dyke's picture, *Belisarius*, is selected as the subject of the first tableau. The others include Poussin's *Ahasuerus and Ester*, Terburg's *Father's Admonition*, and several scenes of Flemish public houses and fair and market days.[11] The method of presentation depicted in the novel is to prepare the tableau behind a curtain which is opened when the tableau is ready to be revealed. Holmström observes that the appeal is "to the simplest ability to appreciate the degree of similarity to the prototype."[12] This appeal, as we shall see, is basic to a large number of tableau presentations throughout the history of the genre. Holmström asserts, "It is generally considered that tableaux vivants first became fashionable after Goethe published *Die Wahlverwandtshaften* in 1809."[13] She continues, "It seems to me highly probable that it was that novel which lay behind this effort to project independent tableaux vivants solely intended to copy well-known paintings with the greatest possible illusion-creating effect; unfortunately, however, I have not succeeded in finding any documentary support for this hypothesis."[14] Nevertheless, Holmström does provide the following excerpt from a review of the novel, published in *Allgemeine Litteratur-Zeitung* (1810, no. 1):

> The fashionable world is also indebted to Herr Goethe for the new kind of pastime which he has invented. After exhausting everything which nature and art can provide in the ordinary way, he has hit upon the idea of getting living people to imitate paintings. These are not pantomime performances..., but attitudes based on the paintings of Raphael, Guido and others. The actors hold the appropriate attitude as long as their nerves and sinews will allow them.[15]

Although tableaux vivants may have become "fashionable" only after Goethe published his novel, there were notable presentations before that time. In 1775, the painter, Mme. Vigée-Lebrun, arranged tableaux vivants based on biblical and mythological works of art during her visit to St. Petersburg.[16] The production of *The Sabine Women* in 1800 has already been mentioned. In 1802, the art historian Aloys Ludwig Hirt, staged a "gala divertissement" entitled *Dadalus und seine Statuen* at the court in Berlin (See Figure 5). It consisted of "changing groupings in tableaux vivants, pantomime, and a concluding dance."[17] Goethe himself engaged in the presentation of real tableaux vivants just prior to his production of *Proserpina* at Weimar in 1813. "On this occasion there were presented three tableaux in imitation of well-known pictures."[18]

All of these presentations set the stage for tableaux vivants to find their way into the theatre, there to become a popular form of entertainment. The early nineteenth century saw French audiences applauding "a Professor Flor, who reproduced famous classical or modern paintings, to which he added plastic representations [*plastiques*]; and Quirin-Muller, specialist in statuary groups."[19] "Living tableaux were used on the English stage as early as 1811, in William Dimond's *The Peasant Boy* at the Lyceum," according to Richard D. Altick.[20] Other early English examples cited by Altick include Belzoni's "Roman Hercules" in 1813 and Planché's Drury Lane melodrama, *The Brigand*, which "was interspersed with several tableaux copied from Charles Eastlake's popular series of 'banditti' pictures."[21]

For the student of American tableaux vivants, the most important English performer of the genre was the great equestrian, Andrew Ducrow. A.H. Saxon points out that, at Astley's Amphitheatre in London, Ducrow "invented and regularly performed a number called the 'Grecian Statues,' which he later incorporated into his pantomime *Raphael's Dream,* a forerunner of the 'poses plastiques' so popular in circuses and variety theatres in the second half of the century. Founded on his study of classic statuary, these 'living pictures' were given onstage and were divorced from the equestrian scenes that usually followed."[22] At a typical performance, the curtain opened to reveal "a picture frame in the center of which, on a lofty pedestal against a pictorial background, stood the motionless figure of Ducrow."[23] The performer then imitated a series of statue-like poses, in which he seemed to take on the appearance of marble, depicting Homeric heroes, athletes, and gladiators. The height of Ducrow's popularity was reached during the 1830's, the decade in which tableaux vivants found their way to the New York stage—in part, at least, as a direct result of Ducrow's influence.

Figure 5. Tableau vivant of *Boreas und Orinthyia* (Berlin, 1802). "The author of *Dedalus und seine Statuen,* Aloys Ludwig Hirt, was a well-known and officially patronized artist, who said that it was Emma's [Emma Hamiltion's] talents which had given him the idea for these *tableaux vivants* surrounded by 'antique dances.' The court solo dancer and ballet master, Constant Michel Telle, was credited with inventing the 'Pantomime, Groups and Dances.' The groups, composed of one to three persons, were 'living statues,' in subjects taken from mythology and impersonated by members of the Court—the Queen presided as Minerva. In the tableau *Boreas und Orinthyia* [illustrated above], for example, Boreas was impersonated by a young officer from a Hussar regiment and Orinthyia by a young noblewoman." (Marian Hannah Winter, *The Pre-Romantic Ballet* [New York: Pitman Publishing Co., 1974], pp. 199, 226.)

2

The Beginnings in New York, 1831-1847

The introduction of tableaux vivants into New York seems to have occurred during the theatre season of 1831-32. George C.D. Odell observes that, in that season, the stock company at the Park Theatre included a Mrs. Barrymore, and that "her physical charm and her ability to pose were utilized in a new form of art, the reproduction of famous pictures in living tableaux."[1] Beginning on 1 September 1831, Mrs. Barrymore appeared in "TABLEAUX VIVANS [*sic*], illustrating Scheffer's beautiful Print of THE SOLDIER'S WIDOW,"[2] the earliest instance of tableaux advertised by a New York theatre.

Mrs. Ada Adams Barrymore had begun her career in England in 1803 as a dancer and had risen to some prominence as a regular performer at the Royal Circus, London. Her husband, William Barrymore, was a prominent stage manager, sometime writer, and scenic machinist. He achieved some notice for his productions of sensational pieces at Drury Lane. Just prior to their arrival in America, however, the couple had spent several years in Andrew Ducrow's company at Astley's Amphitheatre, and they were undoubtedly thoroughly familiar with that equestrian's famous tableaux.[3] Indeed, it is possible that they were engaged by the Park Theatre management specifically to add that novelty to the theatre's offerings. Whatever the motivation, posing and pantomime were clearly Mrs. Barrymore's specialties. She made her New York debut on 29 August 1831 as Pipino, the pantomime role in *The Dumb Savoyard and his Monkey* and in an interlude entitled *Winning a Husband; or, Seven's the Main.*[4] She was a versatile performer, however, appearing in numerous roles throughout the season. In *Winning a Husband*, she played no less than seven roles at each performance. In addition, her tableaux of "The Soldier's Widow" continued to be popular. In fact, so frequent were her poses that one critic was moved to gentle complaint:

> Much has been said of the "dumb show" exhibitions of Mrs. Barrymore.... We protest against making this branch of the drama so prominent. Excellence in this branch requires as much, or more study, than many branches of infinitely more importance. Yet the taste for such exhibition will not remunerate the pains necessary to reach it. We do not condemn the study in toto, but it should never be a prominent aim of a dramatic campaign.[5]

After their success at the Park, the Barrymores moved to the Bowery Theatre for the 1832-33 season, as actress-dancer and as stage manager. Their opening production was Douglas Jerrold's new play, *The Rent Day*, a work especially suited to Mrs. Barrymore's talents as a poseur. Tableau representations of two paintings by Sir David Wilkie were designated by the playwright to be included in the play. The opening stage direction for Act I reads, "*The characters and stage so arranged as to form on the rising of the curtain, a representation of Wilkie's picture of 'Rent Day',*" and the directions for both the beginning and end of Act II specify that Wilkie's picture, "Distraining for Rent," shall be represented.[6] This tableau device was apparently successful enough to merit repetition, for J.B. Buckstone's *The Forgery; or, The Reading of the Will*, which played at the Adelphi in March 1832, only two months after Jerrold's play had been performed there, included representations of two more Wilkie paintings, "Reading of the Will" and "Village Politicians."[7]

In December 1832, the Barrymores left New York for Boston, where Mrs. Barrymore appeared as a dancer at the new Tremont Theatre. The following year her husband was "director of spectacles" at the newly renovated Federal Street Theatre, and the 1836 season found the couple at the Lion Theatre, Boston.[8] Although Mrs. Barrymore performed chiefly as a dancer while in Boston, it is likely that she continued some tableau performances as well, for, in 1838, while touring, she appeared in Philadelphia in *Soldier's Wife and Soldier's Widow*, a pantomime whose title suggests that it probably incorporated her earlier representations of Scheffer's picture.[9]

In New York, another member of the Park Theatre company, who had arrived at about the same time as the Barrymores, was George Wieland, a famous mime and man-monkey from Drury Lane.[10] He had shared debut billing with Mrs. Barrymore and, of course, portrayed the monkey in *The Dumb Savoyard and his Monkey*. At Mrs. Barrymore's benefit on 12 October 1831, Wieland "portrayed Ducrow's Personifications of the Ancient Statues," again emphasizing the influence of the English equestrian.[11] The Wieland "personifications" also continued to be a frequent offering at the Park throughout the season.

In competition with this new form of attraction at the Park, the Bowery Theatre (later known as the American Theatre, Bowery), on 1 October 1831, announced that, as an afterpiece, "Mr. Frimbly will exhibit a celebrated classical scene, bearing the title of the Living Statue."[12] Frimbly had made his debut at the Bowery only three days earlier, playing William in *Black Ey'd Susan*. He continued in this role while also providing the "Living Statue, or Model of Antiques," throughout October.

The only description of Frimbly appears to be a retrospective account written in 1850 by George G. Foster as part of a most uncomplimentary description of later sensational tableaux:

He [Frimbly] was a knotty, knurly, well-formed manikin of a fellow, and used to dress himself neatly in skin tight cotton fleshings, which he then plastered all over with flour, until, at the distance of stage from audience, he really looked very like a statue in plaster-of-paris, by Garbeille—very well modeled, but rather overcharged in outline and exaggerated in position. Thus accoutred, and furnished with pasteboard shield and helmet, Frimbley [sic] would throw himself into all sorts of shapes and attitudes, however, well-chosen, and sometimes really beautiful.... Frimbley was a good artist and studied his attitudes carefully.[13]

Later, John Fletcher took over the tableau act at the Bowery, appearing for the first time on 14 December as the "Venetian Statue."[14] While Frimbly may well have been simply "drafted" as a poseur from his regular line of roles to meet the Park Theatre competition, Fletcher had already appeared as the "Venetian Statue" earlier in 1831 at London's Adelphi Theatre.[15] Interestingly enough, it was the later performer, Fletcher, whom the famous actor, Joseph Jefferson, remembered afterward as the originator of living statues:

About this time—I was three years old—there dawned upon the public a new entertainment in the shape of the "Living Statues," by a Mr. Fletcher. I was much taken with these novel tableaux, and became so statue-struck that I could do nothing but strike attitudes, now posing before the greenroom glass as "Ajax Defying the Lightning," or falling down in dark corners as the "Dying Gladiator." These postures appear to have been so successful with the family that they were, as usual, tried upon the public. I am in the dark as to whether this entertainment was the "talk of the town" or not, but I fancy not: an attenuated child representing Hercules struggling with a lion could scarcely excite terror; so I presume I did no harm if I did no good.[16]

Significantly, Jefferson's memory reinforces the link between early American tableaux and the work of Andrew Ducrow. Fletcher's poses imitated by Jefferson are all included in those performed by Ducrow at Astley's beginning 28 January 1828. Furthermore, the title of Frimbly's act, "The Living Statue, or Model of Antiques," was the same title used by Ducrow for his performance.[17]

With these early performances, tableaux vivants had been firmly established as regular fare on the New York stage. In the summer of 1832, "Living Portraits...from the Life" were advertised by an establishment at 2 Pine Street, formerly the Athenaeum Rooms.[18] Odell (3:592) reports that, on 14 June 1832, Fletcher appeared at Peale's Museum, "a living model of ancient sculpture, whose poses were accompanied by Kendall on the harp." A Mr. Rea is billed in "Venetian Statues" at the Park in 1834, while Barkham Cony performed the same act at the Bowery, joined by Blanchard in 1835.[19] Peale's Museum offered a living statues act in late October 1836, and in August 1837 Eliza Monier exhibited "a classical scene of ancient statuary" at Wallack's Theatre.[20] During the week of 11 September 1837, Louisa Johnson appeared with Fletcher at the Franklin Theatre, "portraying beautiful compositions of the celebrated masters of painting and sculpture, with appropriate music."[21] In the summer of 1839, performances at Niblo's Garden by the famous Ravel Family included "the Attitudinarian, by Francois Ravel."[22] In December 1839, a performer named Cole at Peale's Museum was described as the "accomplished delineator of classic portraiture,"[23] and at the New Chatham Theatre, "Brown, Gibson and Barnes (of course not old Jack Barnes) posed...as Ancient statues."[24] On 16 October 1841, Niblo's billed "REVOLVING STATUES, by the Ravel Family,"[25] and on 3 October 1843, "the beautiful classic groupings of The Three Gladiators, are to be presented in the usual *relief* of the Ravels, by Jerome, Antoine, and *the* Gabriel."[26] Odell (4:602) observes that "Double Ancient statuary (whatever that was)" appeared at the Military Garden on 10 August 1842. Also in 1842, during Charles Dickens' visit to the United States, a "grand Boz ball" at the Park Theatre featured tableaux representing scenes from the Dickens novels.[27] In November 1845, Palmo's Opera House was advertising "Mysterious Soirees in the Temple of Enchantment," featuring "Senor Carrero, the unrivalled delineator of the ancient sculptures."[28]

In 1840, the first of several troupes appeared, whose main efforts were devoted to tableaux vivants. The Swiss Brothers, while they also performed in ballet, made their greatest impression in New York with their "Roman and Italian Portraitures of the celebrated Warriors, Athletae [*sic*], and Heroes of Ancient History."[29] They opened 4 February 1840 at the Bowery Amphitheatre (then called the Zoological Institute), moved to Niblo's in July, and returned to the Amphitheatre in December.

The significance of the Swiss Brothers' performances was that, for the first time, advertising gave considerable emphasis to the fact that these tableaux were presented "with scenery"—they were announced as the "first scenic exhibition at the Amphitheatre"—a feature which was to assume even greater importance in later productions. The Bowery Amphitheatre management was almost apologetic about this feature of their offering:

> In announcing the addition of SCENIC REPRESENTATIONS to the entertainments given at the Amphitheatre the proprietors do not wish to be understood that anything will be offered in the shape of "theatricals," any farther than by giving effect to some of their exhibitions by appropriate scenery, which cannot be so well represented in the circle. The pieces they shall have the pleasure of offering to the public will be strictly confined to Pantomime, Ballet, Pageants, and Tableaux, all of which will be represented by the members of the Arena.[30]

The press justified the management's apprehension, lamenting the introduction of any "dramatic nonsense" into the Amphitheatre program, and preferring the regular circus fare normally offered. Nevertheless, critical comment was generally favorable toward the tableaux themselves, and even noted some scenic embellishment:

We must, however, in candor, admit that the tableaux in the Death of Abel were given with splendid effect. Mrs. Gossin made a most charming Eve—perhaps a little too fashionably dressed for the times of our first parents, but the affair notwithstanding was very creditably done.[31]

In addition to these presentations under generic titles ("Venetian Statues," "Living Pictures," etc.), numerous pantomime productions also included tableaux. "A classical, historical, mythological Drama, entitled RAPHAEL'S DREAM: or, the Artist's Study," was offered at the Park Theatre 11 January 1833, with Richings as Raphael and Rae portraying "Specimens of Art."[32] Again, Andrew Ducrow's influence is to be noted, for this "drama" had been originated by him at Astley's Amphitheatre on 13 September 1830 and was devoted solely to the presentation of living statues in a dramatic framework. In the play, the artist, Raphael, pauses in his painting to comment on several statues which are sequentially revealed on stage. These are represented by a live actor (originally Ducrow) who poses as specified in Raphael's rambling commentary. Various poses are thus revealed, and the performance culminates in a representation of "Coloured Specimens of Art in a series of Living Pictures," presented in a large picture frame and embellished with painted scenic backgrounds.[33]

The immense success of *Raphael's Dream* at the Park resulted in frequent productions there and elsewhere; the Swiss Brothers even produced it on tour in Philadelphia.[34] Success also led to numerous imitations. Odell reports that one of these, *Il Studio, or, The Living Models of Antiques*, featuring Mr. Bennie, was offered at the Bowery Theatre in 1834 (4:26), at the Richmond Hill Theatre in 1835 (4:39), at Vauxhall Gardens in 1841 (4:524), and at the Chatham in 1842 (4:568). Under the title, *Lo Studio*, the production was billed at the Franklin in 1838, with W. Wood as the model (4:306), and another "Master Wood (only seven years old)" appeared in Grecian Statues at Peale's on 12 July 1840 (4:512-13). Another variation on the same theme was the Bowery production in 1834 of *The Dumb Brigand; or, The Dark Gondolier*, in which Mrs. McClure embodied "several Poetic and Classical Tableaux, from Horace Vernet's celebrated pictures of the Brigands."[35] Similarly, on 8 June 1839, the Ravel Family at Niblo's announced "the beautiful Tableau Vivant, called the ITALIAN BRIGANDS," a production destined to become part of that troupe's standard repertoire.[36]

A somewhat different approach was taken by the flamboyant William Mitchell at his Olympic Theatre. On 10 May 1841 Mitchell himself and "every member of his company" appeared in "Tableaux of the Tyrol." Odell reports:

> the scenes represented were at morning, noon, evening and moonlight, and included all the sentimental rag-taggery of peasants, hunters, goatherds, vine-dressers, chamois-hunters, etc., the stock in trade of all second rate writers from time immemorial. But the Olympic audiences liked the pictures, and they were given nightly, almost to the end of the season.[37]

In fact, tableaux, in various forms, ran until 22 December 1841 at the Olympic. On 13 December the pictures there included "Diana and her Nymphs, representing the Goddess and her Nymphs at the moment they are discovered by Actaeon; Napoleon's Bivouac, the night before Austerlitz; and Cleopatra in her Galley."[38]

Thus, by the mid-1840's, tableaux vivants had become a familiar and popular entertainment form in the New York theatre.[39] In the process, several conventions of production had been established. Subject matter included not only classic statuary and familiar paintings, but also scenes inspired by literature, historical events, and similar sources. While some tableaux were incorporated into a dramatic structure, such as *Raphael's Dream,* most were offered for their own sake under generic titles or with no general title at all. As the representation of pictures and "scenes," rather than statues, became more common, there was greater emphasis on the use of scenery, lighting, and costume.

The justification offered for these early tableaux was that they contributed to the edification, refinement, or moral uplift of the audience. Advertising attempted to focus attention on the esthetic, didactic, or moralistic value of the work represented. Advertising for the Ravels' production of *Italian Brigands,* for example, proclaimed that the tableaux would be "as painted in Paris, by the celebrated Cicery—founded upon circumstances which actually occurred in Paris in 1804."[40] The Swiss Brothers' performances at the Bowery Amphitheater were to be "entirely of a moral tendency—designed as well to instruct as delight."[41] Statue presentations were usually called "ancient" and "classical" works by "celebrated masters." Surely the epitome of such labeling is the Park Theater advertisement calling *Raphael's Dream* a "classical, historical, mythological Drama."[42]

Another obvious appeal of the tableau was its similarity to the work of art represented. Such, of course, was the appeal of the Wilkie tableaux in *The Rent Day,* and even Ducrow was praised for having "copied with the most astonishing exactness and fidelity" the ancient statues he represented.[43]

A comparison with the original was easily possible for many audience members, since exhibits of painting and sculpture were readily available and widely attended in New York. Announcements of these exhibits were prominent among the "amusements" advertising of the daily newspapers, and the admission costs were low enough to encourage attendance by those who were also potential theatre customers. The admission charge of 25 cents—50 cents for a season ticket—for the Gallery of Original Paintings at the Academy of Design was exactly the same as the cost of attending tableaux at the Athenaeum in 1832. In addition, familiarity with historical scenes and exotic places—both popular tableaux subjects—was assured by the many panoramas, dioramas, and cosmoramas exhibited regularly in New York. In 1831 Niblo's Garden exhibited panoramas of the battles of Navarine,

Waterloo, and Algiers, while the American Museum offered "the largest Cosmorama in the world, the whole comprising at least 100 glasses through which are exhibited correct delineations of every remarkable place in the world."[44] In 1835 Harrington's dioramas presented "grand moral representations of the Deluge, (being an animated illustration of Martin's celebrated picture."[45] Certainly one of the most spectacular of all was the "Great National Exhibition of the signers of the Declaration of Independence.... This exhibition is not a painting. It consists of fifty-six figures, large and natural as life, dressed in a costume of the day, arranged as in Congress when in seventy-six they signed that immortal paper which has given freedom to our country."[46] Wax museums, too provided popular exhibits throughout the period. The Eden Musée, most long-lasting and prominent of these, changed its exhibits regularly, adding groups of figures based upon both topical events and historical subject matter. One of its major competitors, the National Museum of Wax Figures, opened on the Fourth of July, 1842.

It is not difficult to imagine the atmosphere created by the presence of such exhibits. Tableaux vivants simply provided the logical extension of this trend, presenting the work of art in living, three-dimensional reality. The exhibits of paintings and sculpture provided the audience with a knowledge of source material; the panoramic displays contributed the exotic; and, taken together, they all encouraged that sense of spectacle which could be satisfied by tableaux.

The aura surrounding tableaux vivants from their introduction in 1831 until 1847 seems one of almost child-like awe and curiosity—innocent, well-intentioned, and receptive. All this was soon to change, however, as managers began to capitalize more and more on the sensational possibilities the tableaux offered. The result was to be a running battle throughout the remainder of the century between tableaux artists and the forces of law and decency.

3

Model Artists vs. the Law, 1848

On 22 March 1848 the proprietors of five New York amusement halls were served with bench warrants enjoining them to cease the "immoral" presentations occurring in their establishments. Four of these managers complied at once; the fifth resisted briefly and was held under bail until he, too, succumbed to the official pressure. The cause of this furor was a civic outcry against the "model artists" who presented tableaux vivants, and the arrests of 1848 appear to be the earliest legal action against these productions.

The reasons for this action, and even reliable details of what actually took place are difficult to reconstruct. Official documents are missing or incomplete, there was little critical evaluation or description of the tableau as an art form, and subsequent historians have largely ignored this unique entertainment. Nevertheless, sufficient information is available to provide at least some insights into the changing attitudes toward this popular theatrical phenomenon during the critical years just before mid-century.

By 1848 tableaux were no longer primarily the work of individual performers like Mrs. Barrymore, Wieland, Frimbly, and Fletcher. Instead, productions had shifted to a more grandiose style involving whole companies of performers devoted entirely to the presentation of tableaux vivants. It was after this shift in emphasis that questions of taste and propriety began to be raised. Critics, both during the period and in later years, point to the manager of the first of these tableau companies, a Dr. Collyer, as providing the turning point from moral to immoral performances, and they associate his productions with the introduction of women into tableaux, even though, as we have seen, women had appeared earlier. Revelation of the "female form divine," however, became a major focus of critical attention from Dr. Collyer's time onward.[1] In 1850, while Dr. Collyer's tableaux were still fresh in the public mind, George G. Foster wrote, "Up to this time these exhibitions had been composed exclusively of men, and we never heard of their being immodest; but the moment the ladies made their appearance, an outcry of outraged public decency rose on all sides."[2]

Meade Minnigerode, writing in 1924, assigned the cause of the trouble to the fact that Dr. Collyer's troupe presented a representation of Hiram Powers' statue, "The Greek Slave." Exhibits of the actual statue had caused an "artistic sensation" in New York at the time of Collyer's arrival in 1847.[3] Bernard Sobel, writing in 1956, traces the history of American burlesque and points out:

> Fleshly intimations of the oncoming striptease nudity were bared to the naked eye as far back as 1847. At that time Living Models or Tableaux Vivants drew audiences to at least five New York theatres where they were regaled with bare bodies and posturings that resembled the classic sculpture.
> A Dr. Collyer was the original sponsor of these pseudoaesthetic exhibits, and the participants included shapely women "without a blemish" and handsomely molded men, usually acrobats recruited from circuses.[4]

"Dr. Collyer's Model Personifications" opened in New York at the Apollo Rooms on Thursday evening, 23 September 1847. The event was noted with anticipation in the "Theatricals and Musical" column of the *New York Herald* on that date. Advertising for the performance announced:

> Dr. Collyer will (for the first time in America) commence his colored and Marble Personifications of all the great Masters in Painting and Sculpture.... The strictest accuracy will be observed in relation to the drapery, also to the classical, sacred and modern, events represented. The Artistes are from the Royal Academy of London and Paris.[5]

In addition, it was pointed out that, "to give the greatest possible effect to the symmetrical beauty of the Living Models, they will revolve on CANOVA'S PEDESTAL, and will be illuminated by the DRUMMOND LIGHT. Each Tableau will be accompanied by descriptive music, by a complete Orchestra under the direction of Mr. Dodworth, of DODWORTH'S BRASS BAND."[6] (See Figure 6.)

On the day following Dr. Collyer's opening, the *Herald* critic was full of praise for what he had seen:

> We attended the first exhibition of Dr. Collyer's *troupe* of model artists last evening, and we are free to say that they excel anything of the kind we have ever seen in New York. Before seeing it we were afraid it would not be as chaste and pure as we would desire; but after seeing them a short time, that impression was soon dispelled.... We saw accurate representations of the most exquisite works of the most renouned sculptors of the old world—such as Titian, Van dyke [sic], Rembrandt, and a host of others, equally celebrated: and we learned from persons present who have seen the originals, the personifications of them, last evening, were very accurate.[7]

In the weeks that followed, hardly a day passed without some complimentary remark by the *Herald* critic. He assured his readers that "nothing that could offend the most fastidious" could be found in the personifications, and he recommended that "they ought to be seen by all admirers of the fine arts."[8] The appeal of the tableaux was further insured by

Figure 6. "The Three Graces" as they might have been presented by Dr. Collyer at the Apollo Rooms, 1847. Possibly the circular platform on which the models are posed was actually a turntable, or "revolve," which would permit the grouping to be viewed from all sides.

The illustration bears the inscription, "Entered according to act of Congress in the year 1848 by J. Baillie." (Bernard Sobel, *A Pictorial History of Burlesque* [New York: G.P. Putnam's Sons, 1956], p. 110.)

the use of such patriotic subjects as the "Grand Tableaux in honor of the Heroes of Mexico" and "A Monument to Washington," which took place on the day the cornerstone was laid for the real Washington Monument.[9] On 26 September, Dr. Collyer's troupe was billed for only "another week," but in early October he was still "attracting crowds" to the Apollo Rooms, and on 4 October the announcement for the following week proclaimed: "The entertainments for Monday, Tuesday, and Wednesday, will comprise an entire new series of groups, from painting and sculpture, which are superior to any before offered.—There will be changes in the programmes every evening."[10] Five announcements of additional "new" tableaux appeared between 10 and 30 October 1847. Dr. Collyer seemed determined to provide fresh attractions to keep his audience coming back for more.

Perhaps some intimation of trouble to come may be read into the announcement of new tableaux on 10 October. The *Herald* reporter mentions that there will be "several scenes from Paradise Lost," however the actual list of titles suggests that Dr. Collyer's inspiration may not have been Milton. The Apollo Rooms advertisement headlined "SCENES FROM PARADISE," not Paradise *Lost,* and went on to explain that these were to be "sublime personifications of the scenes from the Garden of Eden, viz;—'Adam's first sight of Eve,' 'The Angel discoursing with Adam,' 'The Temptation,' 'The Expulsion,' 'Death of Abel,' &c, &c, with other interesting groups."[11] By 18 October "Adam and Eve, as they appeared in the Garden of Eden," had become the headline attraction. On 21 October it was noted that fourteen tableaux were presnted, including the Adam and Eve series. One might suspect that revealing Adam and Eve, "as they were in the Garden of Eden," might be designed to appeal more to prurient than to artistic interests. Odell, in his retrospective account, even goes so far as to suggest that the advertising claim that "the strictest accuracy will be observed in relation to the drapery" probably "aroused the interest of the prurient."[12] However, there is no indication in the newspaper accounts that such was the case. Every comment attests to the high artistic and moral quality of Dr. Collyer's presentations. On Monday, 8 November 1847, Dr. Collyer moved to Palmo's Opera House, where the opening was announced "for the benefit of the Washington Monument Association."[13] Success followed the troupe, and the house was consistently reported full.

Dr. Collyer's last New York appearance was on 4 December 1847. The *Herald* critic announced the fact in nearly eulogistic style:

> After a lengthened stay among us, during which they have been patronized "to the top of their bent," as Hamlet says, this troupe take their departure from us southward, in order to fulfill many engagements in that part of the Union. To-night, then, is positively the last time they can perform here for some months to come; and those who miss this opportunity of seeing them will have missed a delightful entertainment. Dr. Collyer deserves credit for

having introduced this novel and delightful species of amusement into this country. From the very great patronage bestowed on him, we have no doubt he has found it quite a profitable affair.[14]

In passing, it may be worth noting that during the ten weeks of Dr. Collyer's run a subtle change in terminology had occurred. When he opened at the Apollo Rooms the term, "model personifications," was used to designate his performances. As the run progressed the newspapers used "living statuary," "model impersonations," and "living models" to describe the production. In his advertising, Collyer consistently used the term, "model artistes," and as the run continued, he gave this term more and more typographical emphasis. In a typical advertisement, the words would be centered on a line by themselves and printed in capital letters. When editors and other writers picked up the term, they dropped the last "e," stripping away the hint of French. "Model artists" then became the common title for this kind of production and for the performers themselves. Furthermore, these entertainments were looked upon as "exhibitions" rather than as acts or performances or shows. Thus, by the close of Dr. Collyer's run, it had become common usage to speak of "exhibitions of model artists," an expression which was to lend itself easily to the adverse connotations which were soon to be thrust upon it.

It is interesting to note that Dr. Collyer's great success overshadowed the tableaux being presented in other New York theatres during the time of his appearance. The press took almost no notice of living models who appeared in an afterpiece at the Park, beginning 15 November 1847, and it commented only briefly on the appearance of the Ravel Family at Palmo's before Dr. Collyer took over that house.[15] It is possible that Dr. Collyer may have taken the inspiration for his "Garden of Eden" series from the Ravels. They had been producing "a series of magnificent tableau vivant [sic], called 'Cain and Abel, or The First Fratricide.' This beautiful representation executed by the Ravels, and taken from the painting in the gallery of the Louvre, in Paris, has been considered, by those who have witnessed it, as the most perfect consumation of the artist's ideas."[16] Reviewing the performance, however, the *Herald* critic observed that, "although we prefer Dr. Collyer's performances, we find the Ravel's [sic] very accurate and excellent in their style."[17]

Some additional competition for Dr. Collyer also occupied the Chatham Theatre, where Fletcher (possibly the same Fletcher who had so impressed the young Joseph Jefferson in 1832) arranged and presented "Grand Tableaux," beginning 9 November 1847. These continued sporadically through February 1848, but were accorded little notice in the newspapers. Odell (5:361) comments that "the living pictures were the one fixture of the Chatham through the season."

After Dr. Collyer's departure from New York, tableaux were being shown regularly at Pinteux' Saloon (also known as the Broadway Odeon), and that house became involved in an incident which sensationalized tableaux vivants.[18] On 26 December 1847 the manager of Pinteux' presented an exhibition of tableaux—living statues—"contrary to law and good order," as the press put it. The ruse of employing Biblical subject matter—"Eve in the Garden of Eden," "Hagar and Ishmael," "Esther in the Persian Hot Bath," "Jacob in the House of Laban"—did not deter the authorities from stopping the performance and arresting the performers. The newspapers reported the event in elaborate detail and with considerable humor:

> The Aldermen, together with a posse of police, were early on the spot, watching the movements and reconnoitering the premises ... when the curtain was drawn aside for the *tableaux,* representing "Hagar and Ishmael." This the Aldermen allowed to pass, but on the second tableaux, representing "Jacob in the House of Laban," just as the pedestal was revolving, with three well-formed females thereon with short skirts, and the audience straining their eyes with anxious imagination, in pounced the Aldermen with police, which movement struck the audience, as well as the artists, with astonishment and fear. One of the artists fainted, throwing herself into a position which resembled the Greek Slave up set, better developed than any marble representation. On passing to the dressing room, a scene of stirring interest took place, as some five or six well formed females were in the act of preparing for the next tableaux; in one corner was seen a very fleshy lady, dressed as *Bacchus,* on a barrel, studying her position; another beautifully formed creature, just drawing on her tights for the Greek Slave, together with others, who were so dreadfully alarmed at the sight of the police, with their clubs in hand, would sieze up a portion of their garments in order to hide their face, forgetting their lower extremities, thus making a scene mixed up with the sublime and the ridiculous.... After they were conducted to the Station House, and detained for the night, Mr. Pinteux sent them a roast turkey and several bottles of wine, to cheer their souls, which had the desired effect.... In the morning they were all taken before Justice Drinker, who held the artists to bail in $100 each for their future good behavior and to keep the Sabbath holy, and the manager, Mr. Greely, in $300 to do the same.... The performances went on as usual last evening, by the same artists. Their sojourn in the Station House neither destroyed nor impaired any of their fair proportions, and the well developed limb and rounded bust were as conspicuous as before upon the pedestal. The scriptural pieces, interrupted by the police on Sunday, will be given this evening, in the original costumes. Crowds visit this favorite place of amusement, and the entertainments are well worth it.[19]

As a more recent observer noted in 1924, "The immediate and inevitable result of this 'singular *emeute*' was to throw 'the whole world of the undercrust of fashion' into a state of great excitement, and to bring out a perfect rash of similar entertainments in every part of the city."[20] The next day the Hall of Novelty at Centre and Pearl Streets added living models to its minstrel program, and in January 1848 model artists were appearing at the Park, the Olympic, and the Chatham theatres."[21] Meanwhile, not far away, at the Brooklyn Odeon Dr. Collyer's troupe had taken up temporary residence prior to its tour of the South and Midwest.

It is important to remember that the offense charged against Pinteux' troupe was "infringement of the Sabbath;" there was no attack upon the morality of the production itself.[22] That attack, however, was soon to come, for on 24 January 1848 "Professor Thier's Model Artists—20 in number—" opened at Palmo's Opera House.[23]

Although his advertising promised "grand historical and classic tableaux," and much of his promotional copy bragged about the "costly dresses and other properties," these were not the attributes which brought the greatest notice to Professor Thier's model artists. During their tenure of two months, first at Palmo's and later at the Concert Room, press reaction shifted from enthusiasm through tolerance to open hostility and moral outrage.

First there were the usual enthusiastic puffs in anticipation of an opening. Then daily comments attested to the artistry and purity of the exhibition, predicting great popularity for the troupe. The *Herald's* comments three days after the opening are typical of the praise lavished on Thier's work:

> The new model artists at this house are succeeding well; they are a finely shaped set of performers, and from the way in which they go through their groupings, are evidently no artists "for the nonce," but regular bred and *bona fide* ones. They give some seventeen or eighteen tableaux; many of them never before presented to a New York audience. We have observed many ladies and families in the dress circle at Palmo's since the present *troupe* have appeared. The perfect modesty and propriety with which everything is conducted, is a guaranty of the purity and beauty of the exhibition, which can be gazed on by the most refined without in any way offending; on the contrary, it will please those of elegant taste.[24]

It is a sad fact for historians that few detailed descriptions of tableaux are to be found in newspaper reviews of them. However, occasional bits of data provide clues, at least, to what the exhibitions must have been like. A commentary about one item in Professor Thier's program reveals such a clue:

> We think the tableau of Samson and Delilah one of the finest we have ever seen. The suddenness with which the second position in it is assumed by the artists forms one of the prettiest pieces of startling stage effect that we have seen for some time; and moreover, it shows how perfect the performers are in their parts; no bungling, no shuffling around; in one instant every position is changed; and again they stand like marble.[25]

This technique of shifting poses seems to incorporate a method associated earlier with what were known as "attitudes," the most notable practitioner of which was Emma, Lady Hamilton. In such performances, the "poseur" would represent a well-known character or type, often drawn from classical art works, and would proceed through a series of poses, revealing a new emotion for the same character in each separate pose. Observers marvelled, for instance, at the ease and quickness of Lady Hamilton's changes from emotion to emotion as she depicted "Niobe" or "a bacchante" or some other subject. The point is that these changes from pose to pose were within a single character, not changes from one character to another.[26]

In the case of Professor Thier's performance, these critical reactions, as has been observed, were highly complimentary. Only a few days later, however, the *Herald* editorialized that legitimate drama did not seem to be holding up very well in the face of competition from such lesser amusements as "melodrama, spectacle, exhibition, horses, and humbug." The writer singled out model artists for special condemnation:

> One of the most curious phases in public amusements that has struck us at this time, is the progress of exhibiting the almost naked figures of men and women, under the designation of model artists, holy groups, and sacred figures, taken from the scriptures, and the old and new testament [*sic*]. It is only a few months since the first of these exhibitions was opened to a New York audience.... They are rapidly degenerating from the taste and propriety which characterized them in Palmo's or Pinteux's, and has, at last, got so low, in some of the by-streets at three, four, or five cents, thereby inviting newsboys, loafers, and the veriest ragamuffins about town to see them.
>
> We remember the rise, progress, and fall of masquerading, as an amusement. The exhibition of semi-naked figures as models of art, seems to be running the same course; and we should not be surprised to see the necessity of the legislature passing a law regarding such exhibitions. In some of the out-of-the-way streets and lanes, these exhibitions are really too bad, and their further tolerance in our city would be a disgrace.[27]

Finally, on 8 February, the *Herald* was prompted to remark: "There was rather a slim attendance at this place of amusement [Palmo's] last evening, notwithstanding the efforts of the manager in purchasing the most costly dresses and other properties. It would seem as though tableaux vivants were on the wane in this city." Again, on 14 February: "The Model Artist fever seems to be on the decline, the public having probably become satiated with the numerous *troupes* which are to be seen in every street almost." Clearly, something had happened to public enthusiasm. The *Herald* attempted to explain the declining attendance on 10 February, and tolerantly suggested a remedy:

> Palmo's Opera House.—Thier's grand Tableaux Vivants are being exhibited at this theatre, every evening. They are represented on a very splendid scale, the manager having gone to considerable expense in the dresses and decorations, yet the attendance is rather slim. We would advise a little more drapery, when, we are convinced, they will take much better, as a respect to the rules of modesty and propriety, in representations of this character should be strictly looked to. We wish the manager success, as he is a perservering, industrious man, and we suggest this matter for his benefit.

Two days later the *Herald* offered to print, "at length," reports of sermons to be preached against the model artists. Although no such reports appeared, there was evidently a rising effort to suppress the exhibitions, and the *Herald* was becoming more and more closely aligned with it, Petitions were being circulated "among many religious and respectable groups in the city," the *Herald* reported, and these were to be sent to Albany, "praying for an enactment for the entire prohibition of such exhibitions in the future." The reporter goes on to note the change in model artist productions which had prompted this action:

> However scriptural or classic those exhibitions were at the commencement of the season, they have become singularly enough, more naked, as the weather grows colder; so, that, in fact, at this time, the most of these exhibitions are got up, in pretty much the same style that Adam and Eve presented in the Garden of Eden. They may be exhibited during the present week, but the model artists will, no doubt, be suppressed after that. Those sinners who want a sight, therefore, won't have a chance beyond this week. Certain.[28]

During this period of only a few weeks model artist exhibitions had grown in number so that competition between them had increased. It seems likely that it was this proliferation, not the objections to nudity or a waning interest in the exhibitions which was the real cause of reduced audiences.[29] On Monday, 21 February, Palmo's partially solved its attendance problem by reducing its admission to "twenty-five cents to all parts of the house," resulting in what was called a "full and fashionable audience." Apparently there were customers available.

The term, "fashionable," may be a misleading description of audiences at the model artist exhibitions. Two incidents which occurred in March 1848 illustrate the somewhat questionable atmosphere to be found in these theatres and exhibition halls. In the first incident, Palmo's aroused public curiosity by announcing that the evening's entertainment would conclude with a cotillion by the ladies of the company. The *Herald* described the evening:

> A large audience was the result; amongst whom were a large proportion of bald and grey headed men, busily engaged before the curtain rose, in drawing their prodigious opera glasses and pocket telescopes into the proper focus. Upon the rising of the curtain, all these instruments were brought into requisition, for the purpose of examining more closely the proportions of the artists.... All the tableaux received considerable applause, and at the conclusion of this part of the performances, great sensation was visible in all parts of the house, in expectation of the grand *finale* of the evening. After considerable delay, the curtain rose and one cotillion set was on the stage.... There was such great extremes [*sic*] in the figures that at the first sight the audience were convulsed with laughter, and the house in a perfect uproar. The head couple consisted of a short, fat, duck legged man, with a heavy black moustache, Hamlet skirt, and white tights; his partner a tall, slim, knock-kneed girl, with flesh colored tights, and very short white skirt. The other three couples were of about the same order of architecture. There appeared to be great dissatisfaction and disappointment amongst the audience, in consequence of the dancers not appearing exclusively in tights; and for a time nothing could be heard but the most horrible groans and cries of "take off those rags." After a while the uproar ceased, the music commenced, and the cry was, "on with the dance;" but, evidently being unaccustomed to trip on the light fantastic toe, they broke down on the first round, and the curtain fell amid roars of laughter, groans, hisses, yells, and all sorts of noises, and a general cry of "Bring on the girls," "off with the rags;" and "to he—ll with the men." In the midst of this confusion the manager appeared, and pacified the audience by announcing that the next set should be all females; and, in a few minutes, the

curtain rose, exhibiting four females, with flesh colored tights, and remarkably short skirts, who may be good model artists, but are very poor dancers. After shaking their half frozen limbs about the stage for a few moments, the curtain fell, and thus concluded the night's performance.[30]

The second incident took place the same night at a different exhibition hall, the Temple of the Muses:

According to the best information that could be obtained, it appears that from twelve to fifteen persons, laboring under the influence of liquor, forcibly entered the before-named place, knocking down the door-keeper, who attempted to stop them from going in. They next proceeded to the barroom, or saloon, and commenced demolishing whatever they could lay their hands upon; after which they hurried to the exhibition room, where their boisterous conduct created the utmost confusion. The rioters... pushed through the dense crowd, toward the stage, tearing off the backs of the seats and expressing their determination to have their passions gratified.... The females instantly fled to their dressing room, and Mr. Williams, the manager, on coming forward, was knocked down with great violence and severely wounded on the head. The intruders then made for the females' dressing room; but their progress was interrupted by several male *attaches* of the establishment, who armed themselves with a musket, sword, and other weapons used in their tableau in honor of the United States.... The female *artistes* having effected their escape by a trap door, and the drop curtain torn down by the ruthless assailants, the exhibition was necessarily brought to a close for the evening.[31]

The day following these events the *Herald* complained, "These exhibitions during the past week, have been worse and worse—more nakedness and less drapery.... It is really astonishing how these exhibitions are crowded; all the regular theatres are nearly deserted."[32] Whether or not the model artists were actually drawing audiences away from the regular theatres is, of course, debatable, but it is certain that there was no lack of interest in the exhibitions themselves. Even when Professor Thier moved to the Concert Room at the end of February, model artists continued at Palmo's, this time under the direction of a Signor Monticelli.[33] Thus, another troupe was added to the many already in operation.

There was enough enthusiasm over model artists to make possible two remarkable ticket swindles in early March. The fact that these were successful suggests that, in addition to the regularly advertised exhibitions in theatres and halls, there must have been other clandestine productions, probably more daring than the regular ones. The first swindle took place on 5 March 1848 and was reported the following Saturday:

PATRONS OF MODEL ARTISTS HOAXED.—On Sunday last, a complete hoax was practised by a speculative genius, on the patrons of the Model Artists, who placed for sale, tickets, at $1 each, in the hands of barbers, bar tenders, and especially the French *cafes*. These tickets were sold in the most secret manner, accompanied with a small printed circular, setting forth that seventeen French ladies had been engaged, at a great expense, for one night only, who would appear in several favorite *tableaux* in nature's costume, without gentlemen. The exhibition was to take place at No. 163 Grand street, and, upon no consideration, would money be received at the door, which would open at 6 o'clock on Monday evening, and close at 7 o'clock, when the doors would be bolted, and no more admitted. This created an unusual degree of excitement among all the young men and the grey headed old fellows around town, who nightly patronize the Model Artists, particularly, as it was announced that no tickets would be sold after 12 o'clock on Monday. However, the secret affair was soon buzzed about and during the afternoon, $5 and even $10 premium, was offered for a ticket. At the appointed time a large party of gentlemen met on the stairway, at No. 163 Grand street, in breathless expectation of the anticipated treat; when, lo, they were informed by the occupant of the building, that no such exhibition, or any exhibition whatever was to be seen in that building. Upon this information, one began to look at the other, and gradually sneak off one at a time, each not wishing to acknowledge he was hoaxed. Some seven or eight hundred tickets were sold.[34]

The second hoax used essentially the same methods, though on a slightly smaller scale—only "five hundred persons were caught" at one dollar each.[35] Clearly, there was a ready and eager market for tickets, and there were entrepreneurs, legitimate or otherwise, who were ready to exploit that part of the public which was more interested in the "proportions" of the female artists than in the "classical" works of art they represented.

Under such circumstances it is not surprising that an increasingly vocal opposition to model artists was developing. Public involvement is suggested by two letters to the editor of the *Sun* on 10 March 1848 expressing feelings of revulsion and calling for official action. One letter laments:

How ill becoming our city? How unprofitable and pernicious to the young and rising generations? I hope sincerely that the city authorities are becoming awake upon a subject of so much importance.... Cannot this great city afford strength enough to overthrow at once these scenes of sin and wickedness?

The second letter observes that "reiterated calls have been made for their suppression; but thus far, to little or no purpose."

In mid-March "the chief officer of one of the criminal courts" was said to have visited an exhibition at Palmo's and to have been "very much delighted with the appearance of the models." In addition, members of the Grand Jury "visited several of those places on Thursday night [16 March], and, rumor says, could find no fault with the exhibitions." All of which led the *Herald* to recommend, "It would be well for some of them to go when they are not expected."[36] A passing reference in the *Herald,* 5 March 1848, suggests that police payoffs may have been partially responsible for the lack of official suppression: "The police have received over $200 to let them alone—and of course do so."

Although nothing had come of the petitions to the state legislature, the Board of Aldermen and the Grand Jury had been conducting investigations (the *Herald's* cynicism notwithstanding). Apparently, too, some investigators did attend when they were not expected, as this report suggests:

> MODEL ARTISTS.—Alderman Purser made a verbal report on Monday, before the Board of Aldermen, on the subject of model artists. It appears that he had been appointed a committee by the Corporation, together with two others, to investigate the decency and drapery of these exhibitions, as they exist in this modern Sodom and Gomorrah....
> This verbal report of the Alderman, on the part of the committee, was decidedly hostile to these exhibitions, and confirmed, in all points, the shocking indecency with which they are said to have been presented to the public in this city. It appers that the committee visited in person all these exhibitions, and they considered them all equally deserving to be condemned and placed in the same category, as decidedly indecent.[37]

Alderman Purser spearheaded an attack which resulted in putting model artists out of business for a short time at least. First, he sought legal opinions as to the City's authority to prosecute exhibitors and model artists. These were provided by M.G. Leonard, Commissioner of the Alms Department, Willis Hall, an attorney, and John McKeon, the District Attorney. Commissioner Leonard simply offered the services of his department in any prosecution the Alderman might undertake, and he expressed his agreement that "the well being of our citizens requires that every exertion be made for the suppression of this nuisance." The District Attorney was more positive, saying that, in his opinion, "an indictment can be sustained against persons engaged in openly outraging decency."[38] A more detailed analysis of available options and precedents was provided by Willis Hall:

> The law of decency and morality is part of the law of the land. It is a well established principle of common law, that any open violation of decency, or any act or performance, tending to injure public morals is a misdemeanor, and the actor or actors may be indicted and punished by fine and imprisonment.
> The most common offenders punished under this principle are the exhibition of indecent pictures, the indecent exposure of the person, &c.
> Setting up indecent exhibitions is undoubtedly indictable under the same principle....
> Such things have been punished in neighboring states, in Pennsylvania...; in Massachusetts...; in Connecticut....
> Our state has no provision relating to this point, except this; "if two or more persons shall conspire to commit any act injurious to the public health, to public morals, &c, they shall be deemed guilty of a misdemeanor."...
> Whether this exhibition of "model artists" is an indecent exhibition, is a question of fact of which the committee must satisfy themselves by such proof as they deem satisfactory.
> If the committee come to the conclusion that these exhibitions involve an indecent exposure of the person, the persons so exposing themselves are liable to indictment....
> Or if they come to the conclusion that this is an indecent, demoralizing exhibition, the getters up of it, and the parties concerned, may be indicted or if they should conclude that two or more persons have conspired to do an act injurious to public morals, the parties conspiring, both actors and getters up, may be indicted under the statute. But if they cannot come to either of these conclusions they may perhaps consider the exhibition as disorderly persons.

> The act is, "That all jugglers, common showmen and mountebanks, who exhibit or perform for profit, any puppet show, wire or rope dance, or other shows, acts or feats, &c, &c, shall be deemed disorderly persons."
> If the committee think the parties guilty of a misdemeanor, by violation of the laws of decency, either at common law, or under our statute, as to conspiracies to injure public morals, the proceeding must be by arrest and indictment. But if they conclude that the exhibitions can be considered only in the light of disorderly persons, they are to be proceeded against by complaint under the oath of the magistrate, whose duty it is to apprehend them and bind them over to be of good behavior for one year.[39]

The *Herald* reporter, commenting on these opinions, remained unconvinced, noting that the statements were "rather evasive, and the laws referred to very ancient, perhaps as old as Sodom and Gemorrah." He then went on to claim, as he had done before, that "nothing but a simple and direct enactment, passed immediately by the Legislature, can reach the present downward progress of public morality, and the upward progress of public drapery."[40]

Meanwhile, the model artist exhibitions continued unabated, with Palmo's advertising new pictures, "produced in a style of splendor and effect hitherto unknown in America, and some of the figures will be represented on Horseback."[41] The horses had hardly reached the stage, however, before, as Odell puts it, "the majesty of the law had stepped in."[42]

> GREAT INDICTMENT OF THE MODEL ARTISTS—TREMENDOUS EXCITEMENT AMONG THE FASHIONABLE LOAFERS—All the exhibitors of the model artists were indicted yesterday by the Grand Jury. The trials will come off in two or three weeks. We hear that several hundred of the fashionable old rakes and ineffable scoundrels about town—some of them bankers and brokers in Wall street, over sixty years of age—who have been visiting these places before and behind the curtain, will be called up as witnesses on the trial, to tell what they saw on each occasion. Their names were taken by the police as they passed into the exhibitions.[43]

At least one exhibition raided was a clandestine enterprise rather than one at the regular theatres and halls.

> THE LAST SCENE OF THE MODEL ARTISTS.—The police office at the Tombs, yesterday morning, presented quite a busy scene, in consequence of a group of female model artists having been arrested by Capt. Carpenter, of the Fifth Ward, and a posse of his officers under the direction of Aldermen Adams and Schultz. Information, it appears, was given to Capt. Carpenter and Alderman Adams during Tuesday intimating that an exhibition of model artists would take place on that night, in a state of nature, at the building formerly called the Eagle Hotel, No. 171 Canal street, where, in the parlors, the exhibition was to be witnessed; tickets were issued and readily bought at $1 each, numbering between two and three hundred.... Early in the evening a watch was kept on the house, when at the appointed time the anxious spectators flocked in and soon filled the room to suffocation, and the doors were then locked. On the mantlepiece of this room was a glimmering lamp, reflecting a miserable light; and near the folding door were arranged three or four benches, which were occupied by the grey and bald headed old men adjusting their pocket telescopes and enormous opera glasses, in order to view more clearly the well made proportions of the fair

artists.... The two parlors were separated by folding doors, in the front of which was a large gauze nailed up, through which the females were shown—the doors being closed and opened formed the drop curtain. Several tableaux were then shown, the females being nude, holding across their figures a gauze scarf thrown over them in a *negligee* manner, so as to create the greatest excitement possible in the audience. The last tableau was a tall, well-formed young woman, with long hair, representing Venus rising from the Sea, which fairly made the audience rise to such an extent that the folding doors closed, the police burst in, headed by the alderman, and five females together with the door keeper, Levy Hamilton, alias Mace, were all conveyed to the station house.... Affidavits were taken, and the girls examined,... which resulted in all concerned being held to bail in the sum of $1000 for their appearance at court for trial, in default of which they were committed to the Tombs.[44]

Another story in another column of the same page specified the other persons indicted as "the proprietors and conductors of Pinteux's Saloon, Broadway [the Broadway Odeon]; Palmo's Opera House, in Chambers street; Thier's Concert Room, in Broadway, Temple of the Muses, Novelty Hall, corner of Pearl and Centre streets, and the Anatomical Museum, corner of Division street and Bowery." The reports say that bench warrants for the proprietors were issued by the Court of Sessions. The proprietors were asked to stop the performances, "which they all agreed to do except the proprietor of Palmo's [Michael K. Burke], who refused to close, but continued the performance in defiance of this request. He was arrested and detained in custody until to-day, when all the accused parties are to appear and enter bail in $500 each for their appearance at court for trial."[45] The trial, set for Saturday, 25 March, was not reported in the newspapers, and an examination of New York City Police Court records for 1848 failed to reveal any information about the case. This is understandable in the cases of all the proprietors except Burke, since they apparently closed their exhibitions as requested. Only Palmo's continued to advertise on 24 and 25 March. In fact, one account of the incident reported that, while indictments were brought against all the proprietors, only Burke was actually arrested for failing to comply.[46] Both the *Daily Tribune* and the *Sun,* in addition to covering the indictments, printed separate articles devoted only to the arrest of Michael K. Burke.[47] Burke apparently enjoyed a reputation as an influential member of the New York community. He was a lawyer, "long and favorably known," with "a large circle of acquaintances and friends."[48] Perhaps it was this standing which, on Saturday, 25 March, prompted him to place the following outraged notice in the *New York Herald:*

A CARD—PALMO'S OPERA HOUSE—(Give Unto Caesar What's Caesar's Due). The public are respectfully informed that scarcely one of the journals of this city have given a correct statement of what took place in court, in connection with the arrest, bail, &c, of myself, the proprietor of Palmo's Opera House; and further, although many other persons were indicted, for apparently a similar offense, yet the newspapers, like the District Attorney, have thought fit, in their high sense of public duty, to throw their paltry and frothy ire more on myself than the others. The position is now evident. My respectability, standing, and influence in the community is alone an eyesore to them, but it affords me this satisfaction, that they corroborate what I have written about myself, by the mere fact of their indulging me with their extra filthy abuse. The public must be well aware that an indictment having been obtained, with the aid of the lion power of the District Attorney's talent, sarcasms, &c, yet it is but an ex parte statement, and I shall be able, before a jury not alone to vindicate my well known character, which has been so unjustly assailed, but prove to the community at large, the perscution that those clothed with a little brief authority subjected me to. Palmo's Opera House will be opened on Monday evening next. For further particulars, see advertisments. M.K. BURKE Palmo's Opera House, March 25, 1848.[49]

This irate gesture seems to have been fruitless, however. No advertising for Palmo's appeared on Sunday or Monday, and on Tuesday, 28 March, a brief notice on page three of the *Herald* reads simply, "Palmo's Opera House to Let—Apply at the box office between the hours of 10 o'clock AM and 2 o'clock PM." Burke had given up the fight, and the *Herald* editor was able to express, with cynicism, his momentary satisfaction:

At length public opinion and moral sentiment have carried the day. The model artists are suppressed for the present. The Grand Jury have indicted all these exhibitors. They are all shut up, with the exception of one or two, which resisted, and the proprietors of them have been arrested and imprisoned, and will be tried, and convicted, and exposed, and pardoned, and patronized, and start again fresh and clean.[50]

Even after the arrests had been completed, the *Herald* continued what, for that paper, had become a campaign against model artists. The editors and reporters never lost an opportunity to decry the "shocking demoralization" caused by the exhibitions. In April there appeared this bit of doubtfully implied causal reasoning: "During the last week or two there was a considerable revival in the legitimate drama, and also in opera and music. This revival has principally manifested itself since the suppression of those obscene exhibitions called model artists."[51]

Certainly the *Herald* editor's cynicism was not entirely ill-founded. The legal opinions, already cited, which were used to support the attack on model artists, were admittedly rather vague and evasive—a fact duly noted at the time they were made public.[52] Furthermore, when the proprietors of the exhibition halls were forced to appear, one of them, the proprietor of the Temple of the Muses, turned out to be a member of the prosecuting body, Alderman McElrath.[53] In addition, one of the proprietors—"and one who has exhibited these model artists in the most natural and naked style"—was provided with bail by the editors of the *Tribune,* according to the *Herald.*[54] It is clear that power and influence could be found on the side of the model artists as well as that of their opponents.

Whatever the reasons, the suppression did not last. In less than a month exhibitions were again being advertised in language similar to that of the earlier ads. Palmo's Opera House reopened on 1 May with "animated and pictorial illustrations by the first foreign artists."[55] The program for these tableaux, under the direction of Signor Monticelli, included:

1. The Warrior's Dream, Dance of Ulysses' Daughter, Diana, Jepthah's Daughter.
2. The Dancers Reposing, Fairy's Revenge, Medusa, Hercules in the Court of the Gods.
3. The Pleiades, Three Graces, Sappho, The Deluge.
4. Greek Slave, Combat between Isis and Apollo, The Four Seasons, Cleopatra.

Finale in honor of the United States.[56]

Clearly, these pictures did not differ appreciably from those seen before the suppression, and one advertisement even exploits the similarity:

> "A rose by any other name would smell as sweet." Is there anyone who has not seen the Model Artists before their suppression? If there be any so far behind the age, we beg to say that the best imitation of them as yet brought out, [is] now exhibiting at Palmo's Opera House; they are very like the models formerly exhibited here; in fact, they look so like, that those who have seen the artists before, assert that they can see no difference, and that they are but more pictorial illustrations. It appears that the manager, during the time the theatre has been closed, travelled all over the States looking for pretty girls, as we observed some decidedly beautiful ones there last night, fit to mount the "pedestal" in the most palmy days of the models.[57]

The model artists at Palmo's continued through 7 June 1848, apparently without any further interruption by the authorities. Occasional brief comments by the newspaper critics indicated that the tableaux were "handsomely" presented and that the performances were well attended. A novelty was introduced in late May when the character of Mose, the Fireboy, was incorporated into the tableaux of "Mose among the Model Artists."[58] G.W. Smith, "the personator of Mose," took his benefit performance on 3 June 1848. Furthermore, during the entire period of the altercation with the police, and extending as far back as January 1847, the Alhambra Saloon at 559 Broadway was billing a tableau performance, though no "raids" seem to have been directed against this establishment. In November 1848 James Nixon headed a troupe there "in their act of tableaux and poses."[59]

Even though there had been no published attacks on model artists since the arrests in March, advertising for Palmo's in late May, as the end of the run approached, stressed the virtuous and uplifting nature of the exhibitions. Certainly "purple prose" reached its zenith in this remarkably stated advertisement.

> PALMO'S OPERA HOUSE—"Grace in every step; heaven in her eyes." Such language in poetry is developed in every attitude of the Living, Life-like, symmetrical, chaste, and bewitching Models, at the Opera House, where Virtue triumphs over Vice—where the "Three Graces" impart ease and delicacy to the popular taste—where the perfection of Art

and Science takes the place of crude abortions and mechanical structures that the intelligence of our free and discriminating people reject as unworthy of a nation possessing every element and every facility for the highest attainment in every organization of society that contributes to improve the social condition.[60]

Michael Burke took his benefit on 23 May, and the final performance on 7 June 1848 was listed as a benefit for the artists themselves.

Meanwhile, beginning 24 April at the Temple of the Muses, "model artists represented The Bathers Surprised, The Maiden's Rescue, The Favourite of the Seraglio, and The Soldier's Dream,"[61] and in May at The Hall of Novelty "beautiful and graceful groupings" were performed by a "Troupe of Beautiful Girls... acknowledged by everybody to be superior to any ever seen in this metropolis."[62]

In the face of such widespread model artist activity at this time, one wonders what could possibly have prompted the *Sunday Mercury* to run the following little verse in May 1848:

> Where are the Model Artists gone?—
> Those nice tableaux vivants
> Of beautiful young ladies, sans
> Both petticoats and pants,
> Who, scorning fashion's shifts and whims,
> Did nighly crowds delight
> By showing up their handsome limbs
> At fifty cents a sight.[63]

The resurgence of the tableaux was not without protest, ineffectual as it was. Although the *Herald* regularly carried advertising for the model artist theatres and noted the exhibitions in its "Theatrical and Musical" columns, it maintained an editorial objection to their presence. The following editorial of early 1849 is typical:

> MODEL ARTISTS AGAIN.—We understand that the exhibition of model artists, which created so great a sensation last year, and shocked the feelings of the community to such an extent, have been again revived at several places in this city, with even less drapery and more shamelessness than ever.—Such sights are not to be tolerated in a civilized and Christian community. The accounts which we have received of these recent exhibitions are too shocking to be noticed in any other way and in the most general terms of disapprobation and denunciation.
> What has become of the police? Where are the authorities of New York? Is there to be no end to these shameless exhibitions?[64]

Dr. Collyer, who had left New York in December 1847, before the police action occurred, returned to the city in November 1848 after a somewhat stormy tour. In Brooklyn, at the tour's outset, he was given grudging praise in comparison with other troupes then performing: "We must state that his company is beyond doubt, the best and most classical."[65] A letter to the editor in Boston condemned Collyer's women artists especially, complaining that they were "willing for filthy lucre to become the gaze of 'the gay licentious crowd'"[66] An article from the Mobile, Alabama, *Herald and Tribune,* reported that in that city "the audience wound up the performances by tearing the benches to pieces and otherwise making an appropriate finale to the season. Happily it was the last exhibition of this vagabond, Collyer, and his indecent troupe."[67] In Cincinnati, Collyer was forced to plead his case before the city council and in the local press before he gained permission to perform.[68]

When he returned to New York in November 1848, Collyer took over the Classic Museum, 252 Broadway, and advertised that "the public may depend on correct personifications, and nothing to offend the most fastidious." As further assurance he claimed that "the artists have been patronised by General Zach. Taylor, Henry Clay, J.C. Calhoun, Daniel Webster, and all the members of Congress."[69]

As the 1840's ended, tableaux vivants had clearly become a popular mainstay of variety entertainment. They had weathered the storms of the first public attacks and had won, at least to the extent that performances were able to continue. Yet, the character of these exhibits had changed. Although the managers still emphasized the "artistic" nature of the presentations and urged "edification" as their purpose, it was clear that growing numbers of spectators were far more interested in the "symmetry" of the "female form divine." As mid-century approached, this dichotomy of sensation and artistry was clearly evident, and in the 1850's strong proponents of both approaches were to emerge.

4

Sensation vs. Artistry, 1850s

Following the lead of such managers as Collyer, Thier, and Burke, numerous establishments soon employed model artists as their primary attractions, and during the next few seasons several houses were given over entirely to tableaux vivants. Most of these relied heavily on the sensational aspects of living pictures for their main appeal, and as time passed, these became more and more blatant in both performance and advertising. Not surprisingly, such approaches were used almost exclusively in the lesser halls which were not part of the mainstream of play production during the period. Few tableaux found their way into Burton's, the Old Bowery, Brougham's (later Wallack's) Lyceum, or the like.

The first of such lesser houses to capitalize on sensation was the Wallhalla at 36 Canal Street, which, in December 1948 began a run of tableaux vivants which continued through 1850. Its first attraction was a representation of Hiram Powers' "Greek Slave," though one wonders what was meant by the claim that this popular marble statue would be presented "in color."[1] The basic company at the Wallhalla consisted of thirty models, though the number varied from time to time, and certain individual performers were occasionally featured.

No attempt was made to describe these tableaux as chaste or morally uplifting; instead, the descriptions seemed designed to titillate. The artists were described as "French," "the most beautiful women in the world," "the pretty ladies." When Mlle. Matilde Riviera was billed as the featured performer she was called "the most perfect model extant."[2] The selection of subject matter also suggested rather sensational performances. In January 1849, when it was announced that "fifteen new Models have been engaged," the tableaux listed in Wallhalla advertising were "The Greek Slave," "Suzanna in the Bath," "The Three Graces," and "Venus Rising from the Sea."[3] The same bill also included numbers by the "Female Acrobats" and the "Female Ethiopian Serenaders." Possibly some of the same performers took part in all three of these attractions, though there appears to be no conclusive evidence of whether or not such was the case. During this period, however, it was common practice for acrobats, minstels, dancers, and similar attractions to augment the bill of tableaux. In addition, it was common for songs, instrumental music, recitations, and the like to be presented as accompaniment for tableaux.

On 24 May 1849 "Professor Hugo Grotius' celebrated marble statues and tableaux vivants" were announced, and shortly thereafter the establishment was known as Hugo's Wallhalla. Under his management, in October, the company was expanded to "50 beautiful ladies," according to the advertisements. However, November 1849 saw Professor Keller's troupe of twenty-four models in the house, and by February 1850 Professor Quiriu Mutter's model artists were being advertised there.[4] In October 1850 the Wallhalla was occupied for a short time by the familiar Dr. Collyer. Although no closing notices were published, the Wallhalla ceased advertising at the end of November 1850.

The Wallhalla's strongest competition arose in the person of George Lea who had earlier leased the tiny Franklin Theatre at 175 Chatham Square and re-named it the Franklin Museum.[5] In the fall of 1849 he remodeled the house "after the style of Madame Warton's Wallhalla, London" and installed "a company of Ladies not to be equalled in the world for beauty and talent," for the presentation of "beautiful tableaux, which will be produced in a style perfectly original." Under this new arrangement the audience was accommodated in a pit, in boxes, and in "stage seats"—the latter at a cost of only fifty cents.[6] The company was Madame Pauline's Troupe of Model Artists (see Figure 7), "twelve ladies of unblemished beauty" who represented such sensational works as "The Rape of the Sabines," "Adam and Eve," "The Feast of Bacchus," "Revolt of the Seraglio," and other fare often duplicating tableaux exhibited by Lea's competitors. Madame Pauline was listed as coming from the Royal Livery Theatre, Leicester Square, London, the location of Mme. Warton's Wallhalla which served Lea as a prototype.[7] So successful were the model artists at the Franklin Museum that by 27 February 1850 Lea was advertising to send a troupe on tour to "places of amusement, hotels, public gardens, museums, theatres, etc., out of New York City."[8]

On 23 August 1851 Mme. Warton, herself, was billed at the Franklin. Though it is uncertain whether or not this was really the London star, the playbill shown in Figures 8 and 9 indicates that the London exhibition was very similar to Lea's offering. Both Mme. Warton and Mme. Pauline, and Miss Pauline, as she was later called, continued in Lea's employ for several years, taking benefits as late as February 1858, and in 1852 another new name appeared when the tableau company was listed as being "under the supervision of Mlle. Cazinet, Premier Model."[9]

During 1852 and 1853 one John St. Luke, with a company of five men and five women, presented tableaux at the Temple of the Graces, 598 Broadway. St. Luke displayed "glaring placards" advertising his tableaux—"The Circassian Slaves, The Ladies' Bed Room, Depravity and Innocence, the Deceiver and the Virgins, &c."[10] On 9 April 1852, after the exhibitions had been running "for

Coal Hole Tavern,
STRAND.

Mme. PAULINE

AND HER TALENTED COMPANY OF

FEMALE ARTISTES,

WILL COMMENCE THEIR

Graceful and Artistic Entertainments
ENTITLED

GEMS OF ART

REPRESENTING

PICTURES

FROM THE

MANCHESTER ART TREASURES

AND SCENES FROM ALL THE PRINCIPAL

TRAGEDIES, DRAMAS, OPERAS.

&c.,

Dresses for which are of the most Magnificent Description,

Open Every Evening at 7,

And after the Theatres.

Mr. HILTON,

THE CELEBRATED VENTRILOQUIST,

Will open his Original, Musical, Eccentrical, Characteristical, and Mirth-provoking BUDGET of VENTRILOQUIAL WONDERS, EVERY EVENING.

Chops, Steaks, Kidneys, &c., always Ready.

Figure 7. Handbill advertising Mme. Pauline's tableaux vivants at the Coal Hole Tavern, London, probably during the 1840s. (Harvard Theatre Collection, Harvard College Library.)

some 3 months," the police raided the hall and arrested most of the models, as well as the manager, St. Luke.[11] This action did not stop the exhibitions, however, and St. Luke continued his performances into May. In 1853 he moved to new quarters across Sixth Avenue from the newly constructed Crystal Palace. Here he featured "Madame Devulti, the most beautiful woman in the profession," appearing "as Titian's Venus, Cleopatra, The Goddess Juno" with "an entire troupe of model artists... composed of Italian, English, and Spanish ladies."[12]

St. Luke's operation apparently was looked upon by George Lea as serious competition, for his advertising carried the following warning:

> FRANKLIN MUSEUM, 175 Chatham Square.—
> Caution to visitors to the Crystal Palace.—
> The proprietor of the Franklin begs to notify strangers visiting New York that he is in no way connected with a place kept by St. Luke, opposite the main entrance, in Sixth avenue, designated "Living Models." He deems that above caution necessary, as it is generally supposed that it is my concern, St. Luke seeming to dislike placing his name before the public as a proprietor. The Franklin Museum is the only establishment I have any connection with, having been established "by myself alone" over five years; and if strangers wish to see the "real genuine Model Artists," and other sights of this great city, they must not forget to visit us in the afternoon or evening.[13]

Such advertisements containing special announcements for the Franklin Museum were part of a consistent publicity campaign. Lea's advertising technique was to run a "standard" advertisement almost every day and to augment that with additional ads. The "standard" advertisement read as follows:

> FRANKLIN MUSEUM, 175 Chatham Square.—Two performances are given daily, commencing at 3 o'clock in the afternoon and half past 7 in the evening. The above is the only establishment in the United States where the Model Artists are exhibited, together with a great variety of unique and original entertainments, such as can be seen at no other place of amusement in the world.[14]

The additional advertisements listed special features of the week, attacked competitors, or announced benefits for members of the company. For example, on 12 February 1854, the following additional advertisement appeared in the *Herald* immediately below the "standard" one:

> FRANKLIN MUSEUM, 175 CHATHAM SQUARE.—Extra advertisement—Monday, February 13, both in the afternoon and evening, a great bill of entertainment will be offered, being for the BENEFIT OF MISS CLIFFORD, on which occasion over THIRTY YOUNG LADIES have kindly volunteered to appear in the "Model Artists," and will introduce a number of favorite pictures, including "Powers' Greek Slave," "The Three Graces," "Venus Rising from the Sea," "Adam and Eve," with fourteen other splendid representations, &c. Prices of admission will be the same as usual.

While Lea's claim, in his standard advertisement, that he was "the only establishment in the United States where the Model Artists are exhibited" may to some extent, be taken as puffery, no other theatre was advertising tableaux at the time. Even John St. Luke's Temple of the Graces had been vanquished by 1854. It was likely, of course, that there were private productions during the period.

In April 1854 Lea transferred his operation to White's Melodeon, 53 Bowery, a house he had acquired by lease nearly two years earlier, in June 1852. For a short time after leasing the property he had operated it under the title, "Palace of Beauty," along the same lines as the Franklin Museum, featuring the "Bloomer Troupe" in songs, dances, and "groupings of living marble statuary."[15] At the end of September, however, he rented the Melodeon to Charles White and concentrated his efforts on the "museum" in Chatham Sqaure. On 22 April 1854 the final performance took place at 175 Chatham Square, and two days later Lea's tableaux began appearing at 53 Bowery which was immediately also named the Franklin Museum.[16] For a short time in November he moved operations to the old St. Charles Theatre, formerly White's Varieties, at 17-19 Bowery while renovation took place at 53 Bowery.

During 1855, the Franklin Museum tableaux continued unabated, with numerous benefit performances announced for Lea himself and for members of the model artist troupe. Among the names which appeared were Miss Mary Moore (7 May), Herr von Spigalin (11 May), Miss Young (23 July), Miss Fannie Coles (31 July), Miss Julia Leslie (1 September), Miss Henrietta Thompson (5 October), and Adolphe Lea (28 January 1856). At each of these benefits it was announced that an especially large company of model artists would perform. George Lea's benefit on 4 August 1855 was listed as the "last day of the season," but the advertisement on Sunday, 5 August, proclaimed "ONE WEEK MORE, and positively the last chance of seeing the 'Model Artists'... Twenty splendid living tableaux, including all the best in original pictures of the season, will be represented." Then 9 August was called the "last chance of seeing the model artists." Yet the house probably never did cease tableau presentations, for the "standard" ad continues every day, and fifteen new tableaux were announced the following week.[17]

In spite of the fact that Lea continued to claim that his was the only establishment where the model artists were exhibited, he was, in fact, faced with serious competition in 1855. As the new year began, a Monsieur or Professor Fleur "of Paris" entered the field with a troupe "just arrived from Europe."[18] He presented "French and Italian Model Artists" at the International Museum, 51 Division Street, and included in his exhibition such provocative pictures as "Bride's Dressing Chamber," "Suzanna Surprised in Bath," "Venus and Playmate in the Bath," and "Rape of the Sabines."[19] On 7 May Professor Fleur, joined by a Senor Gar, moved to the Gothic Museum, 316 Broadway, where they announced "popular groups of flying living pictures."[20] Just what "flying" pictures were is not explained in either advertising or commentary, but the idea certainly suggests a fascinating novelty. In August Professor Fleur again moved with his troupe to Grand Street Hall, 127 Grand Street.[21]

In the meantime, tableaux continued at the Gothic Museum after that house advertised for "a few young ladies wanted" to appear as model artists.[22] Possibly Senor Gar had remained behind when Professor Fleur moved out. The name of the place was soon changed to "Temple of the Muses—Gothic Hall," and by September it was featuring "'Posees [sic] Plastiques,' 'Tableaux Vivants,' 'Classic Statuary,'... by MADAME WARTON'S TROUPE of LIVING FEMALES."[23] Interestingly, at the same time, both Grand Street Hall and Temple of the Muses listed Madame Warton's trope on their bills, and, it will be recalled, she was also listed earlier by Lea at the Franklin Museum. (See Figures 8 and 9.)

Of the three houses competing for tableau audiences during the 1855 season, the Temple of the Muses was decidedly the most sensational in its advertising. Both Grand Street Hall and the Franklin ran "standard" ads, augmenting these from time to time with rather straight-forward announcements of benefits, new pictures to be introduced, and similar special features. The Temple of the Muses, on the other hand, changed the text of its advertisements constantly and emphasized the risqué and daring. Two examples from the *Herald* will illustrate:

> FREE LOVE—FREE LOVE.—DO YOU WANT TO BE amused. Visit the TEMPLE OF THE MUSES, 316 BROADWAY, in the afternoon at 3, or in the evening at 7, and you can see some of the "handsomest women" in the world. Cards of admission, 25 cents, which entitles gentlemen to see the entire performance without extra charge.[24]

> "DO YOU WANT TO SEE PRETTY WOMEN?" IF SO, go in the afternoon at 3 or in the evening at 7, to the TEMPLE OF THE MUSES, 316 BROADWAY, and you can be initiated into the MYSTERIES OF "FREE LOVE," without extra charge.[25]

By the beginning of 1856 Grand Street Hall had ceased to advertise model artists, so that, seemingly, only the Franklin Museum and Temple of the Muses were presenting them. Then in February 1856 George Lea announced that his Franklin Museum at 53 Bowery would be "closed for a short time," and that "during the recess the entire company of Model Artists, with the usual entertainment, will be given every afternoon at 3 and evening at 7, at the Temple of The Muses."[26] In early March the Franklin re-opened briefly, but then Lea announced that "the premises are going to be used for other business, and the last performance will take place on Monday, March 31, being... positively the very last chance of seeing the Model Artistes, when one hundred young ladies will appear, with other entertainments, the whole being a grand closing festival."[27]

THE PROGRAMME IS CHANGED EVERY WEEK.

THE ELEGANT
PROMENADE.

Eighty Feet in Length, will be Open, and between the First and Second Parts, **SELECTIONS** from the Works of the most admired Composers, will be performed by a

COMPLETE ORCHESTRA,
Under the Direction of HERR REDL.

MADAME WARTON
Will appear in VENUS VICTORIOUS, THE EXPULSION FROM THE GARDEN OF EDEN, DAPHNIE AND CHLOE, A NYMPH, ARIADNE, &c., &c.

MORNING PROGRAMME.
PART I.

1. The Infant Hercules	Sir J. Reynolds, R.A.
2. Messalina's Offerings to Venus and Cupid	Angelica Kauffman
3. Mercury Instructing Cupid in the presence of Venus	Correggio
4. The Continence of Scipio	N. Poussin
5. Daphnies and Chloe	Madame Warton
6. Juno, Jupiter, Venus, and the Graces	Flaxman, R.A.
7. A Nymph	Canova
8. Diana and Actoeon	Frost

PART II.

1. The Rape of the Sabines	David
2. Ariadne ...Personated by Madame Warton	Dannecker
3. A Groupe from the Celebrated Oxford Window, Designed by Sir J. Reynolds, R.A. Comprising (Faith, Hope, Charity, Justice, Prudence, Temperance and Fortitude)	
4. Cephalus and Aurora	N. Poussin
5. A Bacchanalian Dance	N. Poussin
6. The Lute Player ...Personated by Madame Warton	Hyldabrandt
7. Tableau, Finale, in Honour to England	Madame Warton

EVENING PROGRAMME.
PART I.
WHITE MARBLE.

1. The Iron Age	Flaxman, R.A.
2. Mars and Venus	Canova
3. Briseis Delivered to the Heralds	Flaxman, R.A.
4. Mercury taunting Argus	Girodet
5. Diana ...Personated by Madame Wharton	Antique
6. The Death of Priam	Canova
7. The Judgment of Paris	Flaxman, R.A.
8. The Death of Virginius ...Now exhibiting in the R. A. Exhibition	Mac Dowell, R.A.
9. Combat between Idas and Apollo ...in three Tableaux	Antique

A QUARTER OF AN HOUR WILL ELAPSE BETWEEN THE FIRST AND SECOND PART.

PART II.
IN COLOURS.

1. Rape of the Sabines	David
2. Venus Victorious ...Personated by Madame Warton	Gibson, R.A.
3. A Groupe from the Celebrated Oxford Window, Designed by Sir J. Reynolds, R.A. Comprising (Faith, Hope, Charity, Justice, Prudence, Temperance and Fortitude)	
4. The Expulsion from the Garden of Eden	Serveline
5. Mercury Instructing Cupid in the presence of Venus	Correggio
6. Juno, Jupiter, Venus, and the Graces	Flaxman, R.A.
7. Amazonian Triumph	David
8. The Lute Player ...Personated by Madame Warton	Hyldabrandt
9. Tableau, Finale, in Honour to England	Madame Warton

Each Tableau will be accompanied with Descriptive Music by a Band of First-Rate Talent,

Conducted by Herr REDL.

Season Tickets, Reserved Seats & Stalls, may be taken daily at the Gallery, from 1 till 3.
MORNING PERFORMANCE AT 3. EVENING, HALF-PAST 8.
ADMISSION, 1s. RESERVED SEATS, 2s. STALLS, 3s.

J. W. PEEL's Steam Machine, 74, New Cut, Lambeth, Nine Doors from Cornwall Road.

Figure 8. Side one of a playbill for the Walhalla, London, listing Madame Warton's tableaux, probably during the 1840s. (Harvard Theatre Collection, Harvard College Library.)

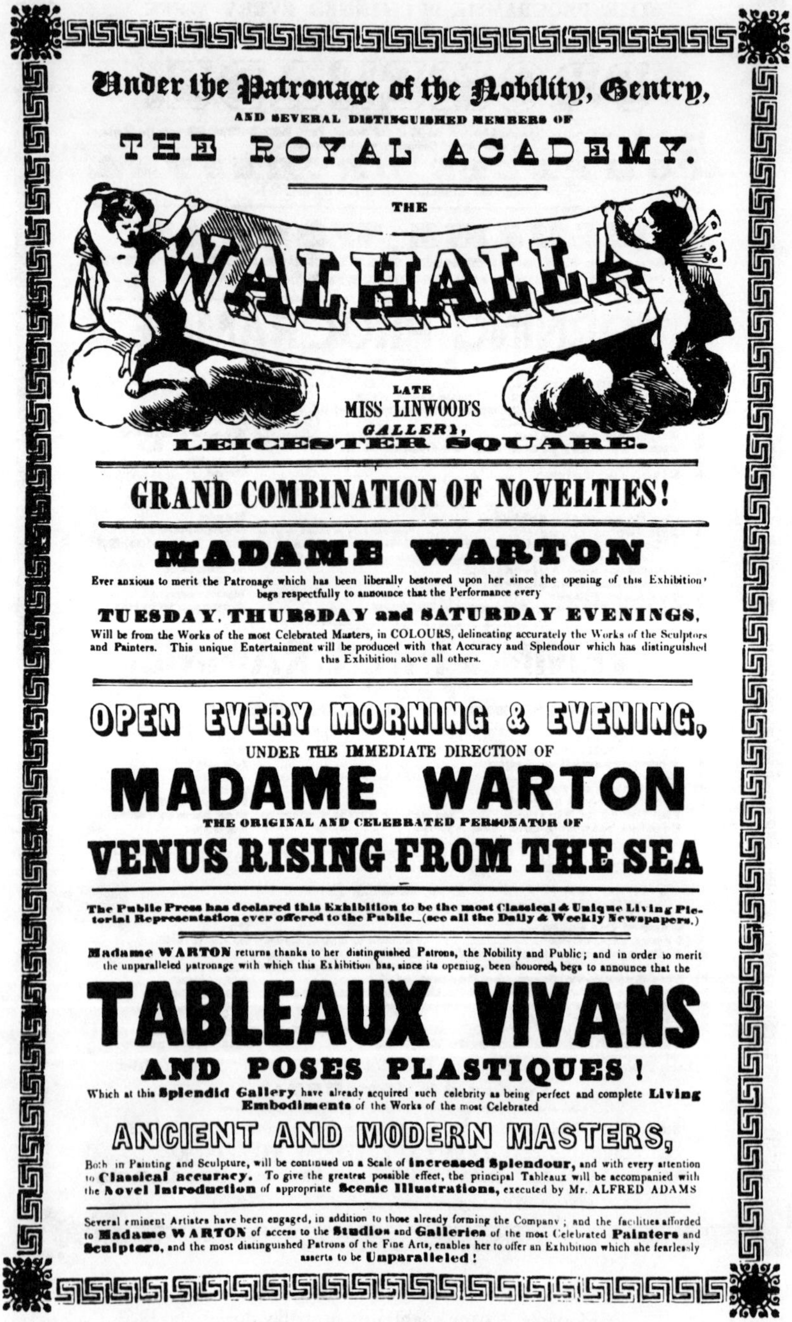

Under the Patronage of the Nobility, Gentry,

AND SEVERAL DISTINGUISHED MEMBERS OF

THE ROYAL ACADEMY.

THE

WALHALLA

LATE

MISS LINWOOD'S

GALLERY,

LEICESTER SQUARE.

GRAND COMBINATION OF NOVELTIES!

MADAME WARTON

Ever anxious to merit the Patronage which has been liberally bestowed upon her since the opening of this Exhibition' begs respectfully to announce that the Performance every

TUESDAY, THURSDAY and SATURDAY EVENINGS,

Will be from the Works of the most Celebrated Masters, in COLOURS, delineating accurately the Works of the Sculptors and Painters. This unique Entertainment will be produced with that Accuracy and Splendour which has distinguished this Exhibition above all others.

OPEN EVERY MORNING & EVENING,

UNDER THE IMMEDIATE DIRECTION OF

MADAME WARTON

THE ORIGINAL AND CELEBRATED PERSONATOR OF

VENUS RISING FROM THE SEA

The Public Press has declared this Exhibition to be the most Classical & Unique Living Pictorial Representation ever offered to the Public_(see all the Daily & Weekly Newspapers.)

Madame WARTON returns thanks to her distinguished Patrons, the Nobility and Public; and in order to merit the unparalleled patronage with which this Exhibition has, since its opening, been honored, begs to announce that the

TABLEAUX VIVANS

AND POSES PLASTIQUES!

Which at this Splendid Gallery have already acquired such celebrity as being perfect and complete Living Embodiments of the Works of the most Celebrated

ANCIENT AND MODERN MASTERS,

Both in Painting and Sculpture, will be continued on a Scale of Increased Splendour, and with every attention to Classical accuracy. To give the greatest possible effect, the principal Tableaux will be accompanied with the Novel Introduction of appropriate Scenic Illustrations, executed by Mr. ALFRED ADAMS

Several eminent Artistes have been engaged, in addition to those already forming the Company; and the facilities afforded to Madame WARTON of access to the Studios and Galleries of the most Celebrated Painters and Sculptors, and the most distinguished Patrons of the Fine Arts, enables her to offer an Exhibition which she fearlessly asserts to be Unparalleled!

Figure 9. Side two of the playbill shown in Figure 8.

Now, the Temple of the Muses was able to gloat, "THE FIELD TO OURSELVES AGAIN.—THE ONLY troupe of Model Artists now exhibiting in New York is at the Temple of the Muses, 316 Broadway, where Madame Warton's original company of artistes, twenty-seven in number, appear every afternoon and evening."[28] In reality, however, it appears that George Lea had simply absorbed his competition, for these productions, too, soon closed, with the announcement that "after May Madame Warton's company will remove to the Franklin Museum, 127 Grand Street, near Broadway."[29] It will be noted that this was the address of the old Grand Street Hall. George Lea had now occupied it, and, following his prior practice, had renamed it the Franklin Museum. Thus, Lea had successfully supplanted his competitor, Professor Fleur, and then adopted the company from Temple of the Muses, leaving himself in sole control.

Lea's exhibitions continued in the same style as before. In the fall he was announcing such tableaux as "The Three Graces," "Adam and Eve," "Judith and Holofernes," "Sappho," "Temptation," and the ever-popular "Venus Rising from the Sea."[30] These once again aroused official objections, however, and in October 1856, another brief attempt was made to close the show:

> Half-a-dozen detailed policemen made a "descent" on Friday night upon a place called the "Franklin Museum," in Grand-street, near Broadway, and arrested four or five young girls who were exhibiting themselves, in a state of semi-nudity, before a crowded and admiring house. The policemen were dressed in citizens' dress, and their presence was not known until near the close of the performance, when, just as "Venus" was "rising from the sea," the policemen rose from their seats, leaped upon the stage and arrested the fair artistes. Neither the proprietor nor any of the masculine assistants were arrested.[31]

One wonders at the methods used by the police in this instance, for the article goes on to report:

> The female prisoners were escorted, attired only in tights and gauze dresses, to the Eighth Ward Station House, followed by a large crowd of men and boys, who wondered much at such a novel exhibition in the public streets, and one for seeing which they had nothing to par [pay].
>
> The next morning they were again escorted through the public streets in stage attire to the office of the Mayor, followed as before by an immense crowd.
>
> The poor creatures seemed to feel keenly their mortifying position, and some of them wept bitterly.

Such treatment was not unusual, however, and the sensational march through the streets became a commonplace adjunct to model artist arrests.

Press reports of the models' replies to police questioning give some details of the performers' lives and the operation of the tableau exhibition. Their pay ranged from four to five dollars per week, and "the variation in pay was governed by the difference in good looks." Although they were employed by

George Lea, they were paid by one Charles Bied, "who sells the admission tickets." They claimed that "they would not be allowed to appear unless clad in a suit of flesh-colored tights and a thin gauze skirt, which they each had to pay four dollars for." Each girl emphasized that she had led a virtuous life, and "they exhibited themselves merely to gain a livelihood." One claimed to have been a tailoress before beginning modeling; another was a paper-box maker; and most claimed to be the sole support of step-mothers, husbands, or other relatives.[32]

Although the models were "held in the sum of $200 for their future good behavior," this did not deter the continuation of tableaux at the Franklin Museum (see Figure 10). The only closing which occurred was January 1857 due to the severe weather, a condition which affected other theatres as well.

Indeed the attitude of the authorities toward model artists, and their attempts to suppress the exhibitions seem to have been rather ambivalent. Such raids were usually initiated, not by the officials themselves, but by the occasional complaints of concerned citizens. A newspaper editorial about the incident at the Franklin Museum characterized the official attitude as "A Moral Spasm," and objected to the city administration's action:

> There are victims of police justice. Poor young girls,—with fathers, mothers, and children to support,—driven by their poverty to earning four or five dollars a week in this way. It certainly is not a very creditable mode of life, and ought undoubtedly to be suppressed, though it is better than the one into which police justice will drive them. But where are their employers? Why are the men who hire them, and compel them to dress in "flesh tights and thin gauze," permitted to go unmolested? Why were their male attendants in the same scenes allowed to walk off unarrested...? Was it part of their orders to let all voters go free?
> ...But such sham displays as these;—which take effect only upon the weak and the poor,—which fall upon women and children, and leave the guilty and the strong to go unpunished,—excite only disgust and contempt. MAYOR WOOD should remember... that we are just upon the eve of an election, and that his acts will be subjected to closer scrutiny than ever before.[33]

Other sporadic attacks were made by the police, but these were to stop more scandalous private exhibitions rather than those in public halls. What was termed "warfare against model artist establishments" took place in January and February 1858. As a result of a raid at August Myer's Francisco Hotel, 13 Howard Street, the proprietor and his wife were each held in $500 bail on the charge of keeping a disorderly house, and four of the female models were given six months jail sentences.[34] When the police "descended" upon a private exhibition at 463 Broome Street, it was reported that the models arrested there "were entirely nude" and attempted to bribe the officers in order to avoid arrest.[35]

In spite of such attacks upon the private, and probably more daring, model artists, George Lea's Franklin Museum was able to continue operations without further interference. In fact, it is interesting to note that the attitude of

Figure 10.
Playbill for the Franklin Museum, dated in pencil 18 August 1858, announcing a program of "Living Statuary." (Harvard Theatre Collection, Harvard College Library.) "The Three Graces," of course, provided a favorite subject for many producers and was probably part of the standard repertoire for George Lea and for Mme. Warton. Several of the statuary titles listed in this bill appear to repeat presentations included in Mme. Warton's London exhibition shown in Figures 8 and 9. Note also the similarity between this illustration and the earlier one shown in Figure 6. Possibly this "Three Graces" pose had become so popular that the picture had been made into a stock advertising cut by theatrical printers.

the press toward Lea's work was quite tolerant. Whether he had modified the sensationalism of his presentations or the attitudes toward them had become more liberal is difficult to tell. Nevertheless, it is clear that, even in reports of the October 1856 arrests, there is little condemnation of the exhibits themselves. Instead, press sympathy is noticeably with the model artists; the police appear as the villains.

While Lea's Franklin Museum hardly provided an atmosphere of refinement, it was apparently looked upon as being within the bounds of decency. The following graphic account of an evening spent at the Franklin seems to strike such a critical balance:

> In a long - narrow hall, with a very low ceiling, the audience come to see the Model Artists assemble.... It is indeed the shabbiest of theatres. The painting is a mass of daub, the velvet looks secondhand, the floor is filthy, and the smell is overpowering. Even here however, there is an aristocracy of arrangements in regard to prices. There are orchestra stalls at 50 cents, boxes at 25 cents, a gallery at 12 cents, and private boxes (Heaven save the mark!) at prices which I did not enquire all comprised in a space not more than twelve feet high at the highest. On the back row a person with obscene books in an oil-skin wrapper covertly offers them for sale, and perhaps succeeds to sell them; but beyond this there is nothing whatever obscene or even lewd in the performances. They are simply coarse, and evincing as much of ignorance as of the lowest kind of taste. Five white girls, of ages varying, apparently, from 17 to 40, sing Ethiopian song.... After the Ethiopian exhibition comes a person with one eye, who, after going through a series of gymnastic evolutions, concludes by breaking a cobblestone by a blow with his fist.... Following this is the principal feature of the entertainment—namely, the Model Artists. Why they are so called would be difficult to determine. Artists they certainly are not, even in the least reasonable acceptation of the term. Models they are not, of anything in the world, except an entire gracelessness and considerable awkwardness. They are by no means well-shaped women; They certainly are not pretty, and their postures are anything rather than elegant. At the same time there is not anything indecent in their costume or in their attitudes. They are dressed very much after the manner of opera girls, except that from the neck to the waist they are habited in what are technically known as fleshings. These however, do not show any more of the natural form than do the *jupons* of the danseuses of the ballet, which nobody deems indecent. Their postures, though inelegant and ridiculous, have nothing prurient about them. The objects selected are usually classical, and therefore entirely beyond the comprehension of these poor creatures who nightly represent "Venus rising from the Sea," and "The Three Graces," without having the most remote idea of who Venus was, or where the Three Graces came from.... It may not be uninteresting to add, as a topographical fact, that Gudney's saloon, ... being directly under the theatre of the Model Artists, the music and applause from the former resort are distinctly heard in the latter, so that I had the gratification of seeing Venus rise from the sea to the tune of "Hopty-Dooden-Doo."[36]

It is clear in this account that the observer takes great pains to distinguish between coarseness on the one hand and indecency or immorality on the other. While he certainly does not deem the Franklin to be a "temple of high art," he is also cautious to state that the performances are not "obscene," "lewd," or "indecent."

George Lea's long tableau vivant career continued until 27 June 1860, when he relinquished management of the Franklin for the last time, and the building was converted into a restaurant. Thus, his activity, in a sense, provides a transition from the sensationalism of the early 1850's to a more acceptable decorum at the end of the decade. This transition, however, was not his doing alone, for other producers had appeared along the way. Two of these, Louis Keller and the well-known and respected Laura Keene, had promoted the artistic approach to tableaux.

Louis Keller entered the arena at the Broadway Theatre on 31 March 1856 with a production entitled *Phanor and Azemas; or, The Two Eras*. Advertising announced that, "in the course of the piece and incidental to the same the great tableaux by the Keller troupe" would be presented.[37] Billed as an "allegorical and mythic spectacle," the reviewer's summary shows it to be a simple plot providing an excuse for the tableaux:

> Phanor, a young and wealthy noble of Athens, loves Azemas, a poor orphan girl, and is loved in return. Agias, a friend of Phanor, loves Azemas, and conspires with Anastasia, Queen of the Isles of Pleasure, who loves Phanor, to entice him to her grotto, where she begiles him with wondrous sights, among which are the tableaux, which are the feature of the piece.[38]

The production achieved some literary stature by virtue of its being a translation of a French piece by Rovere, and to further insure his acceptance, Keller claimed to have the endorsement of "a number of the crowned heads of Europe."[39] In addition, at the conclusion of each performance he adopted the practice of distributing "several hundred bouquets to the audience." The production was an instant success, extravagantly praised in the press and, apparently, heartily applauded by the public. The tableaux included less provocative subjects than those seen elsewhere in New York—"The Triumph of Galatea," "Golden Shower," "Battle of the Amazons," "Faith, Hope and Charity," and the concluding picture, "Washington Crossing the Delaware." "The tableaux by the Keller Troupe are in the highest degree artistic, and utterly free from grossness," sighed the *New York Times*.[40] The *Herald* reviewer said, "As a pure school of art, to gratify the eye and at the same time not to offend the moral sense, Mr. Keller's living pictures are of exceeding value. Certainly nothing half so pleasing was ever seen before."[41]

Keller went to considerable trouble to avoid criticism by surrounding his production with an artistic aura. On Saturday afternoon, 5 April 1856, at the end of this first week, he held a "public rehearsal" of new tableaux to be added to the bill the following Monday. The event was attended by "the *elite* of the learned professions, a large number of artists," and "several eminent divines." All of these "agreed in the warmest commendation of the exhibition." Among the new pictures were the patriotic "True Glory" and "Washington's Triumphal

Entry into Trenton" and the religious "Suffer the Little Children to Come Unto me" and "The Descent from the Cross."[42]

In spite of such caution, it was reported that one "Protestant newspaper" denounced the representation of Rubens' "Descent from the Cross," and to counteract any possible consequences of this, Keller had his stage manager, a Mr. Blake, address the audience before the performance on Monday night. Blake pointed out that "the exhibition has been given in Europe and received with favor" and went on to report the approval of "the *elite* of the city" at the Saturday rehearsal. Finally, "any person who did not desire to see the exhibition" was offered a refund of his ticket cost. The newspaper account of the evening reports that "Mr. Blake's speech was received with prolonged applause, and the exhibition proceeded very successfully." The Rubens picture was said to excite "emotions which the pulpit might envy."[43]

Not only did Keller received the highest of praise from a delighted press, he was also openly lauded by influential members of the community, as the following letter, published in the *New York Times,* attests:

> LOUIS KELLER, ESQ.—Dear Sir: We have seen your tableaux vivants and desire thus publicly to acknowledge our sense of their great classic beauty, and of their position as embodiments and representations of the great world-renowned master-pieces of art.
>
> Will you, Sir, receive from us, artists residing in New-York, a complimentary benefit, as a slight testimonial of gratitude for the pleasure you have given us by your new manifestation of the eternal beauty of those works, by your successful effort to advance and elevate the taste for the divine labors of the painter, the sculptor and the poet.
>
> We will most cordially exercise what influence we may have to render such benefit as beneficial to you as your representations have been delightful to us; and confident of the public taste and love of art, we cannot for a moment doubt that the cooperation of nearly all our citizens will be given to us, and prove to you how well we can appreciate those endeavors of yours to popularize and extend more widely the influence and the knowledge of inspired art.

C.L. Elliott,	W.H. Moore,
Geo. H. Jewell,	W.W. Watherspoon,
Alanson Fisher	Alex. Ransom,
Joseph Kyle,	G. Sicord David,
J.C. Hagen,	Samuel R. Fanshaw,
George Freeman,	F. D'Avignon.

JAMES H. CAFERTY, Secretary,
NEW—YORK UNIVERSITY, April 6, 1856.[44]

After this auspicious beginning, Keller left the Broadway Theatre to open his own house. He took over Empire Hall at 506 Broadway, which had, since 1853, been occupied by the popular panorama exhibit, "Banvard's Pilgrimage to Jerusalem." During the remainder of April, he renovated the hall extensively, installing "about six hundred good seats and five private boxes, very nicely fitted up," and improving the stage arrangements.[45] The opening, which took place on Monday, 5 May 1856, was eagerly awaited. Advertisements for the opening provided the full playbill:

EMPIRE HALL, 596 BROADWAY, two doors above the Metropolitan Hotel.
TRIUMPH OF ART
Louis Keller respectfully announces to the public that he has leased the above place, which has been appropriately fitted up and decorated expressly for the purpose of presenting his second series of
GRAND TABLEAUX SOIREES,
Exhibiting all that is famous and refined in the arts of
PAINTING AND SCULPTURE
Either sacred, moral, mythological, or historical, together with national subjects of more recent interest, forming at once one of the most beautiful and intellectual entertainments for the approval of an enlightened people.

Mr. Keller also intimates, that in order to render the effect of his pictures more perfect by the aid of music and decorations, independently of the enormous expenditure of his own troupe of
TWENTY-SEVEN ARTISTS,
He has engaged talented persons in the various departments of scenery, machinery, &c., including a full and
SUPERIOR ORCHESTRA,
Conducted by .... Mr. Grille
The first performance will take place ON MONDAY EVENING, MAY 5, AND BE CONTINUED EVERY EVENING DURING THE WEEK.

Programme.
Part I
Overture by the orchestra.
"Fra Diavolo" .... Auber
First Tableau
   The Chariot of the Sun ....
Music.
   "Life's Pulse Waltz" .... Lanner
Second Tableau
   Adriadne and Bacchus .... Composed by Mad. Keller
Music, "Pepita Polka" .... M. Grille
Third Tableau
   Famine .... Composed by M. Keller
Music from "Lucrezia Borgia" .... Donizetti
Fourth Tableau
   The Shower of Gold .... Composed by Mme. Keller
Part II.
Overture, "Le Macon" .... Auber
First Tableau
   The Massacre of the Innocents ....
Music, "Musen Quadrille" .... Strauss
Second Tableau
   L'Esperanza .... after Paul Dalaroche.
Music, "Lorley Melodies" .... Strauss
Third Tableau.
   True Glory .... Composed by M. Keller.
Music, "Nationale" ....
Finale.
The Great National Tableau.
   THE BATTLE OF BUNKER HILL, after Turnbull.
Music, "Hail Columbia."

The programme will be changed weekly. The repertoire of Mr. Keller consists of upwards of 3000 pictures, thus enabling him to present an ever varying source of interest and attraction.
Doors open at 7 o'clock. Overture will begin at 8 o'clock.
Tickets 50 cents. Private boxes $5.
Arrangements can be made for the admission of schools and societies, by application at the Hall between the hours of 10 and 4.[46]

Even before the opening, the *Herald* was encouraging "artists, connoisseurs and the public in general" to attend these "beautiful and instructive entertainments,"[47] and expressing confidence "that M. Keller's efforts to present the works of the great masters of *les Beaux arts* will be appreciated and rewarded."[48] Later, Keller's production was called "refined and chastely artistic,"[49] and by the end of May it was observed that his audiences were "steadily increasing."[50]

The second week of Keller's production, the concluding spectacle of "The Battle of Bunker Hill" was replaced by Leutze's "Washington Crossing the Delaware." (See Figures 11 and 12.) Since this painting is so familiar, even today, perhaps it may be useful to speculate for a moment about how this famous work might have been represented as a tableau vivant.

The picture was well-known to New York audiences; it had been painted in 1851 and had been exhibited in the city repeatedly since that time.[51] Its enormous size—twenty-one feet wide by twelve feet high—made it an ideal choice for a tableau, since the figures are nearly life-size in the original.

Empire Hall was not a conventional theatre, but rather an exhibit room which had previously been used for a panorama display. Although Keller's renovations included installation of seats and boxes, the place was still sometimes referred to as a "saloon," suggesting that the arrangement may have included tables rather than regular auditorium seating. Such an arrangement would spread "six hundred good seats" over a fairly large area. Therefore, it seems likely that the stage opening for tableaux might have been rather wide, in order to accommodate the necessary sight lines of a large auditorium. In any case, it probably exceeded the painting's twenty-one feet of width.

Although later tableaux employed an actual picture frame, arranged much like a false proscenium, there is no record that Keller did so. Probably he followed the customary practice of the day by having curtains drawn aside to reveal the living picture.

Of course, before the curtains parted, Keller or his stage manager would be busily checking the poses of the dozen or so models employed in the tableau. To do this accurately, he would have had to secure a reproduction of the painting—no small task in the days before photography and Xerox machines. Perhaps Keller hired an artist to sketch or paint a copy of the painting while it was being exhibited, or, possibly, he was able to purchase an early chromolithograph of the work. Such reproductions were becoming popular in New York during the 1850's, having been introduced to America in 1840.[52]

For the tableau itself, both two- and three-dimensional scenic techniques would be combined. A set piece, constructed to look like an actual Durham boat, would be filled with live models costumed as shown in the painting, and holding actual props—oars, rifles, the flag, etc. For the central figure of George Washington, a model would have been chosen both for his physical resemblance to the painting—especially the profile—and for his ability to project an appropriate look of determined resolution. Fabric used for the flag, scarves, cloaks, and the like, would be stiffened with sizing and paint in order to hold the folds and contours which would make it appear to be blown by the wind. The ice floes in the foreground might well have been papier mâché constructions, although painted two-dimensional profile pieces could also have been used. Three-dimensional pieces seem more likely in this case, however, to facilitate the pose of the soldier in the prow with his pole on one chunk of ice and his foot on another. The water was probably suggested by means of one or more large pieces of lightweight fabric, with holes through which the oars were placed. The background scene would almost surely have been a flat, painted drop, located just upstage of the boat, depicting the distant expanse of river and shoreline, the other barges and boats, and the stormy sky. Lighting for the scene required fairly cool hues and probably made use of limelight, or Drummond lights, offstage right, with general illumination by gaslight to fill in the shadows. Such special effects as the rays of light shining through the storm clouds would have been painted directly on the backdrop.

Finally, the stirring strains of "Hail Columbia" were provided by Mr. Grille's orchestra as an introduction to the tableau and probably as an accompaniment for it. Although musical performers were usually listed on the bills with tableaux at other theatres, Keller made a special point of indicating the selections to be played (See his programme above). In addition, his advertising gave prominent billing to the musical performers—Mr. Grille, the orchestra leader; Madame Lovarny and Miss Maria Duckworth, vocalists; the Germania Quartette; and Alexander Stoepel, tenor.

If the tableau were truly elaborate, it might have included some other refinements, though these are less likely than those described above. For instance, the entire picture could easily have "come to life." A simple rocker mechanism would cause the boat to pitch and dip. The ice floes could be mobile, equipped with wheels, and operated from the wings by means of ropes hidden below the "water line." The water line would then consist of overlapping strips of fabric extending the width of the stage and kept in billowing motion by stagehands in the wings. Actual wind might even be produced by a fan, although that is unlikely, since mechanical, rather than electrical, power would have been required to turn it in 1856. Finally, even the

Figure 11. *Washington Crossing the Delaware* (1851), oil on canvas, by Emanuel Leutze. (Photo by the author of the copy on exhibit at the Memorial Building, Washington Crossing, Pennsylvania.)

Figure 12. Tableau vivant of *Washington Crossing the Delaware*, presented at the fifth Washington Crossing Assembly, held at the Union League of Philadelphia, 29 October 1982. The "poseurs" include prominent business people, government officials, and officers and members of the Washington Crossing Foundation. (Courtesy of the Washington Crossing Foundation.)

painted backdrop might have moved laterally by means of panorama rolls, thus causing Washington to seem to be moving across the river. Of course, in this case, the other boats and barges would have to be depicted on a separate profile piece in front of the moving drop.

All the techniques and devices here described were available to the mid-nineteenth century producer. While there is no assurance that Keller actually employed all of these methods, it seems probable that he must have used many of them. Whatever his techniques, they were sufficient to thrill and impress his audiences—audiences who were undoubtedly familiar with such common scenic devices.

True to his promise made in early advertising, several of Keller's tableaux were changed each week, although the general format remained constant. Few of the traditionally sensational representations were included—"Venus" did not often "rise from the sea" here—and there was a liberal sprinkling of such moralistic and sentimental subjects as "Faith, Hope, and Charity" and "Time and Poetry." The concluding number was always a patriotic spectacle; "The Battle of Bunker Hill" was replaced by "Washington Crossing the Delaware," and later by "Washington Entering New York in Triumph." Clearly, these were selections to avoid the charges of immorality which had plagued earlier living models. The only reviewer who suggested even a hint of skepticism was the writer in the New York *Clipper*, who somewhat cryptically observed, "Keller's Empire Hall is now well under way upon a successful experiment, and we think that the public mind can always correct or manage its own standard of taste, without the interference of self-constituted censors."[53] The "censors," however, made no move in Keller's direction, and his tableaux continued successfully at Empire Hall until 31 July 1856 when the "Farewell benefit and positively last appearance in New York" was held. His concluding tableau for the event was "The American Patriot, or Last Moment in Havana," described as "a vivid illustration of one of the most thrilling events that ever occurred on the island of Cuba."[54]

Keller next took his troupe on tour, returning to New York for an engagement at Niblo's Garden which opened 20 June 1859 for a two-week run. Keller appeared in the cast of *The War In Italy; or, Napoleon I and Napoleon II*, a spectacle which included the following tableaux vivants: "Napoleon at St. Helena," "Embarkation of the French Army," "The Soldier's Dream," "La Alliance," and a "Grand Allegory" which pictured numerous military heroes.[55] Reviews of the opening praised the tableaux but had little to say of the "play." The *Tribune's* comment is typical; "The less that is said of the literary merits of the play the better—it was merely intended as the vehicle for the admirable tableaux of the Keller Troupe, which purpose it answered excellently."[56]

Louis Keller seems to have been especially influential in creating a sense of artistic stature for this form of entertainment at a time when such approval was sorely needed. Subsequent references to "tableaux in the style of Keller" identified a praiseworthy exhibition which did not carry the stigma of either immorality or tawdry production, but indicated artistic spectacle instead. Even the famous Madame Warton described her own tableaux as "arranged after the style of J. Keller's."[57]

At the same time, one other well-known theatrical figure, Laura Keene, adopted the tableau form as part of her introduction to a career in management. She incorporated tableaux into a "rhythmical, musical, scenic, dramatic, extravaganza," called *Novelty*, produced in February 1856 at Laura Keene's Varieties in Tripler Hall. Conceived as a special Washington's Birthday offering, the production consisted of ten tableaux, the last of which was a patriotic spectacle, "The Apotheosis of Washington."[58] On 23 April she produced *The Marble Heart*, an afterpiece reminiscent in format of the old *Raphael's Dream*, including representations of living statuary. Although, in June, Laura Keene lost her lease at Tripler Hall, *The Marble Heart* appeared frequently on her bills for those last two months. In addition, the piece appeared at the Holliday Street Theatre on 6 October 1856 and at Laura Keene's New Theatre which opened at 624 Broadway in November.[59] On 16 March 1857, Laura Keene opened a new afterpiece which Odell (6:543) called her "biggest hit of the winter," *The Elves; or, The Statue Bride*, a burlesque by Charles Selby. In it, Laura Keene appeared as the statue in a variation of the familiar Pygmalion and Galatea story.[60] *The Elves* continued until 11 May, when it was replaced by *Variety; or, The Picture Gallery*, another burlesque, similar in concept to the earlier *Novelty*. Drawing its material mainly from current offerings in the New York theatres, *Variety* contains a series of tableaux which poked satiric barbs at a wide "variety" of targets:

> We have *The Spirit of the Drama* (Miss Reinolds)—very badly dressed—deploring her fate and that of her disciples, whom she dismissed as no longer having the power to attract a house in legitimate business. In the midst of her distress, *Puff* (Miss Manners), a fast young man—"the hope of the living drama"—descends, and undertakes to show the Drama's Spirit the different classes and entertainment which the public of the present day admire and patronize; this is done in a series of tableaux, the intervals between which are filled up with conversation germane to the matters at issue. Thus, we have the scene between *Macbeth* and the Witches, with an imitation and puff of Forrest, and caricatures and sneers at Garrick and Charles Kean. Next comes *Comedy*, with Miss Ada Clifton dressed for *Lady Teazle* or *Lydia Languish* (we could not clearly make out which). Then *Spectacle*, embodied by Mrs. Stoddard, then *Burlesque*, by Mr. T.B. Johnston, next *Ballet*, by pretty Miss Stella, and the choreographic corps; anon modern, original, French, English drama, with an imitation of Borucicault [sic] in *The Phantom*. Then *Melodrama*, personified by Messrs. Johnston and Kent, including a Bowery combat, on which the sailor-hero kills off five of his assailants. This is followed by the *Young American Drama*, which is represented by two Yankee girls, who sing Independence Day and kick up their heels at anything but a delicate style. We have then an allegorical tableau, entitled *The Queen of Roses*, representing a mammoth circle of those flowers, with a pretty rose-queen in the center, whilst roseate nymphs form a complete circle around her. This tableau was exceedingly pretty, malgre one ludicrous effect, caused by the

young lady who stands on the apex, who, to the denizens of the boxes, presents the view only of a pair of flesh-colored shoes and a neatly-turned ankle, whilst those located in the parquette (with the exception of those in the front seats), perceive the hem of a muslin skirt, and the usual leg—all continuations which a lady in ballet costume exhibits—the remaining portion of her figure being entirely out of sight. The effect, we need scarcely say, is exceedingly funny. The *Circus* comes as a matter of course with Johnston and a basket horse, after the fashion of his *Herne the Hunter* over the way, in a daring act of horsemanship. The last scene being the Grove of Palms, groupings of Graces, nymphs in Lama dresses, red fire, and a "shower of gold," after the style of the tableaux exhibited by Keller.[61]

In all, fourteen tableaux were presented in each performance of *Variety*, the selections being changed from time to time during the run.

The 1857-58 season at Laura Keene's saw, first a revival of *The Elves*, and then the introduction of *Blanche of Brandywine*, another piece with "no connected plot," but a collection of illustrative scenes, ending with "a brilliant military tableau."[62] This "play" was the work of Joseph Jefferson, who had just joined Keene's company, and James G. Burnett, the stage manager. Jefferson later recalled that it was the economic panic of 1857 which led to his efforts:

> Business had fallen off and the theatre was in a fair way to follow in the train of bankruptcy that was dragging everything after it, when I hit upon the idea of producing what was deemed a shocking innovation in a legitimate Broadway theatre. Casting about for a novel that might be turned into a strong military drama, I came upon George Lepard's Revolutionary story entitled "Blanche of Brandywine." Battles, marches and countermarches, murders, abductions, hairbreadth escapes, militia trainings, and extravagant Yankee comicalities boiled over in every chapter. James G. Burnett, the stage manager, and I soon concocted a soul-stirring drama from this material and it was accepted by Miss Keene, the manageress.[63]

Jefferson goes on to provide some amusing insights into the difficulties of posing the company for the featured tableau in *Blanche of Brandywine:*

> The second act of our play ended with the battle of Bunker Hill, which I had arranged should be given as a tableau rather than as an action, from Trumbull's picture of the "Death of Warren" or "The Battle of Bunker Hill." It was so well known, and its leading features presented such a fine opportunity for effective grouping, that we decided to have the stage raised to represent a mound covered with grass, and to arrange the figures in exactly the same manner as in the famous painting. On the morning the tableau was to be grouped, Miss Keene appeared with the engraving, which she unrolled with a proud air and Sir Oracle demeanor that was all the more amusing to me as I knew she was in deep water, and likely to sink at the first plunge. We (the company) were assembled and the stage manager eyed us with a sidelong look of anything but approval. After a preliminary cough or two Miss Keene charged up the hill and prepared for action.
>
> Looking over the scroll, which every now and then would keep rolling itself up, much to her annoyance and our smothered delight, she began to place us in our different and, I may say, difficult positions. One would be made to rest upon his elbow while another was arranged to stand over him with an uplifted gun. The next gentleman, a cruel British officer, was then told to be on the point of thrusting a bayonet into the vital regions of some American patriot. The wounded Warren was ordered to lie down in an uncomfortable

position and be held by a friend. This was all very well, and for a brief period these attitudes could be maintained; but by the time Miss Keene had got through the militia the regular army was completely worn out. Then she began to badger Warren, telling him to lie with his head a little more that way, or a trifle more the other way, besides requesting him to look exhausted—which expression, however, under the circumstances, he had taken quite of his own accord.

"You are out of position again," Miss Keene would say to some old soldier. "Now observe, I want you to stand—well, look here," and away would go the scroll again as if it were on a spring roller.

"General Warren, you have got your head all wrong again."

"I cannot stand it," said the hero; "my head has been in that position for twenty minutes."

I do not think that the original general could have suffered more than did his counterfeit on this occasion. By this time every one was exhausted, Miss Keene included, so there was nothing left but to dismiss the army and hold a council of war.

I now saw that the arrangement of a tableau from a picture with so many figures was a more difficult matter than I had at first imagined. Miss Keene declared that it could not be done at all, and I was myself beginning to think we were nonplussed, when Burnett came to the rescue with a simple suggestion which made the way clear at once. His idea was that the characters in the engraving should be cast just as they would be in a play. Thus each figure in the picture was marked with the name of the actor who was to represent it. The engraving was then hung up in the greenroom where each one could look at it and so study the attitude he was to take. This was caught up at once; their names wre then marked upon the mound in chalk, and when the word was given to strike the tableau each one took the position, assumed his attitude, and the picture was complete.[64]

These arrangements apparently solved the problem, for the tableau was an immense success, vigorously applauded in performance and highly praised in the press. In addition, there were other scenes in the play, equally admired, and which depended on their pictorial impact. These were specifically identified in relation to the painters whose works they represented: "an American barnyard by Hawthorne" and "an old church and graveyard by moonlight, by Minard Lewis."[65]

Laura Keene's emphasis on tableaux continued during the 1860's. "The Trial Scene of Effie Deans, after Landers' celebrated picture," provided the focal point for *Jeanie Deans; or, The Heart of Mid-Lothian* in 1860, promising to represent, "with all possible fidelity the forms and formalities, costumes and incidents, of the Court of Judiciary under Charles the Second."[66]

In 1861, the burlesque, *Seven Sisters,* was augmented by a series of "Union Tableaux," many of which had obviously been developed for various earlier productions. Some of these made use of live models, and some relied on the novelty of magic lantern pictured by "Uncle Samuel's stereoscope." The live presentations included:

> The Waking of Columbus, the Four Sections of the Union: The East and her Manufactures, The West and her Agriculture, The North and her Commerce, The South and her Cotton Fields, Washington Crossing the Delaware, Columbia and Columbus at Washington's Tomb, The Happy Plantation Home. The Thirty-four States of the Union, Calhoun's

Dream, and Washington's Army at Valley Forge, The Declaration of the Union, The Apotheosis of Washington and the Union, and concluding with the great scene, The Birth of the Butterfly in the Bower of Ferns.[67]

Some sense of the spirit of the piece may be drawn from the tone of the *New York Times* review of the opening performance:

> A *melange*, or medley, or, in the language of the play-bill, a "grand operatic, spectacular, diabolical, musical, terpsichorean, farcical burletta, in three acts, called the 'Seven Sisters,'" was produced at this theatre last night. Of course, there was no plot to it, or attempt at plot, and equally of course there was plenty of fun brimful and overflowing.... The entire piece is one of those indescribable and admirable absurdities at which we laugh heartily when we see it, while we are almost ashamed of ourselves the next morning for having been amused with such folly. But for all that, we are ready to advise our friends to go and make themselves equally foolish, and for that matter, would not object to a repetition of the folly ourselves.[68]

Later in the same year, the second act of a companion piece, *Seven Sons*, was entirely given over to a new series of these Union Tableaux, plus "the great Watteau scene of Arcadian Nymphs Reclining among their Flocks by the Mountain Torrent of Real Water."[69] These were followed at Laura Keene's by *Peep O-Day* (1862), a revival of *The Elves* (1862), *Fanchon* (1862), and *Jessie McLane* (1863), all of which relied upon tableaux for their primary appeal.

In addition, other major theatres occasionally followed Laura Keene's lead. At Wallack's, military tableaux accompanied *Jessie Brown; or, The Belle of Luckenow* (1858), and *The Irish Boy and Yankee Gal* (1858) included "grand allegorical tableaux." An equestrian piece at the Broadway Theatre, *The Nena Sahib; or, The Demon of Cawnpore* (1858), made use of tableaux to show "the English overpowered" at the end of Act I and "British arms triumphant" at the end of the play. At the Melodeon, tableaux were prominent in *Donnybrook Fair; or, Ireland as It was in 1800* (1859), and at Niblo's, tableaux even accompanied a ballet entitled *The Painter's Dream; or, The Illusion* (1861).

At the close of the 1850's, such places as the Franklin Museum and, undoubtedly, some clandestine enterprises were still presenting fairly sensational model artists. However, these were balanced by the less provocative tableaux vivants of Louis Keller, Laura Keene, and others. Furthermore, it was usually possible for the public to distinguish between one form of presentation and the other. The terms, "model artist" and "tableau vivant," while they were sometimes used interchangeably, carried quite different connotations after the days of Dr. Collyer and Professor Thier in the late 1840's. "Tableau vivant" was a more socially and morally acceptable term. "Model artist" connoted a more sensational, voyeuristic kind of activity in which the focus was on the "artist"—usually on the "symmetry" of the "female form divine," as nineteenth century writers were fond of saying. The terms, "tableau vivant" and "pose plastique," on the other hand, threw emphasis on the works of art represented—paintings or sculpture, respectively—and, thus, carried less social or moral stigma.

By 1858, however, even the still-questionable "model artists," such as those under George Lea's management, were being viewed with considerable tolerance, even though they were not totally approved. Perhaps the attitude was best expressed by the *New York Clipper* reviewer as he looked ahead to the Christmas season:

> Even the model artists are preparing extra attractions for the holidays. Venus will rise from the sea in new and gorgeous, though scanty apparel; the Graces will don new tights, so delicate in their texture and life-like in their make-up, that the oldest reprobate that visits the show will not be able to detect the filmy veil that shuts the Graces' naked charms from view; and Eve, that author of our sin, will sin again in freshly gathered fig leaves and entrance some other Adam with her fascinating and penetrating glances. The Model Artists are an institution in our midst, and will give the show for 25 cents a pop; private boxes, $1; and *seats on the stage* (d'ye mind that, now?) $3. Of a verity, we are a strange people; but our cousins from the country are the chaps that go the $3 pop the oftenest.[70]

Clearly, the public attitudes toward tableaux had changed during the 1850's, as had the exhibits themselves. Although some clandestine enterprises probably still presented sensations to rival those which had introduced the decade, they were, to a large extent, balanced by the less provocative, more "artistic" offerings of Louis Keller, Laura Keene, and other admired producers. The rise of such respectability undoubtedly helped to develop a more liberal public outlook toward tableaux generally. Perhaps tableaux vivants might have built upon this foundation of acceptance, had not other forces, unknown at the time, appeared during the next decade to undermine their popularity.

5

Decline in the Face of Competition, 1860-1875

The period of the 1860's and early 1870's saw fewer tableaux than the preceding decade. This diminishing popularity can be attributed to three major changes in the entertainments available to the public: (1) the popularity of sensational melodrama, (2) the arrival of plays and performances whose appeal was based on "leg art," and (3) the rise of "concert saloons."

Sensational melodrama, exemplified by such plays as *Uncle Tom's Cabin, Jessie Brown, The Poor of New York,* and *The Octoroon* in the 1850's and *East Lynne, Under the Gaslight,* and numerous Boucicault plays in the 1860's, relied to a great extent on the same kind of appeal which had popularized tableaux. The "sensation scenes" in these plays made use of the same elaborate scenic effects seen in tableaux but with even greater attempts at strong visual impact. Often the places represented on stage were local scenes familiar to the audience, so that, as in the case of tableaux, fidelity to the actual subject matter became a source of pleasure for the viewer. Boucicault's *The Poor of New York,* for example, carried this feature to the extreme of using new scenery for each major city where the play was produced. Even the title was changed to *The Streets of London, The Poor of Liverpool,* or *The Streets of Philadelphia.* In Philadelphia it was announced, "The following Local Scenery, has been painted expressly for the Piece, by Richard S. Smith: Chestnut Street, Third Street, Broad Street, during a snow storm, A Fire on Shippen Street."[1] In this way, such scenes made the same basic appeal as tableaux had done.

Even those plays without strong sensation scenes often relied on the tableau as a device to "freeze" and point up situations at significant moments in the play and, thus, used a technique of tableaux vivants without employing external subject matter. The device was so popular that virtually every play of the period called for tableaux at the final curtain and often at several other times as well. The enormously popular *Uncle Tom's Cabin* is fairly typical of this use of tableaux within a play. "*Tableau*" or "*picture*" is actually specified in stage directions at the ends of II, 3; V, 1; and V, 3. However, tableaux are clearly implied by stage directions elsewhere in the play as well. Act II, scene 6, for instance, ends as follows:

> *Marks and Party run off. George and Eliza kneel in an attitude of thanksgiving, with the child between them.—Phineas stands over them exulting.*

At the end of V, 5, when Uncle Tom has just died, the direction reads:

> *Solemn music.—George covers Uncle Tom with his cloak, and kneels over him. Clouds work on and conceal them, and then work off.*

This is followed by a final scene, entirely in tableau, depicting the "apotheosis of Eva:"

> Scene 6
> *Gorgeous clouds, tinted with sunlight. Eva, robed in white, is discovered on the back of a milk-white dove, with expanded wings, as if just soaring upward. Her hands are extended in benediction over St. Clare and Uncle Tom, who are kneeling and gazing up to her. Impressive music.—Slow curtain.*[2]

Such tableaux, since they were the visual focal points of the production, were frequently described in detail in advertising and programmes, and a play was apt to be called a drama "in five tableaux" rather than in five acts or scenes. Indeed, a critic in 1870 ruefully commented that "dramas will soon have no scenes, only 'tableaux'."[3]

Thus, it can be seen that, not only had much of the tableaux vivants' appeal resulting from technique and fidelity to subject been ursurped by the "legitimate drama," but the very term, tableau, had been adopted by it as well.

In addition, there appeared during the 1860's three noteworthy productions which usurped a second appeal of tableaux vivants, the appeal of the "female form divine." The first of these was the revival in 1861 of *Mazeppa*, in which Adah Isaacs Menken created a tremendous stir by appearing in pink fleshings and white trunks. Her costume was considered so risque that when she played on tour at Virginia City, Nevada, she was described as being "stripped to the buff."[4] Her daring appearance coupled with a notorious offstage life titillated audiences for several years.

The second event to give impetus to "leg art" was the 1866 production of *The Black Crook,* described by a reviewer as "a medium for the presentation of several gorgeous scenes, and a large number of female legs."[5] So popular was the production that it played at Niblo's Garden for sixteen months and also spawned a host of imitations.

The third event was the arrival in America of Lydia Thompson and her British Blondes in September 1868. Their special brand of burlesque performances involved songs, dances, jokes, and impersonations, but the feature which caught the public eye and aroused heated controversy was the brief costumes worn by these attractive women. Again, "leg show" was the claim to fame.

Finally, those who attended the old model artist exhibitions simply to admire the "symmetry" of the female models now discovered a new entertainment which served the same purpose in a more personal way. This was the concert saloon with its "pretty waiter girls." These establishments—often called music halls but quite unlike the variety theatres using that name—provided some vaudeville-type entertainment, sometimes including model artists, either free of charge or at extremely low cost. Concert saloons were aimed primarily at male patrons, and the female performers and "waiter girls" were encouraged to mingle with the audience to solicit the purchase of refreshments. Such saloons as the Broadway Varieties, the Canterbury Music Hall, and the Gaities Concert Room were looked upon as scandalous by moral-minded citizens, but they prospered throughout the 1860's. Numerous efforts were made to control or suppress these places, but as the decade began the legal machinery had not been geared for that purpose. In an appeal for more stringent licensing regulations, Wilkes' *Spirit of the Times* lamented:

> What a jolly free-and-easy city this is, to be sure! How everybody can do as they blessed please, without any regard to old-fashioned notions of moral or legal rights. How utterly antiquated have become such ideas as good taste and good neighborhood.... The saloon business is the offspring of Model Artist shows, and is run in some prominent instances by the same men; in other instances by women.... The notorious dealer in Model Artists sets up Aphrodite's Temple in Broadway, stands in the door and solicits customers, and all under the protection of the law.[6]

The complaints were reminiscent of those against model artists themselves in earlier days.

It can be seen that much of the appeal of tableaux vivants was met by other entertainments during the 1860's. The interest in fidelity to source material was satisfied by many sensation scenes in melodramas, and the voyeuristic appeal was satisfied by the "leg art" of *The Black Crook*, the British Blondes, and the concert saloons. The fascination of spectacular scenic display which was an important feature of tableaux was provided on an even grander scale than before both in melodramas and in *The Black Crook* style of extravaganza.

Of these new entertainments, only the concert saloon occasionally preserved the model artists in their traditional form, and these were usually looked upon as fairly scandalous. The Canterbury Music Hall advertised tableaux consistently and prominently during 1861 and 1862, sometimes featuring such famous performers as members of the Ravel Family.[7] The Broadway Music Hall advertised the "Great Carlo Family" in an act labelled "Tableau Motore et Vivant," whatever that was,[8] and the Oriental Free

Concert Hall at 650 Broadway announced that "all the known costumes of modern times are here illustrated by living models."[9]

Strong objections to the concert halls were raised, and an attempt was begun in 1861 to enact legislation to control them. In a published letter, dated 28 December 1861, Henry Lea of the Melodeon sought to rally the managers in opposition to this move:

> TO THE PROPRIETORS OF THE CONCERT SALOONS IN THE CITY OF NEW YORK.
>
> GENTS—A crusade is about to be made against us and the business in which we are engaged. The theatres and others have employed counsel, and have a law proposed to present to the next Legislature, which they will endeavor to have passed. It is our interest to meet them there and defeat their purpose. I cannot, nor can any one person, afford to fight the combination against us, and I therefore propose that a meeting of all interested be called for the purpose of discussing the best course to pursue. I will cheerfully pay my proper proportion of the expenses. If your views coincide with mine, please reply by note to me immediately, and I will call a meeting at an early date.
>
> December 28, 1861   Henry Lea,
>   Melodeon, 539 Broadway[10]

A law was passed in 1862, though not a very effective on, providing only that no one should keep a house of prostitution in his concert saloon.[11] Later, however, licensing procedures were initiated to control the sale of liquor, and these proved more effective in suppressing such places.

Tableaux vivants did appear in a few theatres, museums, and regular music halls during the 1860's. Drayton's Parlor Opera Hall, Hope Chapel, the week of 2-7 January 1860 presented *"tableaux vivants,* representing savage African or Kaffir life, and with scenic illustrations."[12]

The outbreak of civil war in 1861 had little impact on tableau vivant production. Exhibitions extolling patriotic themes, which had become popular in the late 1850's, continued to be produced frequently. However, even this kind of subject matter did not always guarantee success. Patriotic tableaux entitled *Stars and Stripes; or, The Patriot's Dream* at the New Bowery in May 1861 were not successful and ran only a few performances.[13] Only one production appears to have dealt directly with the war: "A tableau from the History of the War," presented by the Ambulance and Sanitary Corps at the Academy of Music in 1863.[14]

In 1862 P.T. Barnum began to exhibit "Commodore Nutt, the smallest man alive," who posed as "Celebrated Grecian Statues: Hercules, Romulus, Remus, Ajax, Achilles, The Slave, Emoloeur, The Child's Prayer, &c."[15] Interestingly, only a year later Irving Hall advertised the appearance of "Tom Thumb and wife,... including tableaux, songs and dances."[16] Even Tony Pastor, in 1866, offered a tableau troupe in patriotic pictures to accompany "a new drama of the present day, Uncle Sam's Veterans."[17] The Olympic Theatre, in 1869, featured "classical groupings by Mlle. Sangali,"[18] and later presented "marble statues" by no less a star than the famous clown, G.L. Fox.[19] From 1869 through 1871 William Horace Lingard appeared in "comic sketches and living statues," first at the Theatre Comique and later at the Grand Opera House and Lina Edwin's Theatre (formerly Hope Chapel). Lingard combined his posing with a quick-change act and for a benefit performance 7 January 1870, advertised that "to remove an impression which appears to prevail in many minds that his rapid changes of dress and character are effected by collusion with a double or confederate, Lingard will enlighten the public on his modus operandi by DRESSING AND UNDRESSING in the PRESENCE OF THE AUDIENCE."[20]

There were, in addition, numerous plays featuring tableaux during this period. The Wintergarden presented *Napoleon the Great* with "pictures of Napoleon on the Rock of St. Helena, Attempted Escape of Napoleon, Death of Napoleon."[21] Kathi Lanner's Viennoise ballet and pantomime troupe appeared at the Grand Opera House during the fall of 1870, and one of their attractions, *Uriella, The Demon of the Night*, included six tableaux.[22]

A rash of "ghost" plays during the season of 1863-64 included many which featured tableaux. *The Ghost of Altenberg; or, The Mystic Harp*, at Fox's Old Bowery Theatre, for instance, listed titles of seven tableaux in most of its advertising,[23] as did *Brunhilda; or Wake Not The Dead* at Barnum's.[24] Douglas Gilbert even sees the "ghost" plays as a direct antecedent to later tableaux. He explains how their effects are produced:

> One of the great scenery-chewers of the seventies was "The London Ghost Show;" this survived in later vaudeville (burlesque too) in a derivation called "Living Pictures." It was done in the seventies with a large plate glass which leaned at a 45-degree angle over a pit lined with black velvet. One or more characters worked on the stage, the others were in the pit. Because of the reflection in the glass (it was not a mirror), those in the pit were seemingly performing at stage level. By clever manipulation of lights-extraordinary if you recall the crude gaslights of the period-the figures in the pit could be made to appear, disappear, fade, or float away during the performances.[25]

When George Wood attempted to revive *The Seven Sisters* of Laura Keene fame, under the title, *The Seven Daughters of Satan*, in 1865, the *Spirit of the Times* reviewer saw it as that theatre's road to ruin:

> This evening that dramatic monstrosity, "The Seven Sisters," which Laura Keene produced when she "fell from grace," and left off producing those charming dramas which gave her name and fame, will be produced. I am sorry for it; Laura Keene lost her prestige by this hodge-podge of sensational stuff, and her one time patrons that vied with the audiences of Wallack, gave way to a different class of auditors. We fear it will be the same at the Broadway, which has established a good reputation, and been patronized by the elite of playgoers; however, that is the manager's business, and not mine, and I will not forestall events. "The Seven Sisters" has for about three years past been tinkered up to suit various localities, and hawked all over the country by Mr. [John E.] McDonough, and I suppose will be dressed up again for a New York audience.[26]

The play was not a success in spite of its "BEAUTIFUL TABLEAUX" and "ZOUAVE MARCH AND DRILL," employing "TWENTY YOUNG LADIES."[27] In 1866 Mr. Wood tried again with another Laura Keene revival, *The Elves; or, The Statue Bride*, featuring the Worrell Sisters, and in this venture he was more successful than before.[28] Odell (8:78) reports, "The piece and the youthful freshness of the stars caught popular fancy, and no change of main piece was required for several weeks."

Late in the decade the only theatre offering tableaux vivants resembling their original form was Tammany Hall which created a minor sensation and generated controversy even before the performances began. The building had been built by the Tammany Society which occupied a hall on the first floor. Another hall in the building was used by Bryant's Minstrels, and there were also smoking rooms, a ladies' restaurant, bar rooms, and some small performance spaces. In addition, the upper hall was a first-class theatre, and it was this theatre that Henry C. Jarrett and Harry Palmer leased as the Tammany Theatre.[29] When their opening was scheduled in January 1869, the *Spirit of the Times* was incensed:

> Messrs. Jarret, Palmer and Grover,—once the controlling spirits of Niblo's Garden and the lamented German opera—emulous of the evil gains of John Allen and the Peter Funk mock auctioneers, have deliberately heralded through the columns of the press their disreputable intention to inaugurate a combined *dance hall, Bazar (sic)* and varieties show in the building once respectably called "Tammany Hall.". . . That the public may not deem us extravagant in our denunciation of this coming infamy, we will briefly state that the *dancehall* is to be adorned nightly by a half-score of girls, whose wardrobe is to be supplied by the management, in order that these complaisant and bewitching creatures may be outwardly presentable. They are to lounge about the place, ready to drink and dance with whoever may invite them;—the pretty waiter-girl system, in short.[30]

The opening took place amid scathing reviews of course, condemning the offerings as little more than leg shows. The house continued variety entertainment of various kinds through its first season. On 20 September 1869, however, the Tammany began an act about which even the *Spirit* could generate some enthusiasm:

> Tammany, under the ambitious and liberal management of Mr. Grover, strides from attraction to attraction with marvelous celerity. The latest feature is the engagement of the celebrated "Jem" Mace, champion of England, whose statuesque illustrations throughout England, Ireland, and Scotland have been the theme of admiration and critical praise from sculptors, painters, and leading art critics in the principal cities of the United Kingdom. Mace is to-day in his highest form, and presents a model of symmetry and physical manhood. He performs upon a pedestal and with the grace of a genuine artist, if we may rely upon the opinions of the English press; makes one transition after another with marvelous celerity, grace, and agility. The most classic and beautiful of his representations are the "Fighting Gladiator." "Dying Gladiator," "Samson Carrying the Gates of Gaza," "Ajax Defying the Lightning," and other classical *poses*. Brody, the sculptor, recommends the study of Mace's performances to artists, both sculptors and painters.[31]

Reviews of Mace's performances were at least encouraging, if they did not laud. Typical is the *Herald* reviewer who begins his evaluation by noting at length that ancient Greek artists looked to the sporting arena for their subject matter:

> ... Greece therefore by her sports made her magnificent men in good flesh and blood before she made them in marble. In the person of Mace, who may, no doubt, be taken as a fair type of the sort of man made by athletic sports in England, we find those sports far inferior to those of the free state of antiquity. Grecian sports perfectly and evenly developed a man for all vigorous exercises—to run, to wrestle, to box, to throw the discus—but British sport trains away all the points save such as fit a man to flourish in the prize ring. Mace is not a figure that the eye rests upon with a peculiar pleasure for any charm of manly beauty, but he could, evidently, have pounded to death the originals of all the fine statues that were made in Greece. His attitude was especially good in the Slave Sharpening the Knife. It was not accurate in The Dying Gladiator, if it was intended to fairly represent the statue. As an indication of popular taste it is notable that the position that brought down the house was the one that presented The Fighting Gladiator "in shape" for the first round. We are glad that prize fighting pays so poorly that a champion is constrained to coin his laurels by report to the stage, and we wish him all success in this new occupation.[32]

The *New York Times* was somewhat more descriptive in its account, suggesting a style of presentation akin to the "attitudes" mentioned earlier.

> A few minutes before the curtain rises the lights are turned down and several bars of music, in *agitato* time, are heard. The drop rolled up discloses a series of screens covered with maroon cloth and hemming in a small platform upon which are centered the rays of a double limelight. Recumbent on the platform is a tall figure of superb lines and white in every part as if hewn from Parian marble.... As the musicians strike up it becomes instinct with life, freezing every now and then into sculptural significance. First we behold Hercules struggling with the lion and overcoming him. The club disappears, the active strength subsides, and a stalwart Roman stoops to fasten his sandal. A strong arm is stretched out again, and Hercules throws the quoit. Other illustrations follow, a soft violet light now falling upon the statue.[33]

By 9 October, in addition to Jem Mace, Tammany was also listing "Professor Roberts" presenting "sensation tableaux" on the matinee bills. These included representations of famous persons—Commodore Vanderbilt, Jay Gould, Lord and Lady Byron, Harriet Beecher Stowe, Benjamin Franklin, General Grant, etc.—and concluded with "a grand Apotheosis of Washington."[34] Mace closed his engagement at the Tammany on Saturday, 16 October 1869, and played in Brooklyn and at the Bowery. The Roberts tableaux continued for another week and then ceased advertising. Mace returned to Tammany for a brief appearance in a sparring match in February 1870 and then the hall closed. The *Herald* expressed triumph at its departure and took the opportunity to lament all forms of "leg drama" and their supposed effect on the legitimate theatre:

EXIT LEG DRAMA.

At length the last stronghold of the leg drama—Tammany—has surrendered at discretion to the indignation of an outraged public and has given up the ghost. Its last essay at nude burlesque was too much for even the indulgence of theatre-goers, and the result was a timely dissolution. Every lover of art will rejoice at the removal of the intolerable nuisance which has so long disgraced our stage, to the exclusion of all that is good and pure in music and drama. The inundation of bleached blondes [Lydia Thompson had recently played in New York] which burst upon us two seasons ago inflicted more damage upon the art than many are aware of. First, one of the leading theatres of the city was monopolized by them, and night after night its stage formed a sort of rostrum for the declamation of childish nonsense, *double entendres* and jokes, which the poorest comic paper would be ashamed of, and became an exhibition hall for unclad beauties and extensively padded limbs. Again the music publishers caught the infection, and threw aside works of genuine merit to make way for nursery rhymes and the off-scourings of London concert saloons. The "Black Crook" was the *avant courier* of this vitiated taste of the public, and its successor, the "White Fawn," only served to strengthen it; but the blondes brought matters to a climax, and the natural result is a revulsion of feeling on the part of theatre-goers. They looked around for something respectable and artistic, and found it in the magnificent temple erected by Edwin Booth. There we find Shakespeare enthroned in all the splendor and glory that a refined taste and liberality could furnish, and the spectacular drame beaten on his own ground. Neither the "Black Crook" nor "White Fawn" can compare with "Hamlet" in stage pictures and accessories. Daly's little *bijou* theatre of comedy and Wallack's standard establishment also aided in the good work of weaning the public from the nauseous dramatic fare they had so long been fed with at the expense of taste and morality. The change from leg to legitimate drama was not effected in a moment. It was a gradual process, but it attained its objective nevertheless. The treasury of a theatre is the surest sign of the feelings of the public toward it, and the returns made by Booth's each month so far surpass anything leg drama ever dreamed of. The demise of Tammany may therefore be taken as an emphatic declaration of opinion on the part of the public that they want no more black crooks, white fawns or bleached blondes. All future efforts in that line can only be spasmodic and result in the financial ruin of those who undertake them. The public are very positive in their likes and dislikes, and it is useless to fight against them on the stage. *Le Roi est Mort! Vive le Roi!* All hail to the revival of art, genius and merit in music and the drama on the metropolitan boards![35]

Though the writer of the foregoing article could hardly have known it, his reference to Booth's financial success as proof of a "revival of art, genius and merit" is indeed ironic. It was only three years later, in 1873, that Booth's artistic reign drove him to bankruptcy, forcing the great actor to give up his theatre and forego management.

The 1860's produced few tableau exhibits, and those which did occur were short-lived and usually only part of a larger offering—a dramatic spectacle or variety bill. No producers concentrated their efforts on tableaux alone, and, with the possible exception of Jem Mace, no noteworthy performers specialized in posing. For the public, the appeals of tableaux were met by other kinds of entertaiments—sensational melodrama, "leg art," and concert saloons. With the closing of the Tammany in 1870, tableaux vivants ceased in New York until 1875, when the craze started all over again.

6

The Fight Begins Again, 1875-1893

After a five-year hiatus, during which tableaux vivants were not advertised to the New York public, the form emerged again. The same battle lines which had been drawn before were quickly reestablished, and the war was resumed with, if anything, increased intensity. Sensation-minded producers soon advertised in even more openly provocative ways than before, and the authorities responded with their strongest attacks. Meanwhile, one devotee of artistry attempted to keep the stigma of indecency from polluting public response to his own production. The major confrontations occurred in the late 1870's, and for a time the forces of purity seemed to succeed.

On Monday, 26 April 1875, a Mme. Blanche opened "for a short season" at Robinson Hall with an entertainment entitled "Two Hours in Paradise." The puffery heralding the opening described her company as "the only authorized troupe allowed to travel through Germany, Russia, France, Hungary and Turkey," and claimed that she "received the special license from the Minister of Police, of Austria, to perform with her troupe in the Prater, during the great Exhibition of 1873, in Austria."[1] The same advertisement quotes the "Vienna Kiktriki" as saying, "It is worth while to spend half an hour in Paradise to see Mme. BLANCHE with her pretty girls." The performance centered around a series of ten tableaux vivants: "La Graz," "The Flower Girl," "Two Statues," "The Empty Pockets," "The Three Greek Slaves," "The Spendthrift Among the Gay," "The Three Graces," "The Roman Combat," "The Butterfly," and "The Champagne Supper, from Mabille." The production went without critical mention in the press but was sufficiently popular to occupy the house for three weeks, after which it was replaced by the opera bouffe, *Girofle-Girofla*, which moved there from the Lyceum on 19 May.

Robinson Hall was closed during the summer months but reopened on 15 September 1875 with a new name, "The New York Parisian Varieties," under the new management of G.A. Henderson. The opening bill included such offerings as an "emotional poem vivant, entitled The Brooklyn Seminary for Finishing Young Ladies, a pleasant combination of terpsichorean eccentricity, modern morality and female beauty, with a jolly termination, entitled The Parisian La Chateau Quadrille."[2] Advertising for the Parisian Varieties proclaimed the place a "Temple of Sensational Amusement" and described the entertainments as "Voluptuous without Coarseness." Press reaction to the new house was complimentary, but not descriptive, and although the *New York Dramatic News* asserted that the managers were "careful to exclude anything of a coarse tendency,"[3] the *Spirit of the Times* observed that they offered "a good and laughable variety show, exclusively for gentlemen."[4]

It is perhaps not surprising that a tableau troupe took up residence at the Parisian Varieties only two weeks after the house opened. Beginning 4 October 1875 it was announced that:

> Having secured the most beautiful living models in America, M. BLANDOWSKI will produce for the first time his exquisite POSE PLASTIQUE.

The Bathers.	Temptation.
Venus and Cupid.	Kisses.
Slave Mart.	Adam and Eve.
Gladiators.	Cain and Abel.
Bad News.	Jealousy and Crime.
Fairies.	Bad Fix.[5]

Within the first week a reviewer noted that "the Poses Plastique appear to be the favorite item on the bill of fare,"[6] and during the following months they received consistently prominent billing, often as "living tableaux" or "living models." Advertising always emphasized that the act was "spicy," "voluptuous," "naughty," or "piquante." At one point the *New York Times* observed, "'Sensational art' is still the order of things at the Parisian Varieties. *Melange de fascination* is one of the euphemistic descriptions which designates the character of the entertainment."[7] This bizarre nomenclature referred to a bill which listed "Free Love Mishaps and Living Classic Models." In January 1876 the manager turned to bits of doggeral for advertising; the following is typical:

> A maze of beauty, music, dance, and pleasure,
> Where taste and fashion spend their hours of leisure;
> Where art, refined, enthralls without offenses,
> And lovely woman captivates the senses.[8]

By this time new tableaux were being added regularly, and the company was said to include twenty female models. Soon the Parisian Varieties were proclaiming, "This cosy temple of Sensational Art has overcome all opposition, all envy, jealousy and ill feeling of weak imitators, and finally established itself as head and front of the variety entertainments of America."[9]

When the last appearance of Blandowski's troupe was announced for Saturday, 18 March 1876, another tableau company was ready to take its place.[10] This company was under the leadership of Mlle. Ninon Duclos, "a name suspiciously like that of Ninon de l'Clos of history," noted the *Dramatic News*. Its engagement opened on Monday, 20 March 1876 with tableaux culminating in the patriotic picture of "Washington Crossing the Delaware."[11] The press repeatedly noted the large attendance at Parisian Varieties as novelty followed novelty on the bill. Advertisements for the week of 10 April announced fifteen new tableaux,[12] and an intriguing comment on 15 April noted, "In one of the tableaux presented,... Pose Mythologique, it is to be noted that all of the girls presented a striking resemblance to George Washington."[13] At the end of April the Duclos Troupe had given way to Signor Novissimo's Grand Tableaux claiming "100 artists of acknowledged merit," and scheduled to appear at "9:40 o'clock."[14] This troupe continued to perform through the summer and into the fall of 1876.

In the meantime another theatre had begun presenting sensational tableaux vivants and similar entertainments on a regular basis. This was the Metropolitan Theatre, located at 587 Broadway in the midst of what had become a notorious district of concert saloons and dancing parlors. In the preceding year this theatre had been raided by police as a result of its "Parisian Can-can" performances and other objectionable dances, so it suffered a somewhat unsavory reputation.[15] In September 1875 on a bill with Mme. Rentz's Female Minstrels, this house featured "THE ORIGINAL GRECIAN TROUPE OF KALIEDAGYNAI, whose vivid tableaux and graceful groupings no true lover of art should neglect seeing."[16] Perhaps the hope was that people would attend in order to decipher the meaning of so prodigious a label. These tableaux vivants ran through 25 September when they were replaced:

> First appearance of Prof. LAWRENCE and Troupe of GOLDEN STATUE ARTISTS, consisting of Miss Carrie Wilson, the most beautiful lady on the American stage; Mlle. Papeta La Frauck, Mlle. Violetta Bourjeaux, Signore Volatti and seventeen of the handsomest ladies in face and form that can be found on the stage. Selected with great care from the theatres of England, France, Italy, and America. They will appear in the REVOLVING MIRROR OF SCULPTURE, classical and artistic female groupings, at once a most fascinating and artistic exhibition ever presented to the New York public. In consequence of previous arrangements they can appear one week only.[17]

One can only guess at the nature of this act, for it was not reviewed or described in the press. True to the announcement, Prof. Lawrence disappeared from public view when the week ended, though he did reemerge briefly at Aberle's New Theatre in March 1883.

Thus, the reemergence of tableaux in 1875 presented the public with sensational productions, sensationally advertised. Parisian Varieties and the Metropolitan were minor houses, however, and the press paid little attention to their bills. Perhaps for this reason they escaped sufficient public notice to generate strong objections. There is, at least, no record of official action directed against these productions until later. The forces of purity, however, were not completely dormant, for they arose in opposition to the next producer of tableaux—a producer, unfortunately, whose work was probably far purer than such censure would suggest.

When *Girofle-Girofla* was produced at the old Robinson Hall in May 1875 the scene painter for that production was one Matt Morgan, who achieved some notice for his work there and at the Lyceum earlier. In November 1875 programmes at the Theatre Comique announced that he would take over management of that house beginning the 22nd. The opening production was *Art and Nature; or, The Spendthrift's Auction,* introducing "Mr. Matt Morgan's Magnificent Classical Tableaux... which will vividly bring before the audience some of the most STARTLING EFFECTS ever produced in New York since the days of Keller. A Corps of Ladies of Unrivalled Beauty have been especially engaged to carry out the Artist's ideas."[18] A newspaper report informs us that the production, "besides presenting a beautiful representation of 'The Birth of Venus,' brought forward 'living statues' of 'The Shaughraun' and dogs."[19] Morgan's tableaux achieved great popularity and drew large audiences to the Theatre Comique. However, although the critics admired their beauty and their fidelity to the works of art represented, questions were immediately raised as to their propriety. This issue was examined in some detail by a reviewer in the *New York Dramatic News:*

> Mr. Matt Morgan made a bold move when he inaugurated his management at this theatre on Monday, by introducing, in conjunction with a variety entertainment, somewhat the same style entertainment which has made the name of Keller famous. He has taken a pleasant little comedy as the vehicle for the introduction of the main idea, which is carried out therefore with some regard for probabilities, though they do require somewhat of a stretch of imagination. But in this he has proceeded with the eye of an artist, selecting some of the most famous pictures for his experiment, such as "Cleopatra before Caesar," the "Trial of Phryne," the "Slave Mart," and "Rising of Venus from the Sea." His tableaux are simply exact reproductions to the life of these well known nude subjects. Artistically, the reproductions are perfect, nothing is exaggerated, nothing overdone. He found models of great beauty, and has utilized them as only a man of genius could. So, therefore, he no doubt comes within the law, and legally, if the authorities should seek to put any stop to the exhibitions, they would be obliged to prohibit the exhibition or sale of the pictures in our art galleries. And they would hardly prohibit Gérôme.
>
> It is therefore solely on the grounds of art, that we differ with Mr. Morgan. As it is true that the vilest objects may become sublime by being produced on canvas, so the sublimest subject on canvas may become vile if reproduced in life. To put it vulgarly, there is beauty and inspiration in the "Greek Slave." But, if the exact reproduction of the Greek Slave in life should walk broadly, she would be arrested. Art is limitless, but realism is not art. A perfect woman is the most beautiful thing in creation. Custom and civilization may have permitted the representation of this beautiful thing on canvas, in bronze, or in stone. Why? Because art steps in to perpetual [*sic*] and make immortal what is only evanescent flesh, corruptible and corrupted. It may be hard to say where art should end, for some lower natures may be affected even by its purest productions. Yet there can be no doubt that a great many lower natures will be affected by the Comique exhibition, and their vilest appetites will be excited.

Mr. Matt Morgan will make a great deal of money, but the more he makes, the more will the proof exist that his *poses plastiques* appeal to the passions of men. If only those who love art for art's sake, went to witness an exhibition of beautiful female models, the case might be slightly changed. But these can, at best, form but a small proportion of his audiences. The majority will be attracted by sensuality.[20]

In spite of this objection, during succeeding weeks new tableaux were added, many of which relied on sensual material. Among the additions were "The Shower of Gold," "Diana and her Nymphs Surprised," "The Slave Merchant," "The Battle of the Amazons," "The Deluge," and "Rock of Ages."[21]

On 11 December the tableaux were given even greater prominence on the Comique bill, and the *Clipper* reported, "The dialogue which hitherto accompanied them was dispensed with, and the tableaux were displayed separately at intervals during the variety olio."[22] It is impossible to be sure what "dialogue" had taken place during the tableaux. Since some of the poses apparently derived from scenes in familiar plays (*The Shaughraun* has been named), perhaps certain lines from the scene were spoken. It was, of course, common practice for musical selections, poetry, or other readings to accompany tableaux. In this instance, removing such auxillary elements surely focused greater attention in the poses themselves, and, at this point the propriety issue came to a head. Morgan felt compelled to reply to the reviewer who had raised the question originally:

SIR:—... You confine yourself in your remarks purely to the artistic standpoint. You deny that the refinement of art can be introduced into the baser material of living models. Yet it would be hard for you or me to say where art shall end, and where it shall begin. I contend my exhibitions are, above all, artistic. They are the exact reproductions of celebrated paintings which nobody has ever dreamed of calling immoral. The fact that I repeat the human pictures from which the canvas pictures must have been taken, only makes my case the stronger. Artists, however great, in painting nude subjects can trust to nothing but the actual sight of the human form from which to paint. It is their model that is transferred to the canvas, and their brush cannot improve upon the works of the Creator. To the lewd mind all things are lewd. I have taken material which may have been put to much worse uses, and have refined it by making it artistic. So may a mere piece of charcoal in the hands of one person be nothing but base matter, and in the hands of an artist be capable of subserving the highest purposes. It is easy to dismiss the subject with a grin and a shrug, but it is much harder to give a good argument against my human statues. The audiences which are now, both matinees and evenings, large and eminently respectable, and composed both of ladies and gentlemen, appear to appreciate my efforts. Since the present series of representations I have not, at all events, heard a word of dissent or objection, and I, personally, have yet to be convinced that any reasonable fault can be found with my performance.[23]

Morgan, however, was involved in more than a simple intellectual debate:

Owing to the instigation of the Young Men's Christian Association, Mr. Matt Morgan was notified through the District Attorney that he must consider himself under arrest for giving indecent exhibitions at the Theatre Comique, entitled "Classical Tableaux." Mr. Morgan was placed under bonds to appear before the District Attorney on Thursday. On Tuesday evening he informed the audience of the above facts, and apologized for draping the tableaux more than usual, and stated, also, that he intends to contest the action of the Young Men's Christian Association. The pictures will soon be exhibited as originally given. The authorities were represented last evening by Captain Allaire of the 14th precinct, who was a silent and apparently pleased witness of the Tableaux."[24]

The reference in this report to "the instigation of the Young Men's Christian Association" is significant, for it indicates that Matt Morgan's adversary in this situation was no less than the notorious reformer, Anthony Comstock. Morgan's strategy in "draping the tableaux more than usual" may well have been an attempt to pacify Comstock, for this reformer had established a justifiable reputation for dogged persistence and frightening effectiveness in his attempts to root out and prosecute those whom he considered to be dangerous to public morals. Comstock himself stated the purpose of his work in language which reflects his sense of mission:

My object is to expose the multitudinous schemes and devices of the sharper to deceive and rob the unwary and credulous through the mails; to warn honest and simple-minded persons; to shield our youth from debauching and corrupting influences; to arouse a public sentiment against the vampires who are casting deadly poison into the fountain of moral purity in the children; and at the same time expose to public indignation the infidels and liberals who defend these moral cancer-planters.[25]

Shortly after his discharge from the army following the Civil War, Comstock became a Special Agent for the United States Post Office Department, and, while in that capacity, he became the motivating force leading to the passage of postal statutes strengthening prohibitions against mailing obscene materials and objects. In 1873, the New York Young Men's Christian Association placed him in charge of its Society for the Suppression of Vice. His commission as a postal agent, which he retained, gave his work with the Society a pseudo-governmental character and considerably enhanced his power and influence.

Anthony Comstock pursued his duties with a dedication which could only come from a deep personal commitment. By 1880, he claimed to have arrested 408 persons, of whom two hundred had been convicted or pleaded guilty. He had confiscated enormous quantities of books, pictures, engraved plates, circulars, and other "articles for immoral use."[26] Such zeal had sometimes led Comstock to employ methods which, today, would not be condoned and which were severely criticized even at the time. He was not above entrapping his victim by posing as a customer or placing orders under fictitious names. Furthermore, his view of obscenity was entirely subjective; whatever he personally found objectionable on religious or moral grounds, he treated as illegal, and he pursued his goals with strong-arm enforcement. "At a meeting in 1880 an astute clergyman introduced Comstock as a man whose work was displeasing to the devil and whose methods were displeasing to saints."[27]

Prior to 1875, Anthony Comstock's efforts had been directed mainly at those forms of obscenity which involved transmission through the mail—books, pictures, articles for contraception and abortion, etc.—and he had not devoted much attention to the offerings of theatres or other places of entertainment. That was soon to change, however, as he found new "horrors" to expose.

In this first attack, however, Comstock's forces were not successful; the charges against Matt Morgan were not sustained. In addition to "draping the tableaux more than usual," Morgan's defense also relied on the opinions of prominent painters and sculptors whom he invited to observe the performances. The entire affair was viewed with amusement by the press and even those writers who did not totally support Morgan expressed their opposition mildly and with considerable humor. The *Spirit of the Times* published the following commentary:

> MR. Matt Morgan does not cater to the blind. You must have good eyes to see his missionary labors in the right light. He has recently been engaged in an eminently moral undertaking, illustrating high art by the means of the most beautiful creature in creation—woman—woman in all her simplicity, and very much unadorned. It is something in this age to see a self-sacrificing mind. The picture of Matt studying out his *poses* and teaching, for the sake of high art, the "lovely ladies" how to attitudinize, without damaging their tights, is worthy of Arcadian days, when simplicity flourished and there was no police. That invitation to the matrons of New York to bring their budding progeny to the Comique was Spartan. To the pure all things are pure; so of course were to the majority of young gentlemen, who have recently crowded the Comique, the elevated living pictures in question. Who could feel otherwise than elevated at the vision of Phyrne's bareness and Cleopatra's gauze vest, which just withhold the secrets. They suggest tights, and if Mr. Morgan gets into trouble through his pictures, he will be a martyr—a martyr to the cause of high art. But the Comique has become more elevated yet in its teachings—in its mission—this week. It has turned pious, and has given The Rock of Ages. There is a threat, they say, of an approaching exhibition up there of Suzanna and the Elders and Bathsheba in the Bath and Adam and Eve before the Fall. Thus the mission will be complete. The Bible will be pressed into its service, you know. By the way, if it's O.K., all correct, to teach higher art by the nude, why not set up a few literary classes and teach the rising generation the beauties of Martial Ovid, Rabelais and Casanova, as well as of Gérôme. Their works flourish in the libraries of the respectable, just as do the nudities of Gérôme in picture galleries. Mr. Morgan ought to get someone from Brooklyn, say, to give readings from a few choice passages of the above classics, and sandwich them in between Phryne and Cleopatra. But a truce to all this gossip. The season is half over and for all we know, between this and New Year, events may happen which may force the serpent of Old Nile to wear petticoats, and Phryne to cease exhibiting herself and to return to the relict of the Baptist minister—her respected parent. We wish her joy. She has nearly made a martyr of a distinguished artist, who, for her sake and that of high art, has narrowly escaped persecution. She did more; she filled the coffers of the Comique, and, we sincerely trust, her own pockets too. Poor Phryne![28]

The *Clipper* even published a short verse about the incident:

> Matt Morgan's statuary
> Think our police a bore

78   The Fight Begins Again, 1875-1893

> Which makes each statue wary
> To wear a little more.²⁹

The *New York Dramatic News* satirized Morgan's plight in a front page cartoon showing him with a tableau artist in "proper costume"—a cocoon-like coat in which only her eyes were visible.³⁰ (See Figure 13.) Finally, the same paper, in its lead editorial, provided a somewhat more serious treatment of the basic issues of censorship of the arts and of Comstock's influence:

> Mr. Matt Morgan has been annoyingly interfered with in the pursuit of his legitimate calling during the week or two past. This eminent artist has been subjected to the persecution of ignorant and mercenary fanatics, who have taken upon themselves to make their own laws and execute them. It seems to have been enough that a Comstock should disapprove of Mr. Morgan's entertainment, and for that precious moral sheet the *Herald*, to egg this fellow on, to cause trouble and perturbation. Comstock it seems went before the Grand Jury and endeavored to get an indictment against Mr. Morgan. The Captain and officers of the precinct were subpoenaed to appear and declared the exhibition not indecent in the most remote degree. Comstock was therefore thrown out of the Grand Jury room. Humiliated and malicious he goes before a police magistrate to get a warrant for the arrest of Mr. Morgan, on the ground that the Theatre Comique is a disorderly house. The magistrate refuses to grant it. But in the meantime the manager, fearful that innocent parties might suffer, stops the entertainment for a time, and thus Comstock is virtually triumphant. Mr. Morgan has been to District Attorney, Judges of the Supreme Court, and the foremost lawyers to obtain an opinion which might be safe to act upon. But these parties all say they cannot interfere, until it comes before them in legal shape.
>
> It is from this very error in our laws that a narrow brained half imbecile like Comstock finds safety in acting. There should be some sensible, liberal, educated authority, whose province it should be to decide upon a point like this. Are Mr. Morgan's actual reproductions of Gérôme's "Cleopatra before Caesar," and Cabanel's "Venus" indecent? Both these pictures were sold at public auction in this city. One of them now adorns the gallery of Mr. A.T. Stewart, and the other is the property of Mr. Wolff, of Fifth Avenue. Comstock shut up a Broadway store two days for selling photographs of Powers' "Greek Slave," a work of which all Americans are proud. Is he to be the judge of matters affecting either art or the drama? If he is, then he may interfere with our best theatres, and the private residences of our best citizens will come under the ban. Let there be a test case. Morgan should go immediately before the Grand Jury, and have Comstock indicted for perjury, based upon the statement this fellow made before the Tombs Magistrate. We should then know who is to be the authority in matters of this kind. As the law now stands it is a simple farce where crack-brained fanatics may work their dirty ends without molestation.³¹

On the same day the *Spirit of the Times* remarked, "Though the drapery of the ladies is rather scant and abbreviated, the posing and general effect is strictly classical and chaste notwithstanding."³²

Thus vindicated, Matt Morgan's tableaux continued as a highly popular attraction at the Theatre Comique. In January 1876 more new pictures were added—"The Disarming of Cupid," "Temptation of St. Anthony, the Christian Martyr," "The New Slave," "Truth at the Helm," and "The Destruction of Pompeii," the latter made especially effective by means of "the steam effect, as done by Mr. Richard Doyle."³³ As the run drew near its close

Figure 13. Matt Morgan with a tableau artist in "proper costume" to depict "Phryne." (*New York Dramatic News,* 18 December 1875, p. 1.)

the *Dramatic News* seemed pleased to observe, "Mr. Matt Morgan's tableaux are still, and always the main attraction of the Comique, and their value becomes apparent more and more. The carping opposition which they at first received has given way to a proper idea of their artistic worth."[34]

Saturday, 5 February 1876, was listed as the final performance of Matt Morgan's tableaux.[35] The following week a troupe of female minstrels occupied the Comique, and they were succeeded by a production of *Uncle Tom's Cabin*. It is possible, however, that some form of tableau act continued in a minor position on the bill even with these features, for on 26 February the advertising again listed "classic tableaux" and announced "five tableaux at matinee."[36] In mid-March Matt Morgan took over the management of the Lyceum where he presented a variety bill and a burlesque but did not include tableaux.[37]

Other producers were ready to take up the slack of Matt Morgan's departure from tableaux, and it must be kept in mind that the provocative advertising of Parisian Varieties had continued throughout Morgan's troubles at the Comique. It is indeed ironic that official objection was levelled at Morgan while other more likely targets were so near at hand. It was not to be very long, however, before Comstock's attention would turn to these producers also, especially since the new contenders employed some of the most obvious sensationalism yet to be seen in New York.

At the end of February 1876 Chateau Mabille Varieties at Thirty-fourth Street and Third Avenue began to advertise *The Seven Beauties* with the same kind of provocative rhymes which had been used earlier by the Parisian Varieties: "naughty but nice/ a sketch full of spice/ once to see won't suffice/ naughty but free from vice/ you'll see them in a trice/ are sure to entice."[38] Although the name of Prof. Lawrence, whose troupe had recently closed at the Metropolitan Theatre, does not appear in Chateau Mabille advertising, it is likely that he was responsible for tableaux during March at this house, also. The name of the act, "The Mirror of Beauty," appeared on the bills at both places.[39] Apparently, however, the bill was changed rather frequently at Chateau Mabille, for names of other tableau producers appear from time to time. On 8 April H.J. Campbell was listed. His act is not given a title on this bill, but during the late 1880's it appeared as Harry J. Campbell's Tableaux Soleil, playing at many major variety houses including Harry Miner's New Bowery and Eighth Avenue theatres and at Tony Pastor's. He also played many engagements in Brooklyn and other suburban locations.[40]

In April 1876, at Chateau Mabille Varieties, Mlle. Zulilia's troupe of twelve Blonde Statuary Artists, echoing Lydia Thompson's Blondes, presented an exhibition of "Roman and Grecian Statuary" composed of the following items:

1. Court of Beauty
2. Defiance
3. Love and Jealousy
4. Slaves
5. Three Graces

6. Peace and Plenty
7. Change in the Lovers
8. Throwing the Quoits
9. Dancing Girl
10. Goddess of Liberty[41]

Chateau Mabille Varieties continued in the same manner through the summer, fall, and winter of 1876, presenting six evening performances and three matinees per week.

Mid-October 1876 marked the beginning of an all-out crusade against those theatres exhibiting tableaux vivants. The tentative beginnings had come earlier, however, for a raid had occurred on 8 April 1876 against the Thirty-fourth Street Opera House where the sensational bill included "College Girls, Female Bathers, Can-Can, A racy story told with more truth than poetry... Mlle. Avery's Female Minstrels."[42] Not surprisingly, the company was charged with giving indecent performances, and for a time the place was closed.

The main thrust of the attack began, however, on Saturday, 14 October 1876, when, on the strength of a formal complaint by one "David Stoddard, a resident in the vicinity of this theatre," the police entered the Parisian Varieties (Robinson Hall).[43] Fifty-three persons connected with the theatre were arrested, including Julius K. Robinson, the proprietor, and W.M. Woodley, the manager, both of whom were sent to the Tombs to await trial. In a statement to the press, Robinson claimed to have requested both the arresting officer and the Superintendent of Police to give him notice if they saw anything objectionable in his performances. Robinson implies that no such notice was ever given, and there seems to be no record of any warnings being issued, either formally or informally. Nevertheless, reports of the arrests indicate that the theatre had long been looked upon as "offensive" and a "nuisance."[44]

The manner of the arrest was questionable at best, and the treatment of the performers was severely criticized by the press, even while the editors approved of closing the hall. It was reported that the artists were "taken off to the station-house, just as they were, in their stage dresses.... The night was intensely cold, and we should not be surprised to hear that several of the wretched ballet girls have been seriously indisposed, in consequence of their having been dragged through the streets without shawls or bonnets."[45] Confined in the Tombs for the night, the proprietor and manager "were together in a bed about three feet wide, which scarcely afforded space for turning, and compelled them to lie uncomfortable close together. Robinson is stout and jovial; Woodley is thin and pallid."[46] The same reporter observed, "In no other country in the world would such inhumanity as this have been practiced," and he attributed the whole police action to a sudden "spasm of morality" on the part of the authorities.

The press correctly predicted that the effect of this arrest would be short lived. Indeed, Parisian Varieties reopened on 16 October, and, although the *Clipper* at first reported that "the program presented was entirely free from what had been hitherto considered objectionable features,"[47] model artists were added to the program soon afterward, twelve tableaux being listed in the December advertisements. In January 1877 the house was proclaiming, "Good old times resumed, with a company sure to startle the natives,"[48] and Odell (10: 289) notes "Living Statues" on the bill as late as 12 March 1877.

This inability of the authorities to close Parisian Varieties was the result of inadequate laws on which to base prosecution, according to the *Spirit of the Times*. Virtually no legal changes had occurred since the 1848 crackdown on model artists, and the laws had been ineffective even then. The *Spirit* editor observed, "It is high time, we think, that a law be passed making it impossible for such shameless shows... to exist.... Then we should not have this horrid class of exhibitions in our midst, and Justice would not be made the laughingstock of the community for her utter incapacity to suppress them."[49]

Although no such law was forthcoming and tableaux continued to flourish, the authorities kept up their pressure. Next in line for attack were the Columbia Opera House and Egyptian Hall. The Columbia Opera House had begun sensational productions of various types in the fall of 1875 and for a time had been known as the American Alhambra.[50] In the fall of 1876, under the management of Jacob Schomberger—known to most as Jake Berry—the Columbia was advertising a troupe of "50 of the finest formed ladies in the world" to appear in "Poses Plastiques," among other acts.[51]

By March 1877 the management of the old Chateau Mabille Varieties had passed to J. Charles Davis who promptly renamed the house Egyptian Hall. The place did not close for any appreciable length of time during this transfer, and performances continued with no substantial change of style or appeal. The regular company then included the "Egyptian Hall Statue Troupe," and their appearances were featured prominently on the bills.

Advertising for both these houses was blatantly provocative, as were their performances, no doubt. Egyptian Hall billed itself as the "sensational palace of America" with "the latest Parisian novelties,"[52] and the Columbia Opera House offered "Thirty rich, rare and spicy naughty Sensations."[53] When police officials did not respond to such provocation with sufficient alacrity, the Society for the Suppression of Vice, led by Anthony Comstock, applied pressure to force them to act. In mid-March 1877, neglect of duty charges were preferred against Police Captain Kennedy of the Ninth Precinct and Captain Murphy of the Twenty-first. Kennedy was charged with failing to raid the Columbia Opera House when there were "entertainments on the stage of lewd, immoral, lascivious, and indecent character, consisting in the public exposure on the stage (in the view of large audiences of men) of numerous females in a state and condition of nudity, or so dressed as to simulate and suggest naked women and girls, ... posing as pretended models for nude statuary in a pretended artist's studio."[54] In his defense, Kennedy argued that he had assigned detectives to attend performances at the Columbia in an attempt to obtain evidence against the house, but his application for a warrant to raid the place had been denied by the magistrate at the Washington Place Police Court, on the grounds that his evidence was insufficient.[55] The complaint against Captain Murphy, in whose precinct Egyptian Hall was located, was similarly stated, and charged that he had failed to execute two warrants until eight days after they had been issued.[56]

This stratagem was sufficient to force action against at least the Columbia Opera House. On 27 March 1877 the proprietor, Jake Berry, was indicated by the Grand Jury of the Court of General Sessions for keeping a disorderly house.[57]

The Columbia Opera House remained closed for only a short time, resuming operation on Thursday, 28 June 1877, with a "New company in naughty novelties and spicy sensations."[58] This time the police responded immediately, and the house was raided on the following Monday night. The event was reported with apparent relish in the press:

> The Columbia Opera House, at West Twelfth street and Greenwich avenue, was re-opened on Thursday last. Last evening in defiance to the warnings they received, "Jake" Berry, the proprietor; Henry Campbell, the stage manager; Louis Decker, the manager; and Charlie Reeves, the treasurer, were at their posts and the theatre was opened. About 400 persons, mostly countrymen, were in the theatre. They did not recognize Detectives Noble and Finnegan and other officers in plain clothes. At 9 o'clock the curtain rose. At that moment Capt. Kennedy was quietly marching to the theatre with thirty police officers. After placing several men at the rear entrance in Twelfth street, Capt. Kennedy quickly marched the rest of the officers into the body of the hall. No sooner did those in the room notice the police than they sprang to their feet. Women screamed, and men leaped over seats in their anxiety to escape through the windows, but they were ordered back by the detectives. Capt. Kennedy pushed his way through to the stage, and proclaimed the theatre closed. Those in the room were told that they might retire.... Some of the performers were locked up with their faces still black, while others were just as they appeared while preparing for the next scene. Charlie Reeves, the treasurer, escaped with the receipts. As the prisoners were marched through the streets, the residents of the ward cheered Capt. Kennedy and his officers.[59]

The next day, however, when the prisoners were examined before Justice Duffy at the Jefferson Market Police Court, the arrests proved to be fruitless:

> The only witness for the prosecution was Mr. J.G. Herold, Jr., of No. 250 West Twelfth-street, on whose complaint the raid was made. He testified that he knew nothing of the nature of the performances at the establishment, and what he complained of was that the members of his family were annoyed by the women exposing themselves at the windows of their dressing-room, which faced the rear windows of his residence. Capt. Kennedy made a statement that he had received a great many complaints from the residents of the

neighborhood in regard to performances at this place of amusement, but after he had made the arrests the people who had been loudest in their complaints declined to come forward to substantiate their statements. He therefore had no further evidence to offer. Justice Duffy said that he regretted exceedingly that he would be compelled to discharge the proprietors, but as no evidence to hold them had been adduced, he had no other alternative. The proprietors were then discharged, and the magistrate called up each of the female performers and questioned them as to the part taken by them in the performance. They were either "song and dance" artists or ballet dancers, and their salaries ranged from $7 to $15 per week. Several of the women were married and three of the young girls said that their earnings supported their widowed mothers. They were all discharged.[60]

During the rest of 1877 model artists appeared, not only at the Columbia, but at other theatres as well with no further interference by the authorities. Frank Bolton's Poses Plastiques, which occupied the National Theatre from 30 April to 16 June,[61] were succeeded in August by "Mme. La Remyas presenting her revolving and transformation statuary troupe of 'the most bewitching young ladies on the stage'."[62] In June 1877 Tony Pastor had jumped on the tableau bandwagon, featuring an "Attraction Extraordinary...the great FORBIDDEN PLEASURE COMBINATION with MME. CORELLI'S PARISIAN STATUE TROUPE, consisting of 50 beautifully formed young ladies, in a series of elegant LIVING PICTURES."[63] Mme Corelli closed at Pastor's on Saturday, 14 July, only to be replaced by the intriguing "Jackits-Chy Japanese Troupe of male and female artists."[64] On 30 July, Mlle Ninon Duclos, formerly of Parisian Varieties, became leasee and directoress of Central Park Garden and offered her "Statuary Troupe" in 'Living Art Pictures" throughout the summer.[65] From late August until cold weather closed the Garden, Mlle Marie D'Est's living models appeared on the bill.[66] Egyptian Hall maintained a statue troupe under its own name and continued the sensational advertising which had long been its hallmark. Finally, the Columbia Opera House featured Marie Connelly's Statue Troupe in such pieces as "That Wicked Parson and his Wife's Beautiful Living Pictures."[67] By early 1878 "Miss Belle Berry and one hundred Dizzy Blondes" had taken over the Columbia and were the featured attraction when the next skirmish with police took place.[68]

That skirmish began on Monday, 25 February 1878, when large details of police interrupted performances at both Egyptian Hall and the Columbia Opera House. Forty patrolmen occupied the Columbia, and, after dismissing the audience amidst "considerable excitement and confusion," the detective in charge arrested twenty-one women and seven men from the performing company. A similar force arrested fifteen men and thirteen women at Egyptian Hall. Although Jake Berry, proprietor of the Columbia, was not in the theatre at the time of the raid, he voluntarily placed himself in police custody the next day. At Egyptian Hall, George Warren, Charles Davis, and George Williams, the proprietors and managers, were among those arrested.[69] The prisoners were detained through the night in precinct station houses, and the next morning, as had become common practice in such cases, they were "marched through the streets to the Jefferson Market Police Court," where the arraignment was held in a courtroom "crowded to its utmost capacity with politicians and other idlers," a group described in one account as "mongrel curiosity-seekers."[70] The *Herald* described the scene:

> The space in front of the prisoners' railing was occupied by a struggling mass of sickly looking females and broad shouldered officers of the law. On the bench with Judge Duffy were Judge Kilbreth, Aldermen Bennett and Morris and Mr. Addison G. Jerome. Inspectors Murray and Dilks [the arresting officers] were also present. The affidavits were made by Messrs. Meeker and Waite, detectives for the Society for the Suppression of Vice. The charge was that the prisoners had taken part in a performance which had tended "to deprave the senses, corrupt the morals, degrade the character and excite the basest sensualities and passions of all who were unfortunate to be present; a performance filthy and vile, apt to entrap the young and corrupt innocence and purity."[71]

All of the performers were released, except two who were detained as witnesses. Trial dates were set for the proprietors and managers, and bail was fixed at $1000 for each person. William N. Paul, the "leading man" at the Columbia Opera House, was placed under bond of $400 to be on six months' good behavior.[72]

The examination and trial of Jake Berry was given thorough press coverage, as the following description of the session on 7 March illustrates:

> The examination in the complaint against Jake Berry, the proprietor of the Columbia Opera-house, in Greenwich-avenue, which was "raided" by the police some weeks ago, was continued before Justice Duffy at Jefferson Market Police Court yesterday. The court-room was densely crowded with spectators, among whom were Rev. Howard Crosby and a number of members of the Society for the Prevention of Crime, and Capt. Kennedy, of the Ninth Precinct. Col. W.P. Prentice, counsel for Dr. Crosby's Society, represented the prosecution, and Messrs. McClelland & Steiner appeared for the defense.
>
> J.K. Kiefner, of No. 90 Greenwich-avenue, near the Opera-house, testified that the place was a perfect nuisance; he was at times so much annoyed by the place that he and his family were prevented from sleeping; loud and disturbing noises and sounds of revelry kept people awake in the neighborhood; he had been often insulted by the frequenters of the theater.
>
> Mrs. Kraft, of No. 94 Greenwich-avenue, testified that she had often gone to the station-house to ask relief from the annoyance created by the frequenters of the opera-house; she could not keep her tenants, and she feared that her children would be corrupted by the obscene placards in front of the place.
>
> Capt Kennedy, of the Ninth Precinct, testified that he had received several anonymous communications in relation to the place complained of, but no specific complaints had been made to him; he had sent officers in plain clothes to the place, and he had gone there himself a number of times; he had never been shocked by the performance. The captain admitted that the Manager of the theater was well acquainted with him, and he had not visited every part of the house. The attire of the women was similar to that worn by females in other variety theaters.

Mr. William M. White described minutely the performance on the nights of Feb. 11, 13, and 15. The attire of the females was immodest, and the language and the acting were indecent and immoral, especially in the play entitled "Mock Modesty." On being cross examined the witness stated that he had not visited theatres 15 times in his life, and had never seen "The Black Crook," "White Fawn," "Round the Clock," or "Antony and Cleopatra," nor did he wish to see them. Mr. Moses S. Meeker corroborated the testimony of Mr. White. Mr. Isaac Odell, President of the Irving National Bank, residing at No. 17 Bank-street, testified that the place was so great a nuisance that he did not deem it safe for the female members of his family to go out after dark. Property owned by him in the neighborhood had greatly depreciated owing to the proximity to the place complained of.

This closed the testimony for the prosecution and the defense called Robert Peterson, of No. 417 West Twelfth-street, who testified that he had visited the place several times and had seen nothing improper or indecent in the performances. Edward Gomez, an engineer, of No. 217 West Thirteenth-street, testified that he had visited the place on several occasions and had taken his wife and daughters there. He did not think it was a bad place to take ladies. The building belonged to the Gomez estate and he rented it to Jake Berry, and accounted for the rent to Dr. Horatio Gomez of No. 245 West Twenty-fifth street, who was one of the trustees of the estate. G.P. Bernard, the leader of the orchestra, testified that there was no more noise in the place than in any other theatre.

This concluded the testimony, and the magistrate then listened to argument made [by] Col. Prentice and Mr. McClelland. Justice Duffy, at the conclusion of the argument, said he would render his decision at a future day.[73]

Justice Duffy rendered a written decision on 14 March in which he held the accused men for trial, continuing the bail figure of $1000. His review of the evidence is interesting for the attitudes toward censorship which it expresses:

This court is of the opinion, from the evidence adduced, that there is probable cause to hold these parties to answer. The exhibitions of lewd plays in some theatres is no defense for their production in others. Theatres were instituted to teach honor and morality, and are now fostered by the greatest in art and literature. And many of them in this city (to their credit be it said) allow nothing to be produced that would give offense to religion or law, and as such should be maintained and protected. The offense does not always consist in reading the text of a play, but it is in the attitudes and gestures of the performer or player, or the omission or the insertion of a word in the text. In conclusion, the court is of the opinion that the representation of such plays has a very immoral and baneful effect upon the youth of our City, and any and every society instituted for the suppression of such plays should have the moral and legal support of all interested in the welfare of humanity, and their officers and agents the gratitude of all good citizens.[74]

All the managers and proprietors pleaded "not guilty" on 25 March, and the trial continued into April.[75] Testimony consisted mainly of conflicting opinions as to whether the performances at the Columbia were indecent and whether the atmosphere created by the theatre was offensive to the neighborhood. Widely varying opinions were expressed by residents of the area, police officers in the precinct, and employees of the theatre. On 29 April, after four and a half hours of deliberation, the jury returned a verdict of guilty against Jake Berry, with a recommendation for mercy.[76] The next day Berry was sentenced to eight months imprisonment in the penitentiary and fined $150, a sentence which ignored the jury's recommendation. This harsh sentence may have been prompted in part by an irregularity late in the trial. While instructing the jury prior to their deliberations, Recorder Hackett, it was reported, "informed them that he had received anonymous letters stating that the prisoner had friends on the jury and that no verdict would be agreed upon."[77] Then, after the verdict had been rendered, one juryman claimed that he did not agree with the verdict of guilty. This incident was discussed in the courtroom on the day of sentencing and reported as follows:

> Recorder Hackett said that he had just had an interview with the juryman in question, who was greatly excited, and said that he had positive information that he was a personal friend of Berry, and an habitue of his establishment. The eleventh-hour protestations of this juryman did not alter his view of the case in the slightest. It was subsequently ascertained that the juryman who had confided his troubles to Mr. Brooke and the Recorder was Martin Brummerhoff, a stevedore, of No. 47 West-street. He admitted that Berry was a personal friend, and said that he had not been able to sleep in consequence of having agreed to a verdict of guilty. Recorder Hackett said that he had never tried a case in which the verdict was so satisfactory for him, save for the recommendation of mercy. He [Berry] had deliberately violated the law, and his witnesses, in trying to save him from the consequences of his crime, had willfully perverted the truth. The jury, he thought, had arrived at a safe conclusion. He considered it one of the most serious charges that could be brought against a man. He was astonished that the police had permitted such a place to exist. As an example to others more than a punishment to himself, he would, while taking into consideration the recommendation of the jury, impose a severe punishment.[78]

Tableau vivant exhibitions at the Columbia Opera House were effectively stopped by this attack. The house was closed when the arrests took place, and when it reopened in early March as French's Vaudeville Theatre, there were no living models on the bill.

Whether Egyptian Hall actually closed during this period is difficult to determine. Only one press report dealt with the pretrial "inquiry into the naughtiness of the Egyptian Hall performances,"[79] and, after the arraignment and the "not guilty" pleas of the managers, press coverage centered on the trial of Jake Berry, with no mention of the fate of Egyptian Hall. Even while the legal proceedings continued, Egyptian Hall advertising appeared regularly. "NEW LIVING STATUES" were listed on 5 March,[80] and on 11 April the performance was again noted in the *Herald's* "Amusements To-night" column. In early June the place was calling itself "the only sensational theatre in the city" and featuring "Our Renowned Statues by Lovely Living Models."[81] Also in June, one newspaper remarked that after the raids of "two months ago the performances were modified. Recently one questionable feature after another has been introduced."[82] Thus, on 15 June, just as the "Egyptian Hall Statue Troupe" was about to present "The Artist's Studio," Captain Murphy and a squad of policemen again stopped the performance and arrested the performers.

In passing, it should be noted that the account of these arrests gives us another small description of a technique of production employed for tableaux. In this case, the method harks back to the "ghost shows" of the 1850's.

> The "bevy of beautiful young ladies" were arranged for the statue scene. This was produced in a peculiarly artistic way, in the Egyptian Hall. The young women were dressed in flesh-colored tights, resembling the skin as closely as possible, with a covering of thin gauze about the waist. The upper parts of their bodies were almost entirely naked. They did not show themselves upon the stage, but reclined in an inclined platform beneath the stage. A large mirror at the back of the stage reflected their nearly nude figures. In this position Capt. Murphy found them.[83]

Nineteen persons were arrested, including Thomas Lacy, the proprietor, and John J. Dawson, the manager. One of the women, Lillie Phillips, turned out to be an eighteen-year-old runaway "whom Capt. Murphy took off the same stage some time ago, at the request of her parents, who are respectable people, residents of Clinton-Place."[84]

At the arraignment the following morning, the prosecution, as usual, was conducted by a representative of the Society for the Suppression of Vice. The performers were released "with an admonition to keep away from Egyptian Hall," but "Justice Duffy announced his purpose to be severe with the proprietors of such shows."[85] They were charged with keeping a disorderly house. Bail was set at $1000 each, with an extra $100 for the additional charge of selling liquor without a license.[86]

Once again Egyptian Hall was closed for a time, but in the fall it again rose phoenix-like with renewed tableaux. Its advertising in November, in fact, is so similar to earlier ads that one wonders if operation was suspended at all. In any case, a new troupe of model artists had assumed residence and the bill appeared thus:

> SENSATIONAL BALLETS. SENSATIONAL SONGS. SENSATIONAL STATUES. Mlle. DECOURS CELEBRATED ART STUDIO. The FINEST FORMED BEAUTIES in the WORLD. An entire new troupe of French Dancers. THE GREAT LADY VAUDEVILLE TROUPE in NEW SKETCHES. NAUGHTY SONGS.[87]

Mlle DeCours remained on the bill through December, but she may have departed in time to avoid the final attack by police, which occurred on 1 February 1879. Her name does not appear in the list of those arrested when, following the same pattern as before, the police raided the place for the last time. The new managers, John J. Reilly and John Clark were arraigned, as usual, and the performers released with reprimands.[88] The repeated assaults had finally proved successful, however, for Egyptian Hall ceased to function thereafter.

During this last season of Egyptian Hall there were a few other theatres which were also presenting tableaux without police interference. These, however, did not promote sensationalism as the targeted places had done, and often the tableaux were only minor features on lengthy vaudeville bills. The only theatre besides Egyptian Hall which advertised its own resident company of model artists was the National Varieties, at Forty-ninth Street and Eighth Avenue, with its "National Art Picture Troupe, Arranged and Directed by F.A. McClane," which appeared during the summer of 1878. Placed at the end of the "Olio of Fun" and bearing the familiar title, "The Artists Studio," the pictures included were: "The Battle," "After the Battle," "The Stray Shot," "Love, Hate and Jealousy," "Jealousy and Crime," "The Battle" (again), "Disappointment," "The Three Graces," "The Last Whoop," and "The Nation's Dependents."[89] Obviously, this feature had little of the provocative appeal which had so incensed the Society for the Suppression of Vice.

Short-run tableau presentations also took place in other theatres during 1878. In July, Tony Pastor's listed "MAY FISK'S FAMOUS AND ORIGINAL TROUPE OF ENGLISH BLONDES. 20 BEAUTIFUL YOUNG LADIES 20."[90] August saw "Mme. Ida Siddons' English Blondes and Statue Troupe" at Cremorne Vaudeville Theatre.[91] This troupe was later seen as "one of the very first respectable burlesque shows...a small family affair, headed by 'Pop' Siddons, his daughter, Ida, and her comedian husband.... This eventually became known as the Ida Siddons Burlesque and Novelty Company and played the Miner Theatres in New York City. [Harry Miner's New Broadway and Eighth Avenue Theatre]"[92]

From 1879 to 1893 tableau production did not usually achieve top billing at the vaudeville theatres, and no theatres appear to have maintained troupes especially for such productions. Several reasons may explain this change. The practice of "continuous performance" which many variety theatres were adopting during the 70's and 80's made necessary a much wider variety of acts and a larger number of performers at a single theatre. To provide such variety, many acts were booked for short runs and, thus, moved frequently from one theatre to another. It became less and less practical for a variety theatre manager to maintain a "house company," as most tableau companies had been. In addition, it is likely that public interest in tableaux waned somewhat during this period. The proliferation of sensational living pictures in the 1870's and the great notoriety they had received may well have exhausted their appeal as a daring novelty. Some of the dance houses and concert saloons of earlier times were still in operation, and though these suffered raids and arrests from time to time they did cater to those seeking "sensational novelties."[93] Furthermore, the intense legal assault on producers in the preceding years must have discouraged some of the more scandalous efforts and even given pause to tableau artists with the best of intentions. The pressure of this legal assault was kept alive during the 1880's, even though it was not always directed specifically at tableaux.

A notorious afterpiece, entitled *Bashful Venus,* aroused the ire of police at Parker's American Theatre, resulting in a raid on 3 October 1882. How extensively tableaux vivants may have figured in the production is impossible to tell, but the *New York Times* reported that "a tableau of 'Bashful Venus' was on when the police entered."[94] The nature of this "tableau" is made somewhat clearer in the *Spirit of the Times* account: "An old man advertises that he will marry the girl who has the finest limbs, and a lot of girls are displayed upon a platform for the examination of the audience, a curtain covering them down to the knees. When the performance had reached this point the police interfered."[95] Fourteen members of the troupe were arraigned the following day and were charged with disorderly conduct for having presented a lewd and indecent performance. They were fined ten dollars each, with the exception of two girls who pleaded poverty.[96]

In mid-decade, Lydia Thompson, considered by many to have originated the "leg show," was dismayed at the less than enthusiastic reception she received while touring the United States. She complained in the *St. Louis Democrat:*

> I do not see so many of the faces that were familiar in the parquet rows when I was here seventeen years ago. They are all young men I have been playing to this week, at the Olympic—evidently a new generation—and, unlike their bald-head old pas, they do not take that overwhelming interest in ballet costumes that was had by their blissful old progenitors. A sad change seems to have come over the spirit of the male population of this country. Limb shows are not nearly the financial successes that they used to be, even as late as the fifteen years ago, and the rage for the blonde burlesquer appears to have perished.... Married or single, we had all mature men—not the giddy, silly, noodle-headed dudes like those of the present day—in our thrall. We were besieged in front of the footlights and at the stagedoor, and had as many admirers in every town as there were voters. But comic opera and farce comedy, with its ballet trimming, nas [sic] divided attention, and now the legitimate burlesque and limb shows receive little or no encouragement.[97]

Such comments as these served to reinforce public awareness of the "leg show" and similar issues related to the morality of the stage. Even "legitimate" actors occasionally became involved in the press debates which resulted. James Murdock, for example, in response to arguments that the theatre was an evil institution, rose to its defense, though not in the way many producers would have wished:

> ...The abuses of the stage were the fault of the public, which applauded and laughed at evil that ought to be hissed down.... Any public institution, not excepting the church itself, if left to the self-aggrandizing influence of individual control would not remain unsullied and pure. All public institutions require a proper moral supervision to restrain the evil and protect the good. This moral supervision may come from the public and the press, for the hiss of an auditor is to an actor worse than the hiss of an adder in the path of a traveller.[98]

Perhaps the most extreme attack on the morality of the stage was that of the Rev. A. Boyle, a British minister, who argued that the very fact that men and women play together on the stage makes the theatre inherently indecent.[99]

Anthony Comstock and the Society for the Suppression of Vice continued to be active. In 1888 they turned their attention to the "dime museums," raiding four of them at once and confiscating what they charged were "indecent anatomical wax figures."[100] Although no *living* models were involved, the legal action resembled closely that which had earlier been directed against tableaux exhibitors.

Actually, the very existence of dime museums and similar cheap amusements was seen as a threat to legitimate drama, and undoubtedly competed for much of the potential tableau audience. Theatre managers openly resented the inroads made by such entertainments and lamented their inability to reduce admission prices to competitive level.[101]

Public sentiment concerning stage nudity, whether actual or simulated, was expressed through two widely publicized actions in the early 1890's. A Minnesota law was passed prohibiting women from wearing tights on the stage. Its strong language attempted to close all loop holes:

> Any female person who shall, upon the stage or platform, in any theatre or opera house, concert hall or other place whatever where other persons are present, expose her nether limb or limbs, dressed in tights, so called, or in any manner whatever so that the shape and form of her nether limb or limbs are plainly visible to such persons present, shall be guilty of open and gross lewdness and lascivious behavior, and guilty of a misdemeanor,...[102]

There was speculation that the effects of this law were apt to extend to New York, since managers made their money by producing in New York what they could then take on the road.[103]

The potential effects of this law extended beyond tableau vivant productions. If enforced, it would also apply to ballet costume, even though the ballet enjoyed more public and official approval as an art than did tableaux. The complaint which the law was intended to address was an objection to the exposure of "nether limbs," regardless of the kind of performance in which it occurred.

The same attitude was also expressed in attempts to control the widespread use of lithographed advertising posters which depicted women in tights or abbreviated costumes. Police in many major cities were being ordered to tear down posters showing such subjects as "Marching Amazons in tights, and ballet girls whose dresses didn't reach the knees."[104] Interestingly, this attack met with little opposition from the theatrical professions and even received support in many cases. The Edwin Forrest Lodge of the Actors' Order of Friendship, for instance, passed the following resolution setting forth both moralistic and pragmatic reasons for their objection to the use of such posters:

> *Resolved,* That we believe that a persistence in this course will prove injurious to the best interests of the theatrical profession, and we hereby, as a body, enter our protest against the continuance of these managerial methods of advertising as not only an abuse of our art, but a menace to public decency and a strong weapon of attack in the hands of the everready and too-willing traducers of the stage.[105]

Even theatrical managers refrained from opposing the ban, since they were anxious to abandon lithograph advertising altogether, on economic grounds. The printing costs themselves were high, but, in addition, it was necessary to give complimentary tickets to shopkeepers who displayed the lithos in their windows. One manager estimated his cost for these free admissions to be over $200,000 per season.[106] It was further agreed that the less expensive newspaper advertising reached more people than did the lithographs. Nevertheless, one may wonder whether Comstockian pressures were having wider effects than the record actually shows.

What was perhaps the most spectacular and notorious incident related to the issue of stage indecency was prompted by the famous appearance of Little Egypt, performing her "Danse du Ventre" at the Chicago Columbian Exposition of 1893. News of the financial success and the intense moral controversy surrounding her performance quickly spread throughout the country and, not surprisingly, spawned a host of Little Egypt imitators. In New York a "World's Fair Prize Winners' Exposition" was opened at the Grand Central Palace, featuring "a reproduction of the scenes upon the Midway Plaisance, including some of the performances which helped to make that portion of the World's Fair exhibits extremely popular with those seeking novel sensation."[107] The exposition opened on 30 November 1893, and the highlight was immediately recognized as the Cairo exhibit which featured four performers in a "dance du ventre." On the third day of performance, however, police arrested the dancers, asserting that, while such indecencies may have been condoned in Chicago, they were certainly not acceptable in New York. When the judge permitted the dancers to post bail and continue to perform, pending the outcome of a trial, it was duly noted in the press, with considerable badinage, that thereafter a police inspector sat in the audience making notes at each performance. The three-day trial was reported in terms suggesting that it was the best comic entertainment in the city, but in the end the show was closed and the indignant performers fined fifty dollars each.[108]

While tableau vivant production diminished during the 1880's and early 1890's, it did not disappear altogether. Though the sensationalism of the 70's was abandoned and the flamboyant style of Matt Morgan was not to be found, there were some notable performers and productions.

As in the past, tableaux were important adjuncts to many plays, and in the 1880's several productions were even built around the "living pictures" or "living statue" concept. On 25 October 1880 Edward E. Rice's company, which he labelled his "Surprise Party," opened at Haverly's Fourteenth Street Theatre in *Revels,* a comic opera very loosely based on the story of St. George and the Dragon. The highlight of the show was the "haunted picture gallery"— a scene in which models, posed as statues and as paintings in picture frames, come to life to startle and poke passers-by and engage in other comic business. Reviewers called the scene "screamingly comical" and even adopted a joking tone while observing that the costumes served more "to discover rather than conceal fair proportions in the human form divine."[109] E.E. Rice had already established a reputation as a successful producer of extravaganza and comic opera and was credited by one critic with making opera bouffe into an American form.[110] He is important to the development of tableaux vivants in New York, for, as we shall see, it was an E.E. Rice production which began the period of culminating glory for tableaux in the mid-1890's.

The Pygmalion and Galatea story had long been a favorite in the theatre and the role of the statue which comes to life became a mainstay in the repertoire of Mary Anderson during the 1880's.[111] (See Figures 14-17.) In 1887 Koster and Bial were advertising a "grand illusion Galatea—From stone to life, from life to stone."[112] In 1885 Henry E. Dixey appeared at the Bijou Opera House as "the Statue" in the burlesque, *Adonis.* (He also played nine other roles in the same play.)[113] Living statues formed part of the attraction of *The Tinted Venus* at Daly's in 1891,[114] and later the same year *Niobe* was described as "a picturesque mingling of 'Galatea' and 'The Tinted Venus,' with a prosaic American home for the scene of action."[115]

Some tableau presentations did not attempt to follow any dramatic structure and often did not even credit by name the artists who performed or arranged them. Tony Pastor's included tableaux regularly throughout the decade, only occasionally naming the artists responsible. In 1881 a James S. Moffit presented "marvelous groupings" in a "beautiful tableau pantomime" called *The Comanches.*[116] In 1887 Sandiland and Ruthden's Golden Statues exhibited "beautiful living pictures in flaming gold and bronze."[117] Professor James Lawrence provided "living revolving pictures" at Aberle's New Theatre the week of 26 February to 3 March 1883,[118] and Mme. Quitsch with the Sheffer and Blakely Company, presented tableaux vivants in several New York variety theatres during 1887-88.[119] From 1884 through 1889 "Professor" Harry J. Campbell, who had been the stage manager at the Columbia Opera House during the 1877 raids, presented his "Tableaux Soleil" at the Miner theatres, Tony Pastor's, the National Theatre, and others.[120]

A few performers during the 80's were truly ingenious in their attempts to provide novelty in tableaux. May Fisk's English Blondes, who had appeared earlier at Tony Pastor's, were "swinging in midair" at Aberle's Tivoli for two months in 1882.[121] At the Bijou Opera House "Alice Atherton's Picture Frame" was incorporated into a burlesque entitled *Dreams; or Fun in a Photograph Gallery.* The act combined living pictures with impersonations of such

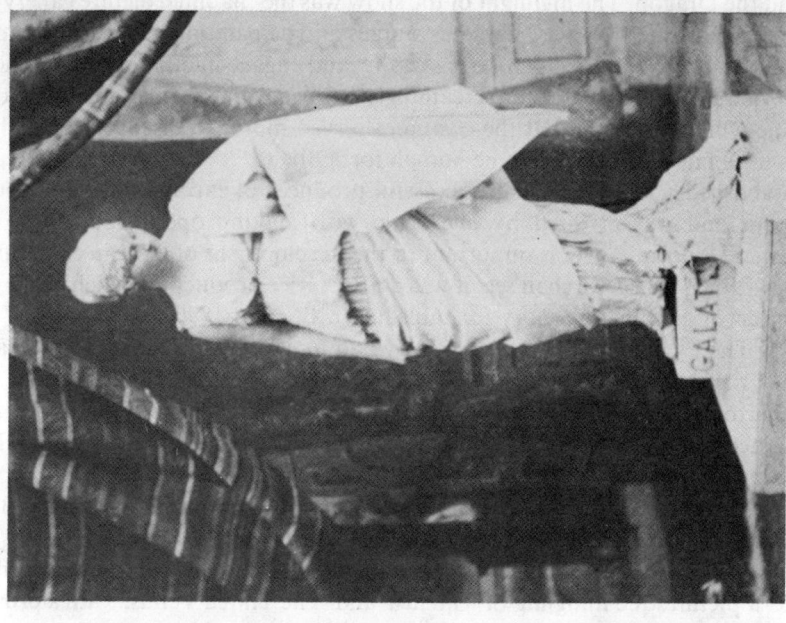

Figs. 14-17. Mary Anderson as the statue, "Galatea." (Courtesy of the Billy Rose Theatre Collection; the New York Public Library at Lincoln Center; Astor, Lenox and Tilden Foundations.)

Figure 14. Photo by H. Rocher, Chicago, 1881.

Figure 15. Photo by Mora, New York, n.d.

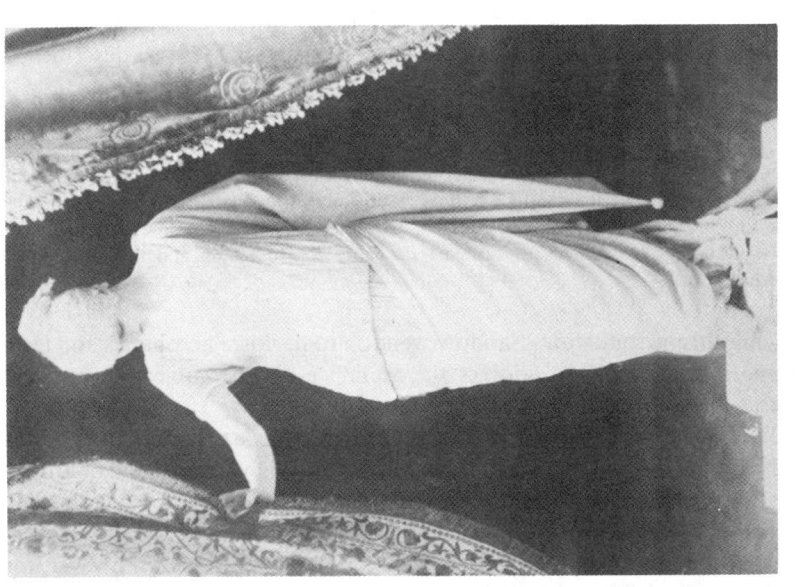

Figure 16. Photo by Napoleon Sarony, New York, 1883.

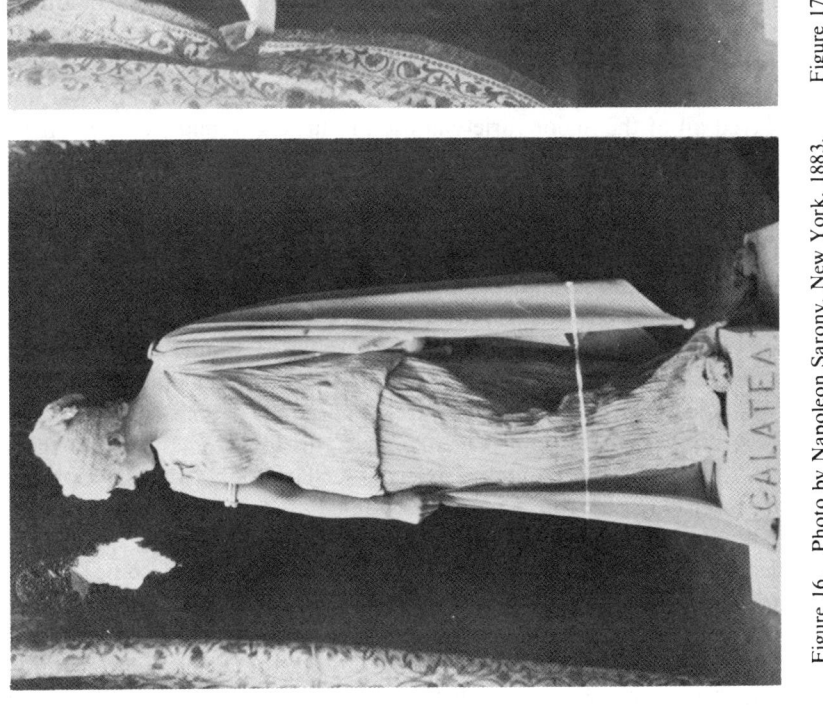

Figure 17. Photo by Napoleon Sarony, New York, 1883.

prominent actors of the day as J.K. Emmett, Mary Anderson, Joseph Jefferson, and Kate Claxton.[122]

One of the most popular and impressive performers then appearing was Sandow, the strong man, who combined tableaux with his athletic exhibitions. (See Figure 18.) One of his performances at the Casino in 1893 was described as follows:

> The curtain went up, revealing the stage steeped in gloom. Then, suddenly, two curtains at the back of the stage were drawn aside, and in a blaze of light stood the "Strong Man," with his mightly muscles standing out in bold relief in the white glare of electric lights. After performing a number of "tableaux vivants," to the accompaniment of slow music and much perspiration, Mr. Sandow left his cabinet, the lights were turned up, and the show began in earnest.[123]

Following this introduction, Sandow went on to perform acrobatics and feats of strength and finally to address the audience on the subject of physical culture.

One of the most durable acts performing tableaux vivants during this period was the team of Jules and Amanda Tissot. They were on the boards of one or another New York theatre virtually full-time from 1880 through 1893, although they generally played engagements of only a week or two and seldom received top billing. Apparently they were a popular attraction, however, for they played all of the major variety houses, returning to many of them again and again. Sadly, critics treated the pair as a sort of "fixture," commenting only that the Tissots "also appeared" or that their performance "elicited uproarious merriment." No descriptions indicate the special appeal of their act; indeed critics seemed to assume the performance was so familiar to their readers as to make description unnecessary. Their performance did not consistently employ a single title and the advertising phrases used in reference to them suggest that they had several specialties through the years. In the early days they were listed as "a troupe of living automatons,"[124] but on 27 October 1884 they introduced their "Cat Duet" act at Miner's Theatre, Bowery.[125] The next year the bills listed "Tissant's [sic] Tableaux Vivants," and this term remained with them afterward.[126] When the famous magician, Kellar, took over the Comedy Theatre for an extensive run in September 1885, Part Two of his program was a short variety bill headed by the Tissots in "Marionettes Vivants (living Pictures)."[127] One indirectly favorable appraisal of the Tissots comes from a critic who disliked Kellar's performance and commented, "As though to make up for this deficiency, he [Kellar] employs...the Tissots to present their marionettes with human heads."[128] When Tony Pastor celebrated his twenty-fifth year of management in March 1889, the Tissots appeared on his bill. In 1887 at Niblo's Garden and again in 1889 at the Standard Theatre the team appeared on the bills with productions of *The Black Crook;* they probably also took part in the main attraction itself. Finally, the Tissots occupied the Casino

Figure 18. Sandow, the strong man, posed as "The Dying Gladiator." (Napoleon Sarony, *Sarony's Living Pictures* [New York: A.E. Chasmar & Co., 1894], n.p.) Courtesy of the John M. Wing Collection, The Newberry Library, Chicago.

Roof Garden during August 1893.[129] After that their career fades into obscurity.

It should also be noted at this point that a new subject for tableaux was introduced in 1886 with the arrival in New York of Frederic Auguste Bartholdi's colossal statue of "Liberty Enlightening the World." The statue was brought to America in 1884, and even before it had been erected on Bedloe's Island, a living representation of it augmented a sacred concert at Koster and Bial's on 8 November 1885, a Sunday.[130] Thereafter it was a popular feature of numerous tableaux. Such a living statue was included in a Bartholdi festival at the Thalia Theatre on 28 October 1886, the date of President Grover Cleveland's dedication of the actual statue.[131]

By the early 1890's, the respectability of tableaux vivants had made considerable progress since the demise of Egyptian Hall and the Columbia Opera House. Even as early as the summer of 1880 tableaux were occasionally noted in the society pages of New York newspapers. *The Daily Graphic*, for instance, published thirteen drawings from "instantaneous photographs taken during the representation" of tableaux vivants based upon Sir Walter Scott's novels, performed at Cromwell House, South Kensington, London.[132]

In February 1891 the prominent Kit Kat Club of New York society inaugurated tableaux vivants as the feature of their annual entertainment to raise money in support of life classes for art students.[133] These were given prominent newspaper coverage on the society pages both before the event (reporting its preparation) and afterward (giving laudatory reviews). The scene painter from the Metropolitan Opera House, T.D. Plaisted, was engaged by the Kit Kat Club, and numerous painters and sculptors supervised the preparation of tableaux to represent their own works. Included in the program were "The Angel of Prayer" by Walter Satterlee, "The Amateur Photograph" by J. Wells Champney, J. Carroll Beckwith's "Ophelia," and "The Death of Minnehaha" by W.L. Dodge. In addition, there were representations of portraits by Franz Hals and Velasquez, works of Greek sculpture, and other familiar paintings. The finale was to be an invention entitled "The Deluge," depicting the "combined cussedness" of the Kit Kat Club itself. "It was a striking scene, showing a score of exhausted men and women endeavoring to climb from an endless waste of waters about a point of rocks that had already been taken possession of by an enraged tiger and her cubs."[134] The same reviewer approvingly observed, "If it were possible to have... the tableaux vivants of the Kit Kat Club last night preserved and put up at auction, they would certainly bring very high prices." Clearly this was a very different sort of response from that which tableaux had received in the more recent past.

The period from 1875 to 1893 had seen the last great legal battles over tableaux vivants. The sensationalism of Parisian Varieties, the Columbia Opera House, and Egyptian Hall had been successfully attacked during the 1870's. The efforts of Matt Morgan had established that acceptable tableaux could be staged, and a resulting state of equilibrium was established. Although the 1880's did not produce any grand tableau spectacles or especially noteworthy productions, tableaux vivants were presented consistently in several forms. "Living statue" characters were the basis of such plays as *Adonis* and *Pygmalion and Galatea,* in which respected actors were featured. Many unsung tableau acts appeared as lesser entertainments on vaudeville bills, and some performers and producers, such as the Tissots and Harry J. Campbell, show up repeatedly throughout the period. Finally, the acceptability of the genre may be inferred from the fact that, by the early 1890's, it was being used as a charity entertainment in the upper levels of society. However, the true proof of its renewed popularity is to be found during the late 1890's in the appearance of more spectacular tableaux than ever before, in the mainstream theatres and music halls. The first and grandest of these productions was provided by a newcomer to New York, Edward Kilanyi.

7

Edward Kilanyi: Master Tableau Artist

The last great era of tableaux vivants on the New York stage was the latter half of the 1890's. Memories of the most objectionable tableaux had begun to fade and more respectable production, both professional and amateur, had diluted the social stigma attached to such exhibitions. By 1893 the time was ripe for a revival of the form, and there were enterprising managers, well established in the theatre, ready to capitalize on what again could be called a "new novelty." The immediate opportunity was provided by a Hungarian named Edward Kilanyi, along with two familiar, talented Americans, manager A.M. Palmer, and producer Edward E. Rice.

Albert M. Palmer, one of the founders of the Players Club, had earned an enviable reputation by developing the highly successful Union Square Theatre company over an eleven year period, 1872-83. Although he had intended to retire after that, he instead assumed management of the Madison Square Theatre and later, in 1888, took over Wallack's Theatre, giving it his own name. On 15 May 1893 he opened a very successful burlesque production entitled *1492*.[1] The next season he leased the Garden Theatre, part of the Madison Square Garden complex, and moved *1492* to that location where it continued to flourish. The producer of *1492* was Edward E. Rice, whose earlier production of *Revels* has already been mentioned. Under the auspices of Rice and Palmer, *1492* had enjoyed a long and profitable run. In March 1894, a novelty was added to the show which was to renew public interest in tableaux vivants and introduce perhaps the most ambitious producer of such exhibitions ever to be seen in New York. That producer was Edward Kilanyi, whose living pictures, entitled "Queen Isabella's Art Gallery," became the highlight of *1492*. A close look at Kilanyi and his work is especially interesting and rewarding because tableaux vivants were his sole concern. There is no indication that, once is "apprenticeship" ended, he was ever involved in any other form of entertainment. His tableaux, however, were highly esteemed.

Little has been reported of Kilanyi's personal life, and there is only sketchy information about his working methods and artistic opinions. Possibly the man shrank from personal publicity; possibly the pressures of developing his ever-changing tableaux, or the state of his health, did not allow the time or effort required for interviews and writing; possibly the lack of "coverage" stems from the simple fact that the press habitually concentrated its attention on a featured play at the expense of the after-piece and on "legitimate theatre" generally at the expense of variety and music hall performance.

It is known that Edward Kilyani came within the theatre's influence at an early age.[2] He was born in Dieben, a village near Budapest. As a young boy, Kilanyi worked as a scene painter at the Victoria Theatre in Berlin, where his mother was the ballet mistress. In the late 1870's he took "an original spectacular production" on tour through the Hungarian provinces. In March 1892, he produced his first "living tableaux of art" at the Reichshaller Theatre, Berlin. In 1893, he produced his pictures at the Eldorado in Paris, appeared briefly in Spain, and then went to London where his troupe played a four-month run at the Palace before traveling to the United States.

The London run was a great success and was lauded, both for its artistic virtues and for its financial achievements. The following notice, which appeared in *The Stage,* is typical of the praise accorded Kilanyi's troupe:

> In the Kilanyi troupe the Palace has an attraction that should draw all London. Their *tableaux vivants* are not only perfect in every artistic sense, lifelike and real, but such as have never before been presented in so complete a form in London. There are eighteen tableaux in all.... if the *tableaux vivants* do not pack the Palace, then the British public must be very hard to please indeed.[3]

A week later the same publication continued its praise, declaring, "Stronger and stronger grows the Palace programme, and larger and larger grow the audiences. The Kilanyi troupe... have, of course, given a wonderful impetus to business."[4] Such observations of business success at the Palace continue throughout the Kilanyi run.

Kilanyi's success had a noticeable impact upon variety entertainment in London. When he arrived at the Palace, tableaux were not listed on any theatre bill in the city, but at his departure a virtual stampede had begun. Two days before the Kilanyi run ended, tableaux were being reviewed at the Empire Theatre: "It appears that *Tableaux Vivants* are to be the order of the day. Kilanyi's pictures exhibited at the Palace turned the fortunes of the house, and now we have a perfectly delightful series of living pictures at the Empire. At other halls preparations are being made to follow suit."[5] By March, the London Pavilion was exhibiting tableaux. Furthermore, the Palace itself replaced the Kilanyi troupe with another similar performance, possibly even developed under Kilanyi's tutelage. The new tableaux were called "another triumph," and consisted of twenty pictures "after works by celebrated English and foreign masters. Arranged by W.P. Dando."[6] W.P. Dando had been at the Palace during most of the Kilanyi run and had "invented" a "ballet divertissement" entitled *The Spider and the Fly* which shared the bill with

Kilanyi from November onward. Thus, Dando had had ample opportunity to observe Kilanyi's techniques, if he had not actually been taught by Kilanyi.

From the Palace, Kilanyi moved on to Brighton before embarking for America. *The Stage* records the Brighton engagement as "unquestionably a great success" and observes that "the Kilanyi tableaux vivants at the Brighton Alhambra have, we hear, brought a great deal of money to the treasury."[7]

In New York, press announcements began to be published two weeks in advance in Kilanyi's arrival and tidbits of information appeared regularly in the theatrical columns. On 11 March 1894 it was noted that "the company sailed for this country on the Majestic on Wednesday," and a week later that "the pictures will be shown preliminary to the third act of *1492*."[8] A description of the company and an extensive list of the offerings were included in one announcement:

> The troupe is composed of a dozen German and Italian girls and is under the management and direction of Herr Von Kilanyi, an artist from Buda-Pesth, who, it is said, has obtained some original limelight effects and has devised an apparatus by which the tableaux presented may be changed with great rapidity.
>
> Among the pictures to be reproduced are "Diana" and "Hebe," by Canova; "Moonshine," by Von Kray; "Sappho," by Spiridon; "The Fairy in the Moon," by Kaulbach; "Idylla," by Pigelheim; "The Daughter of the Sheik," by Sichel; "le Passeur," by Bayard; "Psyche," by Thuman; "Will o'the Wisp," by Lerch; "Springtime," by Cott; "The Flute Player," by Eberlein; "Faith, Hope and Charity," by Coppay; "Pharoah's Daughter," by Delaroche; "Cupid and Psyche," by Bouguereau; "Ariadne," by Danecker; the "Venus of Milo," and Herr Von Kilanyi's original study, a water picture, entitled "Aphrodite."[9]

Kilanyi's tableaux at the Garden, separately titled "Queen Isabella's Art Gallery," were presented between the second and third acts of *1492*. (See Figure 19.) The added novelty seems to have provided a welcome "shot in the arm" for business, because the tableaux soon eclipsed the play itself in terms of both critical acclaim and popular appeal. *The New York Times* review of the opening reads,

> "Queen Isabella's Art Gallery," introducing living pictures by the Kilanyi troupe of men and women, mostly the latter, was the salient, if not sensational, feature of last night's performance of "1492" at the Garden Theatre. It was the introduction of the Art Gallery to America, and it obtained quite as proud a triumph here as it is reported to have obtained in Paris, London, and other European capitals.[10]

Predictions of success led the reviewer to conclude, "This is, by the way, the eleventh month of *1492* in New York. It will now run for more than a year."

The newspaper coverage of Kilanyi's exhibition provides several interesting bits of information about the physical production techniques employed. As in such productions at other theatres, the massive, gold frame was an important element; in this case, it was "set well to the rear of a stage darkened and draped with black. During the arrangement of the pictures, which follow each other with remarkable celerity, this frame is concealed by dividing curtains, which are alternately drawn apart and reclosed by two pages."[11] Other critics were impressed by the "celerity," as well. Eighteen pictures were presented in "less than a quarter of an hour. This rapidity is obtained by the use of a revolving table divided into sections, and having removable backgrounds."[12] Apparently, the mechanism was quite complex, for Kilanyi's opening had to be delayed by a day, "owing to the intricacies of the apparatus employed . . . and the difficulty in arranging it."[13] On 29 March 1894, only a week after the opening, Kilanyi filed for a patent on an "Apparatus for Displaying Tableaux Vivant [sic]," which he had previously patented in Germany.[14] Probably the mechanism used in *1492* was similar, at least, to the patented device. The patent specified a platform which could be rolled into place behind the picture frame. Mounted on it was a turntable, each quadrant of which could present a separate tableau. While one quadrant was visible to the audience, changes could be made in the other three backstage, so that each quadrant could be presented in its turn, providing an uninterrupted series of tableaux. Kilanyi's pride in his invention is indicated by the following notice which appeared in newspapers a few days after the opening:

WARNING!
ANY INFRINGEMENT OF THE RIGHTS OF E. VON KILANYI IN AND TO THE MACHINERY, LIGHTS, EFFECTS, COSTUMES, POSTURING AND CREATIVE DISTINCTION OF THE KILANYI LIVING PICTURES WILL BE INSTANTLY PROSECUTED ACCORDING TO LAW.
HOWE & HUMMEL,   ATTORNEYS FOR
A.J. DITTENHOFER   KILANYI'S LIVING PICTURES[15]

It was noted that both "marbles and canvases" were represented onstage, and that, in a few instances, "the realism was a little too strong to be artistic." Aphrodite's nudity, for instance, "was made more real by the dripping of water over the form." Other realistic devices were approved, however. Snowflakes fell through out the representation of "Winter," and "Pharoah's Daughter" made her way "through imitation bullrushes to a painted Moses." Lerche's "Will o' the Wisp" was made vivid by the use of electric lights which "flashed now and then about the figure floating so gracefully in the air."[16] The use of light was also praised for its ability to make the models appear to be cut from marble. The most ingenious technique mentioned, however, is surely the method for exhibiting the "Venus de Milo." It was reported that "the arms of the woman personating the armless figure were draped in sleeves of the same color and texture as the background. The illusion was so perfect as well-nigh to defy detection."[17]

Kilanyi's production continued throughout the season, receiving regular attention from the press. The *Spirit of the Times* noted in April that "Rice's

Figure 19. "The Daughter of the Sheik," one of Kilanyi's living pictures presented in *1492* at the Garden Theatre. (*New York Herald,* 25 March 1894, p. 4.)

1492, at the Garden Theatre, has been strengthened by the introduction of the beautiful Kilanyi tableaux,"[18] and the *Clipper,* on the same date, observed: "The pictures presented by the Kilanyi Troupe have made a profound sensation, and are drawing crowds to the house. They are moreover being appreciated as they deserve to be, and are receiving much well-merited commendation."[19]

So successful were the tableaux that on 24 March 1894 a Kilanyi troupe opened and played for nearly a month at the Columbia Theatre, Chicago, between the first and second acts of another E.E. Rice play, a comic opera entitled *Prince Kam; or, A Trip to Venus.*[20] (By the way, "Venus," in this case, refers, not to the planet, but to the Venus de Milo.) The pictures presented in Chicago exactly duplicate the titles offered at the Garden Theatre in New York. A June newspaper report indicates how widespread Kilanyi's production had become.

> Kilanyi will be first.—The first series of living pictures shown in Boston will be Kilanyi's after all. Managers Palmer and Rice have leased to John Stetson the series originally seen here in "1492," and they will be exhibited at his Park Theatre, Boston, to-morrow night. The pictures for the Tremont Theatre will not be ready for some time, so that in Boston, as in New-York, Chicago, and Philadelphia, Kilanyi's show will be the original.[21]

Furthermore, a short time later it was announced:

> C.B. Jefferson, Klaw and Erlanger have secured from A.M. Palmer and Edward E. Rice the original Kilanyi pictures to be taken over the circuit of theatres booked and controlled by them. Mr. Kilanyi will go to those cities with the pictures and personally superintend their production. The entire paraphernalia now in use in the Garden Theatre will be carried."[22]

The last performance of *1492,* its 450th, was announced for Friday, 12 October 1894. With no delay, however, it was succeeded the following Monday by *Little Christopher Columbus,* a burlesque which again featured the Kilanyi tableaux. The pictures were shown as part of Act II, set in "the Harem of the Bey of Barataria."[23] One reviewer summarized the plot of the piece as follows:

> The opening scene is in the great square of Cadiz, upon the anniversary of the Columbus fetes. Here are assembled Spanish fisher lads, flower sellers, street venders, and American sailors, bent upon holiday recreation. Little Christopher Columbus, a cabin boy, has deserted from an American liner—the Choctow—being deeply enamoured of Guinivere, a beautiful American girl, the daughter of the Second Mrs. Tanqueray Block, an eccentric widow, whose husband was a rich Chicago pork packer. The widow has a private detective, O'Hooligan, whose mission is to assume quaint disguises and investigate the antecedents of fortune hunting suitors, but he is unscrupulous, and is at the command of the longest purse. Little Christopher Columbus is arrested, changes costumes and identifies with Pepita, a Spanish dancing girl, and is finally released through the bribery of the detective.
>
> In the second act, the tourists, with a party of performers bound for World's Fair, are captured by the Bey of Barataria, before whom they give an improvised entertainment. The

Bey is captivated by the bogus Papita, whose identity is revealed by the detective in self defense. He has posed as Papita's eldest brother until he learns that the laws of Barataria condemn to death the eldest brother of the Bey's bride. Existing complications are straightened out at the World's Fair, where the principal characters, with other foreign visitors from strange lands, are assembled in the Midway Plaisance, represented in the third act. Little Christopher Columbus proves to be the last lineal descendant of the great explorer, and all ends merrily.[24]

Although the tableaux were again praised generously, initial reaction to *Little Christopher,* as it came to be called, was far from enthusiastic. The story was called "complex and dull"; the first act, "unutterably tiresome"; the dialogue, "about as bad as dialogue can be."[25] Two weeks later, however, the *Mirror* declared, "Little Christopher Columbus, having been submitted to heroic revision, has apparently entered upon a prosperous run at the Garden."[26]

In mid-November thirteen new tableaux were added to the production, the final one being "La Cascade," which featured a real waterfall.[27] In this tableau, a naiad was shown, crouching under a torrent of water, which, it seems, almost drowned the poor model at one performance:

After the curtain had fallen, it was found that something was wrong with the apparatus which regulated the flow of water, and it was fully three or four minutes before the torrent could be shut off.

When this was finally accomplished and Miss [Alma] Eggert, who posed as the naiad could be removed she was in a fainting condition. She revived after restoratives had been applied and was wrapped in blankets and dosed with brandy....

Miss Eggert was the Aphrodite in the first series of living pictures presented by Kilanyi at the Garden in "1492."[28]

Perhaps the young lady was a specialist in water poses, for Aphrodite, also, appeared in a real water shower, it will be recalled.

On 15 April 1895 *Little Christopher,* with its tableaux, moved to Palmer's Theatre, where it played successfully until the theatre closed for the summer.[29] The closing was at first scheduled for May 25th, but the show was still running on the 27th with the announcement that "Little Christopher has been doing such remarkable business for the past few weeks Mr. Palmer is seriously contemplating keeping the merry burlesque on for several weeks to come."[30] It was not until 3 June 1895 that Palmer's was finally listed as closed. The listing included the announcement that the Kilanyi pictures would open in Brooklyn in September.[31]

Throughout any engagement, Kilanyi attempted to keep his audience coming back for more by regularly adding new pictures to the bill. Occasionally, when several changes were to be made at once, a "New Series" of tableaux was announced. At the 300th performance of *1492* Kilanyi introduced a new series made up of eighteen previously unseen pictures but retaining several of the old ones as well. A third series, which began 28 May 1894 included at least three new offerings, one of them a very large representation of "The Dancing Hour in the Temple of Dionysus" which employed fifteen models. Another new series ushered in the fall season on 25 August 1894 only one week before the 400th performance of *1492*. This series contained twenty-three tableaux—three more than had been customary—and introduced five new ones.[32]

Little mention is made in the press of Kilanyi's activities during the summer and fall of 1895, though one brief article in June, indicated that he was preparing what was to become the *pièce de résistance* of his tableaux vivants:

> Edouard [sic] von Kilanyi, of living picture fame, is of inventive genius as well, and has recently received from Washington a grant for patented apparatus that will create a sensation in the way of tableaux vivants or living pictures. This new and ingenious contrivance of Prof. Kilanyi's is one by which a number of groups or pictures can be presented in rapid succession and panoramic order; historical scenes, war pictures and art groups of thirty or forty persons can be exhibited with ease, and that without delay of any kind, each picture moving on and off the stage with clockwork precision, and with such rapidity that twenty pictures can be presented within the space of twenty minutes.[33]

In November 1895 a steady stream of news articles, many of them frankly based on puffery from Koster and Bial's began to appear. Living pictures at that house which had been introduced the previous year to compete with *1492*, were to be replaced by a new spectacle arranged by Kilanyi. The "Glyptorama" was thus announced: "The living pictures have been discontinued at Koster and Bial's, and in their place the management promises to introduce a startling novelty in Kilanyi's Glyptorama, which will shortly be produced for the first time on any stage. The preliminary announcements describe it as 'a most marvelous illustration of modern mechanism in the art of stage craft. A moving reproduction of the principal paintings of the great masters of the world.'"[34] (See Figure 20.) Another annoucement only two days later included a more detailed description of this new production:

> The Glyptorama, to begin with, is immense and, in the second place, its mechanism is intricate. Kilanyi will show in frames 14 feet high and 22 feet wide living reproductions of some of the largest pictures ever painted.
> He will use eighty-five models, and in each picture will be from five to twenty-five of them.
> No curtains are to be used. As in the changes of slides in a stereopticon, one picture will dissolve into another. The models are posed on sectional platforms on immense carriages, with double steel tracks, one above the other. The shifting of the platforms is controlled by interlocking switches.
> As soon as a picture has been shown automatic power carries the platform back to its original position, where it is made ready for the next grouping.
> The backgrounds for the pictures were painted by Signor Operti. They are automatically rolled into position behind the frame.[35]

Figure 20. Newspaper illustration of one of the tableaux from Kilanyi's Glyptorama, possibly meant to depict "Michael Angelo and Pope Julius Second" by Julius Pabst, the opening picture in the Glyptorama bill. (*New York Herald,* 3 December 1895, p. 7.)

The mechanism was indeed complicated—an appealing quality to the nineteenth century theatre-goer. Advance notices of the Glyptorama provide just enough description to whet the appetite, but no single story gives a really clear picture of the operation. Reviews of the opening night performance add more details, and from all these accounts taken together a fairly complete explanation emerges. One reviewer supplies this bit of information, for instance: "The carriage on which the models are posed moves along exactly in time with the painted background."[36] The *New York Times* reviewer adds that "the back-that is, the scenery—of each picture is sent into its proper place by the turning of the old-fashioned panorama rolls." He, too, then proceeds to give his description of the whole process:

> The figures in the pictures are posed behind a black screen at the right of the stage. A crank is turned, and out into the 40 [sic] by 22 foot gilt frame it slides, the lights in the meantime being low.
> The picture remains for a minute, and the orchestra plays what its leader has been ordering for every living picture exhibit for two years. Then there is a signal that the spectators do not hear, because the musicians are paid to drown it. A crank is turned, and the picture that has been shown vanishes just as does a stereoptican view when another is sent into the slot to dissolve it.
> So, as far as the mechanical part goes, the pictures push each other along until the first posing platform has been sent to the end of the foundation for rollers.
> Then come interlocking switches. The poseurs are first taken off the used platforms; then the pasteboard palm, the tissue flowers, and the paper marble steps are removed. Finally the platform is let go. It strikes along an iron-bound inclined piece of wood for a time, bends it, and then drops, just as Kilanyi planned, to a second switch piece, which guides it to a chain that carries it back to the place whence it started.[37]

The cost of this remarkable mechanism was announced at $6000; however, when all the bills were in, the actual expense came to $7900.[38] Some of the added cost undoubtedly was brought about by the liberal use of electricity. Shortly after the opening, electric power was added to move the platforms, and it was noted that "several improvements have been made in the lighting."[39] On 10 December, the *Herald* observed that "showing the pictures by electric light has greatly increased their beauty," the clear implication being that gas lighting had been used earlier. Such may well have been the case, for while electric light was installed in most theatres during the 1880's, many continued to use gas jets and calcium along with the electric lights.[40] Furthermore, reviews of Oscar Hammerstein's tableaux at Koster and Bial's the previous year refer specifically to the use of calcium light in that house.[41] Whatever the case, frequent press comments about Kilanyi's tableaux attest to the effectiveness of the lighting techniques, although none are described specifically.

So impressive was the scene-changing mechanism itself that few comments dealt with other production features. It was, however, noted that "the backgrounds are painted and the figures in the foreground are living models."[42] The scenic artist was "Signor Operti," apparently the resident artist for the theatre, since his name appears in connection with other productions at that house.[43] An oblique reference in one review suggests that the figure of Moses in the bullrushes was actually made of *papier mâché,* though no further description of the picture is given.[44] The same account notes two mistakes which marred the opening night: "the Pyramids were shown for a minute in the Roman bath scene," and a scene in Switzerland appeared instead of "Old Vesuvius" in "The Bay of Naples." Such errors were readily excused, however, and the production was deemed "the most colossal thing of its kind New-York has ever seen."

The Glyptorama was an unmistakable triumph. The *Dramatic Chronicle* called it "the greatest effort of his [Kilanyi's] life, and the result of years of study of mechanical devices and of color and light effects," and the *Mirror* said it was "the most important production of the season so far at Koster and Bial's."[45] Indeed, it was spectacular and successful enough to encourage a rush of anecdotes in the press. For example, one sad story of the "stage cat" at Koster and Bial's being crushed under the big rollers on which the scenery was moved.[46] Another reported that a trained sea lion from one of the vaudeville acts had escaped from his tank and wandered into a living picture model's dressing room, frightening her into hysterics.[47] Still another story told how "one of the male models... got rattled one night last week and stepped from his platform to the one occupied by the women in 'The Roman Bath' in full view of the audience. When he discovered his mistake he beat a hasty retreat, while the audience laughed."[48]

A few anecdotes reveal useful information about the Glyptorama's operation. The last picture on the bill, entitled "The Deluge" used a real waterfall effect, probably similar to the one used earlier for "La Cascade." The reviews repeatedly refer to this effect as the high point of the evening. The *New York Clipper* called it "a rather daring grouping in the nude, but the models were cleverly arranged."[49] The *Mirror* described it by saying "the light and scenic effects were superb, and the real rain, falling upon the sixteen shapely maidens grouped about on the mountain top, in all sorts of picturesque attitudes was a triumph of stage realism."[50] From the other side of the footlights, however, the scene was less glamorous, if more revealing. As the platforms moved along, one pushing the other, "it is not possible that there should be absolute evenness of action." In other words, the platforms shook— probably one reason for installing motors to move them.

> "But, oh, my gracious!" exclaimed a young woman who poses in the last and greatest picture, "The Deluge," "the shaking isn't anything to the sprinkling we get in that last picture. You know a dozen of us lie around on the rocks....
> "Well, up at the top of the frame is a tank full of water. I think there's ice in it. The man on the light gallery opens the whole tank when we are in the frame and lets the ice water down into a receiving tank at the bottom of the frame.

"Some of it—yes, I am willing to admit that the most of it goes all right; but B-r-r-r-r! we get our share."[51]

While praises for the Glyptorama seemed universal at its opening, there were a few mild expressions of dismay about the "shaking" mentioned above, and about a few mistakes in coordinating platforms with the proper backgrounds. Most remarks were indulgent, ascribing the minor problems to the newness of the machinery and the usual opening night jitters. Additional practice and the installation of motors to "turn the crank" soon improved the smoothness of operation, and the Glyptorama continued its successful run through the week of 11 January 1896.[52]

Herr Edward von Kilanyi, as the newspapers had begun to call him, never saw a performance of his greatest invention, it is sad to note. He died of "rapid consumption" on Wednesday, 4 December 1895, in his house at 221 West Fortieth Street, New York City.

> The deceased had been ill for several months, and but for the artificial stimulation caused by his production of his Glyptorama at Koster and Bial's he would have succumbed long ago.... Although in a dying condition, Kilanyi stayed on the stage night after night, working for the preparation of the production of the Glyptorama. He was at the theatre on the Friday before his death. On the Monday night when the Glyptorama was seen for the first time there were loud calls for Kilanyi. He was on his death bed at home.[53]

An autopsy was performed at the request of a "close personal friend," Abraham Gruber, who was concerned over the suddenness of Kilanyi's death. The authopsy "showed conclusively that Kilanyi had died of consumption. Coroner Hoeber said that it was a wonder the man had lived as long as he had."[54]

The Glyptorama continued to be advertised at Koster and Bial's through the week of 6 January 1896. On 13 January the listing read simply "Living Pictures," and this form continued through the week of 9 March.[55] By February, apparently, Kilanyi's mechanism for changing the pictures mechanically had been removed, for its was reported that "living picture are continued, but are now posed on a stationary platform."[56]

On 27 April 1896 "Edison's Vitascope" became the new novelty at the house. Interestingly, the advance notices for the Vitascope proclaimed, "By this invention veritable *living pictures* are thrown upon a screen...."[57] Soon similar motion picture devices were the new rage in virtually every New York vaudeville house.

During his brief New York career of less than two years, Kilanyi had re-established tableaux vivants as a major theatrical entertainment. His success was amply demonstrated by the fact that the same proliferation of living pictures which had characterized Kilanyi's London run soon took place in New

York. Odell (15:572) observed that these "artistic tableaux... started a new 'craze' in our crazy town, and before long, 'living pictures' breathed and had their being on many stages within the purlieus of New York." Among the imitators were some of the most successful and respected managers in the city. As a result, the late 1890's saw a blaze of tableau glory such as had not occurred before and was not to be seen again.

8

The Final Blaze of Glory: 1894-1899

The first manager to imitate Kilanyi's successful tableaux was no less than the famous entrepreneur, Oscar Hammerstein. In 1894, although his name did not appear in the name of the theatre, Hammerstein was a part-owner of Koster and Bial's Music Hall, and he was active in both management and artistic direction.[1] At first, an attempt was made to attract Kilanyi himself to Koster and Bial's, to which, as we have seen in the previous chapter, he did not move until November 1895. The after-effects of this attempt erupted suddenly at the end of March 1894 into the much publicized threat of a lawsuit. The newspaper accounts, however, lead one to suspect that most of the shouting was really a good publicity agent's method of gaining some free notice for Kilanyi and for A.M. Palmer, manager of the Garden Theatre. Under the headline, "Mr. Palmer Calls it a Bluff," the *New York Times* reported Palmer's version of the incident:

> "I think" said Mr. Palmer, "that this alleged suit against Kilanyi for $50,000 damages for breach of contract, which is absurd on the face of it, is simply a 'bluff' on the part of Koster and Bial to cloak their already announced intention of attempting to infringe on Mr. Kilanyi's rights by presenting a bad imitation of his pictures at their music hall. Kilanyi contracted with me originally by cable to present his pictures at the Garden Theatre in connection with *1492* on March 19. When I forwarded the written contract for his signature, a slight misunderstanding arose in the question of terms, and it took quite a little cable correspondence to straighten it out. While these cables were going back and forth, Koster and Bial made a proposition to Kilanyi to come to their music hall, instead of to the Garden, and I became aware of the fact. I sent for Mr. Bial, and he came to see me. I showed him my contract with Kilanyi, and, after seeing it, he not only wrote a letter to me withdrawing from all competition to secure the pictures, but he cabled Kilanyi, withdrawing all claims in behalf of Koster and Bial. This letter and cable would be an unanswerable defense in any suit against Kilanyi for breach of contract. The fact is, now that the pictures have proved such a wonderful attraction, Koster and Bial, like everybody else, wants them, or something like them. They were offered to Koster and Bial in Europe, and they did not want them then. Things have changed now that their value in New York has been demonstrated."[2]

Whatever the truth of the case, Kilanyi remained in residence at the Garden with continuing success, and Oscar Hammerstein began exhibiting his own living pictures in early May 1894 at Koster and Bial's.

Oscar Hammerstein announced his living pictures for nearly a month before they actually appered at Koster and Bial's, and, as was common for such productions, the opening itself was postponed "to allow more time for rehearsals with the settings."[3] Apparently, public anticipation was effectively whetted, for when the pictures were finally shown, on Thursday, 10 May 1894, one reviewer commented, "The assurance of the pictures was enough to crowd the house. As the successive pictures were displayed the upper part of the house became more than pleased; it was excited."[4] Another reviewer noted that the "throng of people" included "a surprising number of people whose names are addicted to the getting-into-the-paper habit," including socialites, politicians, and artists.[5] The *Herald* reviewer concentrated his enthusiasm on the pictures themselves, and gives us some idea of the subject matter and its treatment:

> Much, very much, might be said in praise of the productions, and the objections could be dismissed in a few words. Fifteen representations of pictures, some well-known works of art, and three reproductions of sculptured figures were given. Among the most successful was Knille's "Tannhauser and Venus." The voluptuous splendor of the original was represented with remarkable and most artistic fidelity. Gernier's "Arabian Pastime" was another exceedingly effective picture, in which the sympathetic background, the easy, graceful poses of the figures and the charm of the subject contributed equally to its success. Vinea's "Queen of the Flowers," a delightfully artistic reproduction; Sanders' "The Nymph of the Wave," Fedro's "Truth"—almost literally the naked truth—and Tojetti's "The Three Muses" were greeted with wild applause, while a war scene, "General Grant at the Battle of the Wilderness," called forth a genuine ovation. Much merriment was evoked by a pretty little "Orchestre d'Amour," in which the tiny conductor changed his position in the most delightfully nonchalant way.... Of the sculptural groups, the "Hommage à Edison,' and the "Romeo and Juliet" of Moulin were singularly effective.[6]

The same reviewer, however, noted two tableaux which seemed to him less effective than the others, and his criticism of them provides some insights into the techniques of staging:

> One or two of the backgrounds are rather rough. The peasants in Millet's "Angelus" seem to be standing against a wall, so incorrect is the perspective, and the support for Diana's knee is so plainly visible that it resembles a black garter. Experiments with the lights should not be tried since the most effective tone has been secured.

The knee-support mentioned was undoubtedly a device similar to those used today to steady the models who ride on parade floats; perhaps tableaux were where the idea originated. In the "Angelus," apparently a painted backdrop was used. Such was not always the case, however, even at Koster and Bial's. An announcement of tableaux for the following season declared that for a representation of Gerome's "Le Gladiateur," the arena galleries would be "on a large scale and full of living people," and that "the stage carpenters have been at work ... on the special scaffolding required for two months."[7] Obviously, both painted and three-dimensional scenery appeared in tableaux.

The concluding picture of Hammerstein's opening series was apparently a rather elaborate production. Three pictures were exhibited simultaneously, "with 'Truth' comfortably cooling herself in a fountain for its central figure, while on one side of her a 'Diana' took deadly aim at something not specified, and on the other an 'Aurora' rhythmically attended to the dawn of a calcium light."[8]

Another noteworthy feature of these Koster and Bial tableaux was the frame through which the pictures were seen. For the May production, "the tableaux were disclosed in a large gilt frame. Black curtains were draped in front of it, and were drawn aside at the proper time by pages."[9] For the next season, the frame was thirty-five feet wide by eighteen feet high, and was described as "nearly as wide and as high as the stage itself."[10] Clearly, the use of a large, elaborate picture frame had become a mainstay of such exhibitions, for the same practice was followed at other theatres. At Proctor's, the "massive," "Louis XIV frame of gold and tufted velvet" was backed by a "satin lined cabinet," in which, presumably, the pictures were displayed.[11]

On 10 June 1894, the *New York Times* observed that Oscar Hammerstein's exhibits "have proved the best drawing card since the house opened,"[12] and the music hall remained open all summer. The first series of living pictures lasted until 20 August, though numerous substitutions were made during that time. The second series, which followed immediately, included only three tableaux carried over from the preceding group. This series attempted to rival Kilanyi's gradiose style more directly, through the use of the new, large frame, thirty-five by eighteen feet in size, and by the addition of large groups of live models in "The Gladiator," as has already been mentioned. *Leslie's Weekly* singled out one tableau from this new series for special attention:

> Messrs. Koster and Bial have put on almost an entirely new programme, in which we notice an ambitious attempt to produce Hans Makart's huge picture of "Diana's Hunt," which hangs in the Metropolitan Museum of Art, consisting of some fourteen figures.... In some respects the vivid realism is more satisfactory than the picture itself. In this production, the difficulties of grouping, etc., have been successfully overcome, and the added realistic interest produces a result that is really artistic but not necessarily sensuous.[13]

A third series of tableaux was inaugurated on 22 September 1894. The highly favorable reviews especially praised "Custer's Last Stand," which was introduced by "a roar of musketry."[14]

At the end of 1894, Hammerstein was becoming less involved in the operation of Koster and Bial's owing to a rift between the managers.[15] In February 1895 the partnership was dissolved, Hammerstein departed, and the house listed "Original Living Pictures," which were made up of selections from past series. On 15 April 1895 Koster and Bial introduced a dramatically different series of tableaux in which all the pictures represented scenes from

Goethe's *Faust,* accompanied by appropriate music from the Gounod opera. It is perhaps ironic that this series took place after the departure of Hammerstein, who, throughout his life, tried so hard to foster the presentation of opera. The scenes represented in this series included: "three scenes in 'Faust's Study,' 'The Kermese,' 'The Meeting of Faust and Marguerite,' 'Three Scenes in Marguerite's Garden,' 'Valentine's Death,' 'The Church,' 'The Prison,' and 'The Apotheosis.'"[16]

The *Faust* tableaux continued until the final week of the regular season, in June, when a series of twenty "re-run" pictures were staged. During this summer, performances continued on the Roof Garden. The fall season got under way on 9 September with a new series of living pictures, "several of which have not been seen before at this house."[17] Critical reception was tepid at best, as this fairly typical comment in the *Times* illustrates:

> The new living pictures included half a dozen of real beauty, but on the whole are hardly as good as their predecessors. One called "Sea Gulls" was the best of the lot. "The Kiss of the Wave" should have been the most startling, if anything in this line could startle New Yorkers nowadays. The rest ranged from inanity, through sentimentalism, up to what usually passes for patriotism.[18]

The fortunes of Koster and Bial were seen to improve, however, for these mediocre tableaux were replaced in December 1894 with Kilanyi's highly successful Glyptorama.

Meanwhile, Oscar Hammerstein, of course, was far from idle. He was busily engaged in "creating Times Square" as the future theatre district of New York, by building his ambitious Olympia theatre complex. This he opened in November and December 1895, with "Marblesques" included as a minor item on his variety bill from May 1896 onward.[19] In August 1897 "the three Vinette sisters" appeared at the house in an unnamed specialty, and the following week "Mme. Vinette's Marblesques" appeared on the bill. The *Clipper* noted that the act "failed to create any enthusiasm," yet it remained into September.[20] In October, Hammerstein attempted something more in keeping with his love of grand opera:

> What may be called "singing pictures" formed the decided novelty at Hammerstein's Olympia for this week. They are something wholly new. Superbly mounted tableaux from grand operas are to be shown in frames, as if they were huge oil paintings. As each tableau is displayed the orchestra will play a selection from the appropriate operatic overture. Then, at the conclusion of the overture, the artists of the picture will come to life, as it were, and sing the music of the scene from which the tableau is taken. "Faust," "Tannhauser," "Lohengrin," "Sonnambula," "Lucia" and "Rigoletto"—a varied and popular selection—are the works drawn on for the first evening of this interesting experiment.[21]

This offering was favorably reviewed in the press, but its success was insufficient, apparently, to stave off the financial difficulties which faced

Hammerstein. In early November the Olympia was closed and the rights to it assigned in order to meet debts of nearly $75,000.[22] Thus ended this busy manager's association with tableaux vivants.

At about the same time that Hammerstein was first contemplating competition with Kilanyi, while the latter was at the Garden Theatre, the Imperial Music Hall added living pictures to its bill on 23 April 1894.[23] In the beginning the advertising by this house suggested a return to the days of Egyptian Hall and the Columbia, with its emphasis on "sensational pictures" and "thirty beautiful girls." However, it very soon engaged the services of Albert Operti, chief scenic artist of the Metropolitan Opera House. Operti designed the Imperial's tableaux, and his preferences ran toward patriotic and inspirational subjects rather than more daring fare. On 5 June 1894 it was reported:

> By far the most successful of them all was a reproduction of Operti's 'The Fireman's Dream,' being a representation of a vision in which a fireman wins the Bennett medal by a deed of conspicuous gallantry. The original painting was, curiously enough, destroyed at the fire at the Metropolitan Opera House a couple of seaons ago. Operti painted the background and arranged the figures in the picture shown last evening and managed to secure a lurid, hot effect that was extremely natural."[24]

The bill was sufficiently successful to warrant being increased on 11 June by the addition of "Undine," "Judith and Holofernes," "Phryne," and "Cleopatra."[25]

A brief moment of difficulty arose at this time when George K. Kraus, manager of the Imperial, was called into court for having shown tableaux on a Sunday. Kraus indicated that "he has been informed by the best authority that there was no section in the penal code covering the exhibition of living pictures," and he chose to fight the charge.[26] Interestingly, there appears to be no further report of the case in the press, and, in spite of Kraus' claim in court that he intended "to discontinue the pictures until next fall, owing to the warm weather," tableaux continued at the Imperial throughout the summer. Regardless of the heat, audiences flocked to the performances, attracted perhaps by some of the more sensational additions that regularly augmented the bill. One critic observed:

> The most comfortable people in the house were the "living pictures," their costumes being nothing if not seasonable. The greatest applause of the evening was divided between the old favorite "Comrades" and a new picture, which proved to be a daring and ambitious bit from the nude with a wave in the background which gave a chilling effect not to be found even in a mint julep. The picture is after "The Daughters of Meysthe," by F. Le Quesme. As produced at the Imperial it represents nine decidedly nude young women either coming out of a cave under the sea or ranged in a circle above it in various postures of abandon, waiting for the crest of a great wave to burst over them."[27]

21 August marked the 150th performance of tableaux at the Imperial, and 1 October saw the opening of an entirely new second series of pictures:

> A most pretentious set of Living Pictures, all new, will be put on at the Imperial Music Hall to-night. They will be unique and very interesting, in as much as they will embrace views of men who are known as heroes of America. The subjects chosen by Sig. Albert Operti, chief scenic artist of the Metropolitan Opera House, who put on these pictures, are: "Admiral Farragut at Mobile Bay," "The Life Saver," "The Artic Explorer," "The Fireman," "The Soldier," "The Scout." Other and lighter pictures will be, "The Materialization of Venus," "Leda and The Swan," "The Coral Reef," "Only a Fly," "Veronica Gazing at the Head of her Rival," and "Return of the Prodigal Daughter."[28]

One week later a new "heroic" tableau capitalized on a dramatic rescue which had made headlines throughout the country. In early September serious forest fires in the Northwest had encircled a small town, threatening the lives of its residents. One James Roote, an engineer on the St. Louis and Duluth Railroad, loaded over three hundred townspeople aboard his train, and ran the train through an inferno of smoke and flame to deposit his passengers safely at a nearby lake. "A tableau representing the engineer and his now historic engine" was added to the Imperial bill on 8 October where it acheived high praise.[29]

Living pictures continued as the featured variety act at the Imperial until 10 December 1894, when they were absorbed into a new burlesque entitled *Old Age and Youth*. This production employed the familiar device of a flimsy plot which served merely as an excuse for presenting the tableaux. The *Herald* review provides a brief summary:

> "Old Age and Youth," a new burlesque in one act and many scenes, was the principal attraction at the Imperial Music Hall last evening. As a vehicle for the introduction of beautiful costumes, tableaux and handsome women, it is likely to be popular, though its literary merits may be questioned....
>
> The plot tells of an aged sculptor, who is rejuvenated and his statues endowed with life, by a fairy queen, to whom he gives a ring with the understanding that he is to marry the woman who returns it. The Queen, disguised as an old woman, tests his fidelity by handing it to him. He keeps his word, and is rewarded when she throws off her disguise, with her hand.[30]

Old Age and Youth continued until mid-January 1895, after which living pictures disappeared from the Imperial Music Hall advertising.

Another theatre to enter the tableau competition in the spring of 1894 was the Casino, under the management of Thomas Canary and George W. Lederer. On 8 May they opened *The Passing Show,* a burlesque treatment of the current theatrical season, which placed heavy emphasis on tableaux vivants. At first, the tableau portion of the show was used as a comment on attempts which had been made to suppress a New York production of Gerhart Hauptman's play *Hannele*. The play had been attacked as immoral and blasphemous and the youthful actress banned from performing, under the child labor laws. Hannele's visions, dramatized in the play, were repeatedly likened to tableaux vivants by the press; thus, the two concepts were linked in the public mind. When *The Passing Show* made sport of this issue, the *Times* reported, "The demure countenance and wonderful mimetic ability of Mabel Stephenson, who, as suffering Hannele, has droll visions of the 'living pictures,' go a great way toward the entertainment of the audience."[31]

The topical nature of *The Passing Show,* however meant that its content was constantly changing, and the living pictures in it were altered almost as frequently as those on the actual tableau bills at other theatres. "Another trio of characters of living pictures" was added 4 June, including "Lady Godiva," "The Bather," and "Cupid and Psyche,"[32] and on 18 June four more were added.[33]

In addition, as summer approached, the Casino Roof Garden offered its own series of living pictures, quite separate from those of *The Passing Show* which continued to occupy the main theatre. The Roof Garden production was termed "Fin de Siecle Tableaux" and consisted of fifteen groupings designed by Max Freeman. Caricature was the mainstay of these tableaux, also. Indeed, one entitled "The Passing Show" was, itself, a burlesque of the burlesque in the Casino proper. A *Herald* review provides some flavor of the production:

> Four very pretty young women in the latest modes and negligee to a refreshing degree this warm weather smoke cigarettes around a table, and don't seem at all disturbed by public scrutiny. They have been playing poker, perhaps. 'Chips That Pass in the Night.' That's what the picture is called in the fin de siecle tableaux vivants given on the Casino Roof Garden for the first time last night.
> There was another picture of four more girls in the abbreviated skirts of the ballet, who smoked, too, and when revealed again had their saucy noses turned toward the stars, while they drank supposititious wine from metal goblets. This must be a solecism in New York, but in Paris, where this was a peep into "The Green Room," many strange things are possible.
> But the Garden gasped when it saw "Neptune and the Summer Girl." It wasn't down on the programme, but it was anatomically much in evidence. In the first pose the girl is facing the old sea god, and his usually red face seemed to grow apoplectic over the array. Such a predicament would cause any man much embarrassment, and Neptune seemed measurably relieved when the young women turned their backs upon him and faced the audience.[34]

Both the Roof Garden tableaux and *The Passing Show* in the Casino enjoyed great popularity through the summer and early fall. During September and October *The Passing Show* moved to Brooklyn to open the season at the Columbia Theatre there, but afterward it returned to the Casino, advertising a "fresh assortment of living pictures."[35]

On 28 February 1895 management of the Casino was assumed by Rudolph Aronson who immediately introduced a new tableau act which was surely one of the most spectacular to be seen.[36] Even its introduction to the public was unusual.

> If public appreciation of stage development in the line of living pictures is to be gauged by the favor of artists, a distinct success may be assured the reproductions of bronze figures and groups which will become part of the programme at the Casino beginning to-night.
> There was a private exhibition yesterday afternoon, to which artists only were asked. About sixty responded, among them such adepts in high ideals as F.F. Church, George W. Maynard, J.G. Brown, M.F.H. De Hass, James D. Smillie, Frederick Dielman, J.S. Hartley, Carroll Beckwith, and Wells Champney.

> The curtain rose on two figures in bronze, representing the statuary group, "After the Bout." The figures were posed within an arch under a gilded pedestal, with a black velvet stand below. A black curtain in the background threw them into fine reliefs, displaying in bronze the lines of life with most striking effect.
> An outburst of admiration and applause followed the display, and lasted for several minutes. The figures had made an instant success.
> In turn, other figures and groups were shown, representing "Achilles," "The Fisherman," "The Wrestler," "Narcissus," "The Gladiator," "The Sprinters," "The Dying Gaul," "The Disk Thrower," "Ajax and Patroclus," "The Adorant," "Gladitorial Group," "Ariadne," and "Truth."
> The exhibition is made by Oscar Nahl and William Kohler, the athletes, both good specimens of physical culture. Giles Bradley, their manager, is the inventor of a process of converting his subjects into imitations of bronze.
> It consists of coating them with a bright bronze powder after their skin has been prepared with an oily application. The figures are thus almost entirely nude, and they are exhibited to the best artistic advantage. Mr. Bradley first exhibited them in San Francisco, where they made such an impression that he decided that his invention deserved a New-York indorsement at once. He brought his men across the continent, feeling assured that his homeward journey will meet with calls from every large city.
> The men have been so well trained to statuesque postures that they seem like pieces of fine sculpture. To relieve the audience of this illusion they execute a change of pose in the "Gladitorial Group." A young woman was shown yesterday as "Ariadne" and as "Truth."[37]

In the first public presentations by the "Nahl-Bradley Troupe," as it was called, only male performers appeared, but on 11 March the "young woman" again joined them, first as "The Liberty Statue" and later in a group representing "Hagar and Ishmael."[38] By 18 March the full bill included twelve tableaux: "Apollo Belvedere," "The Wrestler (new)," "The Vestal Virgin," "The Gladiator," "Ajax and Patroclus," "Phryne," "The Disc Thrower (new)," "The Fisherman," "Eve," "Paris and Helen," "Gladitorial Group," and "Diana."[39] The "innovation" of displaying a woman in several of these groups soon led to objections, even though it was reported that she "was stout and wore fleshings."[40] The performers and managers were brought into the Jefferson Market Police Court on 25 March. The performances continued, "although not quite as usual—rather in a veiled condition."[41] "All the female figures were draped. The males wore tights."[42] In spite of this modesty, attendance was strong at the performances, leading one critic to observe, "The free advertising given to this feature through the columns of the newspapers and in the courts last week has roused the curious, and a big attendance is the result."[43]

At the trial the defendants mounted a spirited defense, as the following press report shows:

> Detective Titus and Rogers, who witnessed the exhibition and made the arrests, gave testimony. The former did not regard the display as immodest. The latter evaded the question by saying he had never seen living pictures before.
> William B. Chase, President of the Society of American Artists, thought the bronze statues were modest in the extreme, and did not consider the exhibition of copies of paintings on a public stage more immodest than the exhibition of originals in a public art gallery.

"Do you not consider such an exhibition injurious to public morals?" asked Justice Simms.

"No, Sir," replied Mr. Chase. "I would gladly take my wife and daughters to see the statues."

"It does not impress you, then, as being immoral?"

"No, Sir; I cannot see how it can occur to any but a depraved taste that there is anything out of the way."

"You would not, then, object to having the figure of a nude woman posed in a shop window?"

"No, Sir, I would not. I think it might be a very good thing for the public. There is nothing immoral about the human frame. It only exists in the mind, and that, I think can be educated."

"Those figures," said Artist, J.G. Brown, "look no more human than the bronze statuettes seen on the mantles in every house. I do not see how they could impress anyone as being human."

The defendants caused some surprise by swearing that on no occasion had the figures been undraped. Manager Bradley produced a piece of cheesecloth fashioned something like a linen duster, which he and Miss Stanton declared was worn by the woman in a pose in which Titus had sworn she was nude.

Titus was recalled, and he reiterated his assertion. Justice Simmons said, at the close of the case, that he thought somebody had committed perjury.[44]

Two detectives were stationed in the Casino audience during the course of the trial, but the models continued to be clad in tights beneath their bronze power. Apparently this was sufficient to avoid further objections to the tableaux. "Nobody has been heard to say that they were immoral," reported the *Tribune*.[45] So great was the popularity of the act that the dancer, Papinta, who was the featured performer on the Casino bill, inaugurated a "Living Picture Dance" in her performance. "The living picture element is represented by a complete set of fleshings from the neck to the toe. The dance is a series of graceful and artistic steps, somewhat of the serpentine order, and the illusion is furnished by a dress of jet black chiffon, as transparent as glass, and only manipulated by the ever-moving arms of the dancer, concealing her figure only when she permits it to drop in folds about her."[46]

On 17 April, after lengthy testimony, the Court of Special Sessions dismissed the charges against the Nahl-Bradley Troupe for lack of evidence. Even one of the detectives who had witnessed the presentations testified that "his sense of decency was not outraged" and that he "considered the representations excellent." The defense attorney concluded his case with the observation that "the statues on the Criminal Court building are more immodest than the Casino bronze statues."[47]

Legal troubles for the Nahl-Bradley Troupe were not over, however. Their engagements at the Casino ended 4 May "on account of non-payment of salary," and Manager Aronson attempted to prohibit the troupe from using the same act elsewhere. Aronson claimed that Bradely was liable for half the costs of the recent litigation, and he looked upon the bronze statue act as the property of the Casino management. He, therefore intended to continue the act with another troupe after Nahl-Bradley's departure. Giles Bradley, however, secured a court injunction prohibiting Aronson from carrying out this plan, and the troupe left for a tour engagement.[48] As an alternative, Aronson attempted to substitute a new tableau production entitled "The Gardens of Seneca," under the direction of one Mr. von Prittwitz Palm, another member of the Casino company. For this novelty, "instead of showing statues in a frame at the back of the stage, the models, five ladies, posed on pedestals place in a scene representing a garden. Eighteen groups were presented in all, in five sets, the lights for each set being changed so as to represent sunrise, noon, afternoon, sunset, and night. 'La Cigale,' 'Venus,' 'The Lovers,' 'The Dancers,' and 'Naiad' were among the most striking of the poses."[49] The production opened 16 May 1895 after a three-day postponement "as the preparations could not be completed in time."[50] It was to be a short run of only two nights, however, for on Saturday morning, 18 May, Aronson was dispossessed for the non-payment of $3000 in rent and $9000 in back taxes.[51] The house was again taken over by Canary and Lederer who opened their new burlesque, *The Mimic World*, on 6 June 1895, thus ending tableaux vivants at the Casino.

Another major tableau vivant competitor to enter the field in 1894 was the highly successful equilibrist-turned-manager, F.F. Proctor, who controlled more than a dozen theatres between Boston, Massachusetts, and Lancaster, Pennsylvania.[52] His Twenty-third Street Theatre in New York had operated as a "continuous" vaudeville house since January 1893.[53] On 21 May 1894 the Wilbur Opera Company, "with Suzie Kirwin as its prima donna," opened at this theatre.[54] Although comic operas by the Wilbur company provided the main attractions throughout the summer, various tableaux appeared regularly on Proctor's bills. William and Ida, the Austins, were listed as "character statue artists" in May,[55] and in mid-June Lew Dockstader, of minstrel fame, was presenting "living pictures in charcoal!"[56] By the first of June Proctor's was prominently billing "exquisite high art examples, living pictures.... Thirty reproductions of classical, allegorical, realistic and humorous masterpieces with the most charming of models... Vivid object lesson in art."[57] The introduction of this "First Series" of living pictures reportedly met with enthusiastic approval and was reviewed in the press as the focal point of Proctor's variety bill. Three or four new pictures were added weekly as the run progressed, and after only one month a whole new series was introduced. This second series, "under the artistic personal supervision of Miss Suzie Kirwin," was even more grandiose than before and was shown through "a massive Louis XIV frame of gold and tufted velvet" in a cabinet "hung with satins." The pictures included "London's latest sensation, 'The Doctors;' the thrilling war tableau, 'In the Trenches,' and 'An Affair of Honor and its Sequel,'" all of which touched the audience's patriotic fervor.[58] Miss Kirwin expressed the "general aim" of the tableaux as being "to follow as closely as possible the original work of art, to the exclusion of the exaggerative license usually permitted in stage representations."[59] As before, new pictures were added weekly—sometimes as many as six at once—and audiences flocked to see them. The *Tribune* reported that "people were turned away frequently at Proctor's," resulting in the addition of extra performances each day. A noontime exhibition attracted "throngs of women from the adjacent shopping district."[60]

The fall and winter season at Proctor's began officially on Labor Day, 3 September 1894, and advertising for the opening proclaimed, "PROCTOR'S THEATRE. Fall and Winter Season. AN ENORMOUS SUCCESS resulting from the introduction of LIVING PICTURES in the continuous performances at this POPULAR FAMILY RESORT, has determined Mr. Proctor to retain them as A PERMANENT FEATURE, New subjects being added in rapid succession."[61] Retain them he did, adding new subjects at a dizzying pace and even enhancing the effect with music: "For example when 'Coming Thro' the Rye,' and 'The Village Blacksmith' are shown, with living figures, the appropriate melodies will be song [sic] by invisible soloists and quartettes. The Latest Sensation in London."[62] The quartette was soon increased to a chorus, and "realistic battle effects" later accompanied "Comrades."[63] In November it was reported that "more than seventy living pictures have been produced during the last few weeks," but even then the pace did not slow as more and more additions followed.[64] The range of subject matter was remarkable, including patriotic works, such as "Comrades" and "1776;" scenes of local interest, such as "On the Bowery;" romantic and classical works, such as "Venus and Tannhauser" and a host of mythological figures; domestic groups like "A B C," which showed a little child teaching its pug dog the alphabet; and numerous sentimental inventions and traditional nude studies. In January 1895, inspired by A.M. Palmer's popular production of *Trilby* which had just taken New York by storm, Proctor even offered a "Trilby" tableau.[65]

On 2 September 1895 Proctor opened his huge Pleasure Palace on Fifty-eighth Street, at the same time continuing production at the Twenty-third Street Theatre. It was not long before tableaux became a mainstay of the new house, too:

> A series of historical tableaux vivants, depicting "Before Vicksburg," "The Blue and the Gray," "Custer's Last Battle" and other patriotic themes, will be presented at Proctor's Pleasure Palace next week. There will be sixty living figures in each tableau, and incidental music by the singing comedienne, Myra Davis, and a quartet. The tableaux will be posed and supervised by Joseph J. Dowling, the well known melodramatic actor, and the original effects have been copyrighted and protected by letters patent.[66]

The scenic artists for this production included Joseph Physioc, Lafayette W. Seavey, and Augustus Voegtlin, the last of whom had been scenic artist at Niblo's Garden in the 1870's. At the Twenty-third Street Theatre, meanwhile, tableaux were provided by the La Fleur Sisters, who "posed prettily as marble statues."[67] Their appearance continued into 1896 but did not attract any extensive critical commentary.[68]

In March 1896 the strong man, Sandow (see Figure 21), was the main attraction at Proctor's Pleasure Palace:

> Standing in a calcium-lighted shadow box, he reveals his superb muscular endowment, the mighty muscles, contracted and extended, being revealed vividly against a black background. And his new act, never seen upon any stage, and assuming a dramatic aspect, portrays a mythological episode in the life of Hercules. The five tableaux are entitled "The Theft," "The Flight," "The Revenge," "The Interruption," and "The Triumph."[69]

The climax of the act presented Sandow in the picturesque setting of a rocky pass, "with his back to the floor, and resting on his hands and feet, supporting a bridge over which a horse is led by a man carrying a woman on his back. The bridge is said to weigh 1000 pounds."[70]

Following Sandow's appearance, tableaux at the Pleasure Palace were replaced by Professor Abt's stereopticon views rather than live presentations. Nearly a year later, living pictures again appeared for a short time, under the auspices of the Cherry Sisters, a unique team of performers reputed to have come from Cedar Rapids, Iowa. They capitalized on a "hayseed" image which both managers and the press seemed delighted to foster. F.F. Proctor announced that "a cloak room will be provided, where turnips, cabbages and other tributes to the great Western actresses may be checked, as in no instance will it be permitted to pass these over the footlights."[71] A review of the Cherry Sisters' opening suggests a truly raucous evening:

> It was impossible to get into the theatre at half-past seven last night, so great was the crowd of would-be spectators. The bill was a good one, but of course the Cherry Sisters were the chief feature. They were greeted with a storm of cheers, and only those who were very close to the stage heard anything of what they said, so deafening was the noise from the audience all the time they were on the stage. Two apples were thrown to them and quite alot of small coin. Later they sent word to the manager that unless order could be maintained in front they would not go on again.[72]

In the face of such a reception, one wonders at their tableaux of "Clinging to the Cross" and "The Goddess of Liberty," "with plenty of patriotic music and red calcium lights."[73]

Tableaux did not appear again at Proctor's until the fall season had begun. Then Proctor announced for the Twenty-third Street Theatre:

> GRAND PRODUCTION OF HIGH ART LIVING PICTURES, the perfection of animate art, reproducing the greatest masterpieces displayed at the recent Paris, Berlin and Vienna exhibitions. BEAUTIFUL MODELS. NOVEL LIGHT EFFECTS.[74]

Figure 21. The popular Sandow, revealing his "superb muscular endowment" for photographer Napoleon Sarony, n.d. (Courtesy of the Theatre Collection, Museum of the City of New York.)

The pictures included "Mermaid," by Wertheimer; "The Sirens at Play," after La Lyre; "The Salve," after Normand; "Shooting Star," after Charpentier; "Companions in Mischief," by Morpail; and others.[75] As in the past, frequent additions of new pictures kept the tableaux prominent in the press, and attendance was reported to be strong. Although by the end of 1897 they occupied lesser billing in Proctor's advertising, tableaux vivants continued to be shown through 19 February 1898.

The last projected entry into the 1894 tableaux competition was B.F. Keith's New Union Square Theatre, but his turned out to be an abortive attempt. With five other major houses and, doubtless, many lesser halls running tableaux successfully, Keith felt compelled in June to commit himself to a production of his own. He, therefore, appended the following announcement to his regular advertising:

> SPECIAL—In preparation, absolutely the most artistic, high class and brilliant series of LIVING PICTURES ever put forth. To be devised and produced by Mr. Edward Stedle and M. Eugene Castel-Bert, famous for their work at all the great productions at the Metropolitan Opera House, Abbey's Theatre, &c.[76]

Keith's New Theatre in Boston became the try-out ground for his tableaux, but in spite of repeated announcements that they were soon to appear in New York, they still had not arrived by the end of the 1894-95 season. Press puffs enlarged the prospective production at every announcement. Originally scheduled for 17 September 1894, it was described as costing $15,000. "The scenic detail has been painted by M. Eugene Castel-Bert, of the Metropolitan Opera House, and the costumes have been prepared and designed by Mme. Castel-Bert." Another release placed the cost at $20,000.[77] The next projected opening date was 24 September, the postponement "owing to the phenomenal success of Mr. Keith's Living Pictures at his new Boston Theatre."[78] Finally, it was stated that a duplicate series of tableaux was to be arranged for New York production, and that these would not be seen "until considerably later in the season."[79]

Actually, Keith's tableaux never did arrive in New York, and it seems doubtful that any separate production was ever mounted. Even his Boston offering was plagued by postponements. The performance there was originally announced for the week of 3 July 1894.[80] Possibly this attempt was an effort to capitalize on the recent popularity of Kilanyi's living pictures which had completed a successful two-week run in June at Boston's Park Theatre.[81] Keith's opening was postponed, however, as were several subsequent openings. Finally, the exhibition did take place, beginning on Monday, 30 July 1894. Although the performacne was reviewed favorably, there was no great enthusiasm expressed. The writer in the *Evening Transcript* seemed to prefer a human interest approach rather than a critical one:

Mr. Keith has made the child element quite prominent in his pictures, and with a keen understanding of what "takes" with the people, and the tendancy of the little ones to do something "cute," to move a limb or to turn a head, only lends additional color to the tableau. In the picture, "Good Night," for example, there was something irresistibly winsome last evening when kitty pranced out of the frame and meandered demurely toward the footlights, and the little tot made a motion as if to stop her, and then sank back to a sitting posture, in sweet self-consciousness.[82]

This exhibition continued into September, when it was announced that the tableaux would move "to Mr. Keith's Providence house on their way to an exhibition of them at his New York establishment."[83] Again, the plans were changed, however, for, on 24 September 1894, they returned to Boston "for a brief engagement," and there they remained until 1 December.[84]

Perhaps B.F. Keith was satisfied with the business at his theatre in New York; it was reported to be well-filled, and his bills were extensive and varied, even without living pictures. Since other elaborate tableau exhibits were available at such prominent competitors as Proctor's, Koster and Bial's, the Imperial, and the Casino, possibly Keith simply considered the market to be saturated in New York. Whatever his reasons, Keith never did fulfill his promise to add living pictures to his bill at the Union Square Theatre.

In addition to these tableaux vivants presented by the major producers and managers, numerous less prestigious houses also offered living pictures during the 1890's. The Eldorado began tableaux on 16 July 1894, under the direction of "Professor von Palm"—possibly the same person who later staged them at the Casino. Only two pictures were offered—Hans Makart's "Diana's Hunt" and an adaptation entitled "The Sacking of Nineveh," but these were large productions employing a frame thirty-one feet by eighteen feet, and each picture used "more than twenty persons." "New light effects" were advertised, along with "elaborate costumes" and backgrounds claimed to be "reproductions of the originals, and will be painted in oil colors." Furthermore, this was said to be "the first time that the living pictures will be shown in the open air."[85] In spite of all these attractive features at the Eldorado, the reviewer later observed that "nobody goes there all the same."[86] Nevertheless, the exhibition continued on the bill throughout the summer of 1894.

A somewhat more ambitious production formed part of the bill for the fall re-opening of Huber's New Palace Museum on 30 July 1894. A review of the event concluded by saying, "The triumph of the entertainment was the series of living pictures, which Prof. Hooker has made into gems of art."[87] Although virtually no description of these "gems" appeared in the press, they were apparently quite successful and well attended. On 27 August, Prof. Hooker introduced a second series of pictures, "twenty in all." A third series began on 25 November and continued into December.[88]

On 18 May 1896, less than a month after the Vitascope's arrival, Koster and Bial's again offered living pictures, this time with Mlle. Suzanne Duvernois, a young woman with a remarkably fine figure, and she has been astonishing Paris recently by exhibiting herself clad only in tights in a series of rather startling tableaux. Mr. Albert Bial saw her and at once sent her to America. The tableaux she will present a week from tomorrow night are entitled "The Pearl," "Phryne," "The Slave," "Spring," "Summer," "Autumn," "Winter" and the "Triumph of Venus." In this last, with the assistance of a property Cupid, a chariot and an abundance of flowers she impersonates realistically the mythological beauty at the acme of her career.[89]

In spite of its obvious appeal, the act was not successful and held the stage only four days. One reviewer observed:

Some of the poses were really startling, but even the hardened rounder failed to applaud them, and the entire act passed in comparative silence, as far as the approbation of the audience was concerned. This state of affairs continued until Thursday evening, when Mlle. Duvernois was withdrawn. This means that the living picture craze is dead and buried as far as New York is concerned.[90]

In spite of such a dire prediction, Koster and Bial's tried one more living statue act late in 1899. It employed the prizefighters, James J. Jeffries and Thomas Sharkey, in "living statues of ancient and modern gladiators, showing new views of a boxing contest posed in by these champions." The act was part of "The Merry, Joyful Skit on City Life in Eleven Scenes, entitled ROUND NEW YORK IN 80 MINUTES," a revue which had been running since 6 November 1898. The two fighters "covered themselves with white powder and additional glory and appeared in several poses, some of a gladitorial and others of a fistic nature. They stood within a living picture frame and were silhouetted against a background of black cloth, which showed their marvelous biceps, triceps and other muscles to perfection."[91]

The Jeffries-Sharkey addition was a great success, though it seems likely that the cause was more the celebrity of the two men than the appeal of the tableaux. "The crowd howled its approval, and the two gentlemen were brought before the curtain several times after the final pose, which showed the solar-plexus and knockout blows being delivered at once."[92]

Many other tableaux appeared as lesser features of the wide-ranging vaudeville and variety bills, and were never described or evaluated by the reviewers. Tableaux occupied a minor place on Tony Pastor's bill from time to time. For the week of 27 August 1894 Professor Charles Osten's "European Art Pictures" was the incidental entry.[93] During the same week it was noted that "Mme. Eugenie Lineff will add living pictures to the entertainments of her Russian choir this season. These pictures will illustrate phases of Russian life, and all the persons will wear clothes."[94] At Doris' Musuem "a series of living pictures and a crank convention"—intriguing combination—were among the features in early September.[95] In October, St. James Hall, following Lew Dockstader's lead, advertised Comstock's Minstrels presenting "living pictures in black."[96]

At the Columbus Theatre, the famous magician, Herrmann, even employed the tableau vivant approach in one of his spectacular illusions, entitled "The Artist's Dream:"

> "The Artist's Dream"... is a pathetic little sketch telling the story of an old French artist who had painted the portrait of his little daughter, who has died. His work has become a part of his life, and every night as he falls to sleep before the easel, the child seems to come to life again, and to sing and dance around him as she used to do. Of course when he awakes he finds it has only been a dream.
>
> The stage is set to represent the old artist's studio. There are one or two easels, with empty frames, and at one side stands the young girl's portrait. An Irish lackey enters, and in his dusting manages to show the painting to the audience from every side. Then the artist comes in, and after adding a few touches to the picture with his brush, sits down in front of it. He gazes at it awhile, and then apparently drops off to sleep. In a twinkling a fairy appears in one of the empty frames, and as she waves her wand the portrait of the child literally comes to life before the eyes of the spectators. She steps down from the frame and dances and sings around her father's chair. Suddenly he awakes and—presto! the child is back in the frame, a picture once more.[97]

During the summer of 1895 "living marble statues" appeared at the American Roof Garden,[98] and in November Daly's was offering *Miss Pygmalion,* a silent pantomime in which Jane May played a sculptress who made a statue of Pierrot, and the statue came to life.[99]

Finally, from April until July 1898, living pictures formed the first part of *The Ballet Carnival* at Sam T. Jack's burlesque theatre, but these did not attract the slightest critical comment or description.[100]

Inspired by the tremendous success of Edward Kilanyi's tableaux in *1492* and later in *Little Christopher Columbus,* the late 1890's blazed brightly with elaborate tableau vivant productions. The most successful variety managers of the day—A.M. Palmer, Oscar Hammerstein, George Kraus, Koster and Bial, Rudolph Aronson, and F.F. Proctor—all competed for audiences by means of tableaux. Led by Kilanyi, with his fabulous Glyptorama, and productions were ingenious on a grand scale and became the focus of the variety houses where they played.

For all practical purposes, "artistic" tableaux had emerged victorious, for they operated virtually without interference, but with high praise instead. It was not moralistic condemnation which brought about the downfall of tableaux vivants, but a new form of "living pictures"—moving images on a screen. Edison's Vitascope and its numerous imitations replaced tableaux on one variety bill after another at century's end.

Yet, the forces of purity were not sleeping during this final period of living pictures, nor did they share the general enthusiasm for even the most grandiose tableau productions. The opposition wave, however, lacking the zeal formerly provided by Anthony Comstock, proved to be more effective in debate than in action.

9
Morality Debate in the 1890s

During the final period of tableau production in the late 1890's the morality of this entertainment continued to be called into question. The issue was hotly debated in the press, but there was less official action than in the past. Fewer exhibitions were raided, and fewer managers and performers were hailed into court.

Kilanyi's troupe, while in its third series of pictures, closed at the Garden Theatre on 7 July 1894 with the announcement that its tableaux would resume in the fall. On the same date *The Illustrated American* published one of the few truly scathing attacks upon model artists to appear during the decade. The occasion was a refusal by New York City Mayor Gilroy to permit a six-year-old girl to appear in the *1492* tableau. The issue had been raised originally by the Society for the Prevention of Cruelty to Children—the "Gerry Society," as it was known because of its leader, "Commodore" Elbridge Thomas Gerry. However, the mayor justified his refusal by saying, "The fact that the child's mother appears in the living pictures is the strongest reason why the child should not be allowed to continue posing. It is horrible to think of a child looking at her mother in an almost nude condition before an audience night after night."[1] In a two-page editorial, the *American* lamented the "Contamination" brought forth by such "libidinous monstrocities" as tableaux vivants:

> In the first stage of the craze for this wretched device of shameful diversion, there was little to foreshadow the extreme degredation that has rapidly become its most conspicuous characteristic....
> The descent, however, to the Avernus of recklessness and depravity has been rapid to the degree of being headlong. Exploiters of this particular form of spectacle have fairly tumbled over one another in their zeal to attain some novel display of flagrant indecency. They have stopped at nothing in their efforts to be nasty; not even at outright nudity.[2]

That there existed a potential for indecency was nearly always noted by the reviewers of tableaux vivants, but in the 1890's their comments were usually tempered by assurances that the pictures were not offensive. In this respect, the pattern which had been established when tableaux first appeared in America was maintained, and even strengthened. It was pointed out, for instance, that Kilanyi's tableaux in *1492* included "a number of works in which nude figures appear." However, the writer was quick to add, "The realism in these, while remarkable, was in no way offensive, the actual flesh appearing in the reproductions of the paintings only where its uncovering is not unusual...."³ Another reviewer of the same performance observed, "The subjects chosen are all more or less studies from the nude, but while at the first glance some of them are somewhat startling, they have been so carefully selected and so cleverly arranged that they have no taint of grossness, nor do they offer offense to any pure mind that is governed by practical intelligence."⁴ Still another author commented, "There is nothing in the exhibition to offend anyone whose sense of propriety is not shocked by the canvases that the Kilanyi troupe simulate. Prudery may look askance, at it, but that will be because prudery is composed largely of pruriency. A pure, artistic tone pervades this novelty that removes it from the vulgar line of the 'living statuary' shows of a decade or more ago."⁵ The same attitude was expressed in virtually every review of Kilanyi's opening night.

Even Hammerstein's opening was called, "in all probability, for most observers, innocuous enough," though the writer felt compelled to add that in some of the pictures the "revelations were extreme enough to make an inexperienced, and perhaps more than ordinarily unsophisticated observer catch his breath for an instant in sheer amazement. Certainly frankness could go no further than did that of the 'Nymph of the Wave,' for there is no further to go."⁶ Yet, while subjects represented by Hammerstein included several nude figures, apparently less daring tableaux overshadowed them in audience response: "Perhaps the most enthusiastic approval of the night was bestowed upon a representation of General Grant at the Battle of the Wilderness, given to patriotic music."⁷

Kilanyi, shortly after his opening, attempted to circumvent any possible official objection to his pictures by inviting Superintendent of Police Byrnes, "as an expert, to come and look at them."⁸ The Superintendent did so and apparently found nothing amiss, for no action followed.

One reviewer even went so far as to suggest that there was insufficient nudity:

> It should be clearly understood that there is nothing in these "living pictures" to offend the most fastidious. Indeed, I am of opinion that prudishness on the part of someone connected with the management, or else an ill-founded fear of Dr. Parkhurst's myrmidons has prompted the unnecessary draping of some of the figures. I may be right or I may be wrong, but some of the gauze trappings seemed to me strangely out of place. These pictures, besides affording pleasure to the public, are calculated to educate the public taste.⁹

Some reviewers even saw the tableaux as superior to the paintings they represented, since they employed "shapely girls in place of the counterfeits of the human form produced by the artists in the original works,"[10] and one writer indicated his impatience with those who complained about nudity in living pictures, comparing their attitude to "the spirit that put tin fig leaves on the Vatican statues; that rejected St. Gaudens' classic medal; that blushed when Diana was put on the Madison Garden tower."[11]

When Hammerstein originally opened his tableaux in May 1894, the *Spirit of the Times* was prompted to remark that "at Koster and Bial's, the first series of Living Pictures is so beautiful that even Comstock would applaud."[12] That was high praise indeed, for it was Anthony Comstock (as we have already seen) who, as Secretary of the Society for the Suppression of Vice, had spearheaded the attacks on tableau producers in the 1870's. During the 1890's, however, Comstock did not actively fight such productions. It was not that the man had become more tolerant, but, rather, that his attention was focused elsewhere—mainly on those who sold or displayed obscene pictures, kept slot machines, or sold articles for abortion or to prevent conception.[13] In 1894, his attempts to suppress the novel, *Tom Jones,* were earning him the dislike of a somewhat liberal press.[14] Furthermore, as Bremner puts it, "His manner, at once sanctimonious and rambunctious, aroused respectable opposition almost as readily as Bohemian derision. . . . Unable to cooperate with other reformers, and unwilling to accomodate his views to theirs, Comstock took no part in the campaign against civic corruption waged in New York in the 1890's. . . ."[15] Thus, it fell to other forces to take up the struggle to protect the public from the supposed ill effects of tableaux.

An intriguing "human interest" story, published in December 1894, provides a series of pictures which depict a young lady arriving at a theatre to prepare for her role as a model artist. The illustrations show her transformation to glamorous showgirl as she dons makeup and costume. Then, in Picture Number Six, the stage manager is shown telling her "that he will have to omit her 'turn' this evening, as Lady Henry Somerset's watchers are in the theatre."[16] Lady Somerset had been an active crusader against living pictures in London. She arrived in America during the summer of 1894 to serve as a kind of "campaign adviser" to the local protesters who were under the leadership of Mrs. Emilie D. Martin, "National Superintendent of the Department for the Production of Purity in Literature and Art" of the Women's Christian Temperance Union. These women mounted a campaign to condemn living pictures as immoral and to take legal action against them, based on a law which prohibited indecent modeling. One difficulty encountered by this group was that official response to the crusaders seems to have been something less than enthusiastic. Newspaper accounts repeatedly describe attempts by the ladies to interview police chiefs and other city officials, with the usual result that the group is politely put off by an "assistant" or some other minor figure. Lady Somerset's arrival in America was marked by interviews in which she expressed her opinion that New York's tableaux were even worse than those she had opposed in London. Interestingly, it was Suzie Kirwin of Proctor's Theatre who became the outspoken defender of tableaux. Her statement of the case seems surprisingly modern today:

> ...Lady Somerset begins her manifesto by disclaiming at the outset any desire to consider the question from the point of view of demoralization to the spectators. She rightly concedes that they are present of their own volition and that if they did not want to see the pictures they would not pay to visit places of entertainment where they are shown. Their act, as she truly remarks, is purely voluntary. It is the "degradation of the sex" that calls for Lady Somerset's severest condemnation. "The models pose for dollars, for bread and butter, not to educate the public taste for art, but to pander to vitiated tastes." At the very outset, therefore, it is evident that Lady Somerset proceeds upon the assumption that the nude in art is vicious and that the public goes to see living reproductions of some of the grandest creations fashioned by the genius of painter and sculptor simply for the gratification of prurient taste.
>
> It is idle to waste discussion upon the nude in art. It has held an exalted place for ages and it will exist as long as the world turns upon its axis. Every year people are becoming a little more liberal and practical and advanced in their art views as well as in other things. Surely there is no warrant for the assumption that the audiences which assembled to see living pictures are animated by sensual longings. Look about the theatres in New York where living pictures are shown, and you will find assemblages of well conducted human beings, the heads of families, the mothers of children, the flower of the young flock, bent upon rational, wholesome enjoyment. What effect do these pictures have upon them? Is it not one of respectful admiration? What is the expression most generally heard? Is it not one of amazement that painting and statuary can be so wonderfully counterfeited, with occasionally an openly expressed disbelief that the figures are really alive? The human model, to the audience (as to the artist, to whom, from the very necessities of art, she must pose in private), is an inanimate thing, no more than so much paint or canvas or marble.
>
> It is preposterous to assume a degradation of the sex because female models pose for hire. The sordid considerations of bread and butter and vulgar dollars, and even paltry pennies, dominate most of us who are toilers. The "clear cut commercial situation," so pointedly referred to by Lady Somerset, presents itself to most of us born without titles and estates. No doubt, some of the young women in living pictures would gladly exert themselves solely for love of art if worldly circumstances would permit. To certain fashionable functions living pictures have become of late a popular addition. Young women and matrons of fair repute have freely displayed such charms of feature and form as Heaven has favored them with in the cause of charity. The professional model, whether in the studio or the living picture cabinet, is less fortunate in worldly entertainment.... The honorable avenues of employment open to women are none too many. Lady Somerset, as a philanthropist, must know this. Why seek to close any one of them? Why, as the stern champion suggests, should it be "made an impossibility" for a woman to earn her bread and butter as a living picture?
>
> To me has fallen the selection of many models for living pictures. I have studied them with care mentally, morally and physically. I have yet to find one whose womanhood has suffered degradation, or one whose delicacy and modesty have become blunted because of her vocation. Upon the contrary, I have found them clear headed, modest, well behaved young women—self reliant and courageous enough to fight the never ceasing battle for support—women who prefer honest toil to vice. They and other women of this type, no matter what vocation in life, in my humble opinion, lend to the glorification, not to the degradation, of their sex. And here is where I am radically at variance with my philanthropic sister from across the sea.[17]

In succeeding weeks, however, the opposition to living pictures persisted, with the W.C.T.U. requesting the aid of New York police authorities. The responses from that quarter were sympathetic, but vague. One reason, perhaps, was that the law did not provide a suitable foundation on which to prosecute model artists. Although Mrs. Martin sought to invoke a state statute prohibiting indecent modeling, as she herself recognized, "The great question is the one which had to be settled by the courts: What is and what is not indecent?"[18] Of course, that question remains unanswered to this day. Anthony Comstock recognized the legal difficulties involved in such a matter, and actually opposed the W.C.T.U. attack on tableaux. He believed that the campaign served only to draw public attention to the exhibitions, thus undermining the crusade's purpose.[19] Comstock's views notwithstanding, the W.C.T.U. continued its appeals to the law, but no action was forthcoming. In November 1894, however, the campaign strategy appears to have changed. In an interview, Lady Henry Somerset described the group's plan of action: "In general, we shall try to arouse public opinion. To that end we shall use the press and platform, and will aim to crystallize the awakened public sentiment in statutory enactments."[20]

The promise "to arouse public opinion" provoked the model artists and managers to defend their art in terms quite as strident as those of their opponents. In the same column, immediately following the report of Lady Somerset's interview, another article reported the artists' reactions:

> When the news of Lady Somerset's crusade reached Mr. A.M. Palmer's ears he was completely surprised. "Well, that is certainly the work of a foolish woman," he said, and refused to say a word beyond remarking that he considered that quite definite enough.
> Mr. Price, who is one of the management of "Little Christopher Columbus," was completely disgusted. "The pictures are no more than plastic representations of great masterpieces. The figures who take part are no more regarded as flesh and blood than the other stage properties."[21]

The same writer went on to report interviews with other managers and with several of the models themselves. The models expressed pride in their profession: "I think it's a great compliment to be considered beautiful enough to take the part [of Psyche]," one commented, and another remarked, "I do not want blame or pity or condonement for my art. It is art, and so needs no excusing." Some of the models attributed the source of trouble to depraved tastes among the audience: "On what grounds, I should like to know, does this English lady charge the living pictures with immorality? If it is because men come to see us with impure thoughts, are we to blame? When a masterpiece is painted who can object to it? Only those who are not pure in mind." Kilanyi himself was quoted as asking, "... what could be more beautiful than a graceful and handsome woman? Are you going to drape your statues in the museums and put trimmings on the pictures in the shops?" In general, those interviewed expressed indignation that an English-woman had come to America to make such trouble. One of Kilanyi's models expressed the very practical foundation for her feelings: "Wouldn't it be better if she fed the hungry and clothed the naked, than if she shut off another avenue of honest employment? Surely, there are few enough open to women." The attitude was echoed somewhat more cynically by C.B. Cline, the business manager at Koster and Bial's: "It is queer that some persons are never satisfied unless they are hindering others in the business they are carrying on." He concluded, "It will only advertise the pictures, that is all," thus reiterating Anthony Comstock's original objection to the crusade.

In spite of such protestations, the model artists and managers took no chances. When a rumor circulated that a W.C.T.U. committee was planning to visit the tableaux at the Imperial, the Garden, and Koster and Bial's, the curtains rolled up to reveal carefully draped female forms in the living pictures. The managers had no definite information concerning the visit, so they said, "but they thought it best to be on the safe side."[22] The next day Police Superintendent Byrnes was prevailed upon to send police into the theatres to look for evidence to be used in prosecution of the model artists, yet this failed to result in any arrests.[23]

The W.C.T.U. opposition was doomed to continue as a largely ineffectual protest expressed in occasional letters to the editors and now and then through organization spokesmen who temporarily managed to get the ear of the press.[24] Even its attempts to secure legislative bans proved ineffective. When in 1895, a new law was actually proposed, though never passed, it was "so sweeping in its provisions that," according to one New York theatre manager, "it would not only put a stop to all ballets and burlesques, but it would prevent the performance of many of the plays of Shakespeare, would compel the removal of many of the pictures from the Metropolitan Museum of Art and other public exhibitions; would prevent the publication of some of the standard monthly magazines, as at present issued, and would bring Diana down off the tower of the Madison Square Garden."[25]

For a time the questions of nudity and morality overshadowed almost all other commentary about living pictures during the mid-1890's. There was, however, one notable exception to this preoccupation—a review which analyzed living pictures on the basis of art theories, however naive. The critic cited examples among both the Hammerstein and the Kilanyi tableaux:

> Nothing is absolutely artistic, or at least is not in the truest sense artistic, which is not the direct product of an artst using a medium selected by himself as best expressing his conception of a form, of an idea, or of an emotion. If he has no impulse forcing him to choose for it the brush rather than the chisel, or the chisel rather than pen—or the poised models surrounded by accessories, half painted and half real, rather than pen, or chisel, or brush—

then he is no real artist and his work is pretty, perhaps, beautiful possibly, but to a certainty not great and not original art.

Here is the explanation of that something wrong, that vague incompleteness and incongruity noticeable in all the "living pictures" now on view and it will continue to be felt as long as the people having them in charge reproduce the work of artists who, for good reasons, have chosen other media of expression.[26]

This, however, was the voice of one "crying in the wilderness," for the viability of tableaux vivants as an art form never did receive any serious consideration by critics. Perhaps one reason for this omission was that there were other issues which seemed to divert the attention of critics and reformers and the public away from both the artistry and the morality of tableaux. The projected production of *Hannele,* mentioned earlier, was being opposed by the Gerry Society, but many people saw the attack as an attempt to censor the play rather than simply to protect the young girl who was to appear in it.[27]

The propriety of nude figures in painting and the use of "undraped" models by painters and sculptors was also called into question during this period. In October 1894 a painting by the English artist, George Frederick Watts, which had been commissioned by Congress to be hung in the White House, was refused by the Superintendent of Public Buildings on the grounds that it was too risqué.[28] Such situations as these led the *Herald* to speculate, "The reason for the spasm against the nude unquestionably is found in the extraordinary moral wave that is now sweeping around the world, permitting professional reformers to carry out their favorite hobbies and to test their theories on the busy people of the earth."[29]

Finally, as bad as tableaux vivants seemed to some people, there were other theatrical entertainments which incensed them even more. These were early forms of striptease burlesque.

On 5 April 1896, Doris' Gaiety Theatre advertised the arrival of "PILAR-MORIN. Subtle, Delicate, Expressive, Graceful, Refined, a Gifted and skilled exponent of the Maxim 'Actions Speak Louder Than Words.' IN THE DELICIOUS MORCEAUX ORANGE BLOSSOMS. HER VERSION OF THE PARIS SENSATION FOR 3 YEARS. LE COUCHER DE LA MARIEE (Wedding Night)."[30] This intriguing French import was suggestive in the extreme. After a lengthy preliminary scene between a bride, her parents, and the groom, the pantomime then proceeded to depict the bride preparing for her wedding night:

> The pantomimist first removed her veil, then busied herself over taking out various pins, and next removed her bridal dress, remaining in the attire of many corset advertisements. After laying these garments away she unlaced and removed her corsets, afterward vigorously scratching the flesh they bound. Next she removed a layer of white skirts, and then stood by the bed in a single garment that bared the arms and neck and that was so thin that the pink fleshings beneath showed through wherever it did not hang in folds. Following this she

> donned an elaborate night robe, arranged her hair, and seated herself on the bed. With her feet on a chair she removed her shoes, and one stocking and a showy garter were brought to view. Again the pillows received attention, one being placed on top of the other till a sight of the wedding ring led to their rearrangement. Then the pantomimist got into bed, drew the bedclothes over her, turned down the lamp beside her, and bade the bridegroom come in, which he did as the curtain fell.[31]

Such a provocative display raised the hackles of press and police alike. A week after the opening, the *Sun* remarked that "Mlle. Pilar-Morin's 'Orange Blossoms' is continued with the same degree of nastiness that characterized its first showing."[32] The large audiences which attended were soon to be disappointed, however, for Manager Doris was arrested and the disrobing scene banned from the performance. In this truncated form, "Orange Blossoms" continued to run for a short time, spawning several imitations:

> I am told that the Pilar-Morin show is being duplicated in the Miner variety houses, and it is likely that the police will have their hands full in the striving to check the thing before they get through with it.
> At Miner's Bowery Theatre the same exhibition was provided by the Washburn Sisters' Company, I learn, under the title of The Bridal Night. At the Trocadero Fra Diavolo is being burlesqued, apparently for the sole purpose of giving Zelina a chance to disrobe in front of a looking-glass.[33]

In May, while Doris and Pilar-Morin attempted in court to reverse the ban on their "Orange Blossoms" disrobing scene, they introduced a new "Parisian novelty" which was equally provocative. Entitled "The Flea," it depicted a woman awaiting her appointment with a gentleman. "She is all dressed and ready to leave the house when she discovers that there is a flea in her clothing. Piece by piece the articles of apparel are removed and searched until— well,until there are hardly any more to take off."[34] Such provocation did little to advance the Gaiety court case, and, in spite of supporting testimony from critic, Charles Byrne, and producer, David Belasco, both productions were held to "go beyond the legitimate object of a theatre in furnishing wholesome entertainment and instruction," and "to excite in a spectator impure imaginations."[35]

A somewhat more successful attempt at this type of performance was made in July 1896 at the American Roof Garden. Surprisingly, the performer was Hope Booth whose arrival in America had been heralded by dismal reports of unsuccessful appearances in England.[36] Nevertheless, she appeared in "Ten Minutes in the Latin Quarter; or, A Study in the Nude," and managed to provoke unanimously uncomplimentary reviews in New York. Police attempted to close the show, but the "altogether" scene was made more respectable after opening night by the addition of "an extra layer of fleshings" to hide the original "thin covering of flesh-colored stockinet."[37] This time the court favored Miss Booth and Manager Hamilton, so that the performance, with its extra fleshings, was allowed to continue, though "watched by the police nightly."[38]

Following this incident Hope Booth's fortunes rose. She continued as the sensational attraction of the American Roof Garden throughout the summer and in the fall moved to the Trocadero with the same act. By this time she had added "dances and posings" to her accomplishments, and at the end of September it was noted that her "new pose—'Eve'—was the pièce de résistance."[39] Nudity was the main appeal of her act, however, for when the end of her engagement was announced patrons were advised that "few more opportunities remain of seeing her in her 'altogether' specialty."[40] In January 1897 Hope Booth was booked at Tony Pastor's, that bastion of "family vaudeville." Here, she appeared in "chaste and beautiful reproductions of famed art pictures, mythological, classical, poetical and fanciful, presented with electrical effects postively beyond reproach and without offense to the most critical taste."[41] Critical response was tepid at best. The *Herald* observed that Hope Booth "had achieved more clothes since she was last seen in this city."[42] The *Dramatic Mirror* was more descriptive: "Hope Booth posed in various positions, with calciums thrown on her from every point, even through a glass trap. She wore a suit of white fleshings which showed every line of her figure. A little more drapery and some of the pictures would not be amiss."[43] A week later the same reviewer dismissed her act summarily: "Hope Booth continued to present her travesy on 'art' by posing in various attitudes in a suit of white fleshings. Her engagement finished on Saturday night. Her performance caused no great stir, as the living pictures craze died a natural death several months ago."[44] Hope Booth next appeared at Proctor's Pleasure Palace where Chief of Police Coulin requested that her picture be removed from display on the front of the theatre. The press noted that "the pictures had been displayed in Boston, Chicago, St. Louis, and Baltimore without attracting the attention of the authorities."[45] Summer of 1897 saw Miss Booth at the St. Nicholas Music Hall posing "on an ebony pedestal, against a background of thousands of yards of vaulted velvet, with the poses sheened by floods of varicolored light."[46] The engagement continued throughout July.

Through all of this, Anthony Comstock's Society for the Suppression of Vice, with support from certain factions in the Women's Christian Temperance Union, had continued its attempts to secure passage of a more stringent obscenity law in the state legislature. These attempts were consistently frustrated, however, partly due to the conflicting efforts of separate reform forces. The 1897 *Annual Report* of the Society summarized their unsuccessful efforts in this direction:

> Early in January [1896] this Society prepared a bill to amend Sections 316 and 137 of the Penal Code. This bill was practically the same as the one that passed the Senate in 1895, but failed in the Assembly, because of unwise interference on the part of certain persons interested in another bill....

> Unfortunately another bill bearing upon the same subject, making it a general law instead of amending the Penal Code and keeping the offenses codified, was introduced in the Assembly and came before the [Judicial] Committee at the same time.
>
> This adverse bill, as we pointed out to the Committee, was very loosely drawn and contained certain very improper provisions, to wit, one that would have permitted any female to appear in public places in an entirely nude state. We were obliged to oppose this general law bill.
>
> We regret exceedingly that we have to report that our bill again failed. The result has been that our state has been flooded with most worthless and shameful publications, most atrocious displays in theatres and low playhouses, and with open and flagrant indecencies in private halls of entertainment.[47]

In fact, neither bill was passed by the legislature, leaving matters virtually unchanged. No further efforts to gain passage of such legislation were reported during the remainder of the century.

One final attempt at sensational posing illustrates the more tolerant attitude which had developed toward such performances. In April 1898 Koster and Bial's billed Adele Ritchie in a new operetta. The *Herald's* facetious treatment of the announcement is revealing:

> So the lady is going to bathe, is she, and sing while she is "partially submerged, apparently in real water?" That's what they say of Miss Adele Ritchie over at Koster & Bial's, where she is to appear to-morrow night in an operetta with the suggestive title "Au Bain" (At the Bath). And there is to be a man in the moon, or rather in the shrubbery.
>
> Quite piquant all this promises to be, though the picture which shows Suzanne running her fingers through her loosely hanging hair while standing in the pool exhibits her in a costume quite long enough to pass muster with Grandfather Bradley, the moral censor of Asbury Park.
>
> But if the costume is too long it may be diaphanous. Perhaps it is one of those draperies which, as the saying goes, "reveal more than they conceal." So the prudes may find something to cavil at after all. But what business have prudes in a music hall anyway? If they don't like the announcement that Suzanne's costume will be "appropriate to her liquid surroundings," or are shocked at that detail of the opera which shows a man peering through the shrubbery while she is preparing for her ablutions—why, let them flock to a Lenten lecture. And yet it may be ducats to doughnuts it's not half as risque as it is pretended and that when it comes to the "shedding of the silken lingerie" Charmion will still win out hands—or rather head—down.[48]

The *Dramatic Mirror* review the following Tuesday confirmed that "Au Bain" was, in fact, "not up to expectations of sensationalism."[49]

Such a comment illustrates the distance puplic reaction to suggestive performance had travelled. From the vehement attacks and police raids of 1848 and the 1870's, opposition had turned to bemused deprecation in the press and verbal debate among the reformers. While, throughout much of their history in New York, tableaux vivants had been at the center of the controversy over public morals, the opposition had never been successful in suppressing them completely. Although the 1890's were years of noteworthy reform movements, these did not prevent tableaux from reaching their brightest hours.

10

Retrospect

As one looks back on tableaux vivants in New York, from their beginnings in 1831, it is clear that this entertainment formed a significant part of nineteenth century theatrical fare. The major efforts of numerous performers and producers were focused on tableaux. The genre functioned in several ways—as afterpiece or an attraction on a multiple bill, as part of a play, or as the featured event. Tableaux found their way into the most respected theatres as well as the lowliest concert saloons and music halls, and were even presented as "society fund-raisers."

While the productions of tableaux vivants might be more or less elaborate, they held certain characteristics in common. Tableaux generally represented some separate source material—a painting, sculpture, or scene from literature, or a familiar concept or event. They often made extensive use of theatrical techniques of realistic staging, including elaborately painted backdrops, three-dimensional scenery and properties, authentic costumes, and spectacular special effects. Nudity was often suggested by means of "fleshings" and, in the case of statue representations, by body paint and other devices. A large picture frame frequently replaced the conventional proscenium in theatres, thus enhancing the "living picture" image. Finally, tableaux vivants were usually accompanied by music or recitation designed to contribute to the appropriate atmosphere.

The history of tableaux vivants may be viewed as a struggle for acceptance on moral grounds. Although tableau producers invariably emphasized the artistry of their productions and justified their performances on the basis of the great works of art represented, many of them adopted sensational advertising methods and clearly relied on the appeal of female nudity. Such exhibitions flew in the face of moralistic nineteenth century attitudes, resulting in outraged protests and official attacks. Repeated attempts to close tableau exhibitions were made by police authorities, at the instigation of such groups as the Young Men's Christian Association, though its Society for the Suppression of Vice, under Anthony Comstock, and the Women's Christian Temperance Union, inspired by the British Lady Henry Somerset. Yet many producers were able to stay within the bounds of public acceptance and were able to generate an aura of "true artistry" about their productions.

Aside from the obvious sexual appeal of some tableaux, which led to the controversies just mentioned, there were other, more conventional sources of the popularity of tableaux vivants. To some extent, living pictures and statues "borrowed" their popularity from the works of art represented. Many producers capitalized on recently exhibited paintings and sculpture or scenes described in favorite novels of the day. There was an implied sense of status in the ability to recognize great masterpieces—and even those which were not so great. Tableaux vivants were frequently seen as valuable educational aids for adults and children alike. Indeed, tableau artists often expressed an almost missionary zeal in describing their artistic purposes, and critics recommended the exhibitions as a means to achieve cultural improvement. In addition, for the nineteenth century viewer, the sheer love of spectacle was satisfied through grandiose presentations with large casts, exotic subject matter, and elaborate scenery and costumes. Finally, and perhaps most importantly, nineteenth-century audiences were fascinated by verisimilitude. Newspaper reports of tableaux were filled with wonder at how accurately the live representation of a painting duplicated the appearance of the original; conversely, the lack of accuracy in even minor details justified the severest condemnation. Whatever the source of their appeal, tableaux drew a large and enthusiastic following during the nineteenth century.

In spite of their enduring popularity, however, by the end of the nineteenth century tableaux vivants had all but disappeared from New York theatres and music halls. Their appeal was being taken over by the budding motion picture industry, by the leg show and striptease burlesque, and by the theatrical spectacle of musical revue and operetta. Only occasional tableaux appeared in the new century, and notable as they were, they took forms different from their progenitors. The great revues of Ziegfeld, Earl Carroll, the Shuberts, and others exhibited tableaux designed to "glorify the American girl," and many of these employed actual nudity, even without fleshings. Seldom, however, did these attempt to represent actual paintings or sculptures.[1] Living statues occasionally served as gymnastic presentations and were favorites of some school physical education programs. In a few cases, these did employ classic statuary as a source.[2] In the legitimate theatre, the practice continued for a time of ending key scenes with a tableau which froze a significant moment in the play. These, however, were seldom related to paintings or sculpture, as had been the case in the 1831 production of Jerrold's *The Rent Day*.

A somewhat more traditional approach was maintained for a time in circus tableaux, which may be seen occasionally even today. Depicting such subjects as "The Dance of Life," "Victory," "The Spirit of Flight," and "The Rainbow Fountain," gilded or whitened figures posed in the circus rings and even aloft in the rigging of spectacular ariel acts. The subject matter was usually fanciful, rather than based upon recognizable artworks. Circus historians, John and Alice Durant, observe that such exhibits "were a delight to the ladies and some men but a never failing bore to all small boys who must have been glad when the display was discontinued in 1935."[3]

Tableaux vivants, produced for their own sake, occur in the contemporary theatre in only a few isolated instances; these, however, are notable. An annual "Festival of Arts and Pageant of the Masters" has been presented nearly every summer since 1932 at Laguna Beach, California. In a spectacular exhibition involving some five hundred volunteer models and backstage workers, the Pageant offers tableaux representing a wide range of painting and sculptural styles and subject matter. The works of art are represented with extreme fidelity, and audiences are able to compare the tableaux to large, full-color photographs of the originals, published in the Pageant's *Official Souvenir Program*. The techniques of posing and the uses of costumes, makeup, and scenery are fully as ingenious and elaborate as their nineteenth-century precursors.[4] (See Figures 22-24.)

A special tableau vivant production, which attempted to recapture some of the spirit of late nineteenth century exhibitions, was presented at the Brooklyn Museum, 20-21 October 1979.[5] Based on the Midway Plaisance entertainment at the 1893 World's Columbian Exposition in Chicago, the tableaux were part of the "Festival of Fairs," which opened the Museum's exhibit, "The American Renaissance, 1876-1917." Figures 25 and 26 illustrate one of these tableaux and the painting it represented. This tableau shows the combination of two and three dimensional scenic techniques frequently found in nineteenth century production. The flat, painted backdrop represented all the detail of the walls of the "inn," the floor was steeply raked, and the furniture was especially constructed to provide the sense of perspective in the original painting. Red curtains within a large, gilt picture frame were drawn aside to reveal the tableau. (See also Figures 1-4.)

A more theatrical use of tableaux may be found in the contemporary production of the *Passion Play of Oberammergau.* "Living Tableaux" were made part of this play in 1811, though the tradition itself began in 1634. These grandiose tableaux, which depict significant events in the action of the play, are presented on a wide stage flanked by large portals and backed by a panoramic view of the Bavarian Alps. The grandeur of the scene is further enhanced by a formal chorus which breaks from a line across the stage to form two units flanking each tableau. While these tableaux are not rooted in specific paintings or sculpture, they illustrate vividly the biblical source material which inspired them. The first tableau, for example, depicts "The Expulsion from Paradise" and is inspired by the account in in *Genesis* 3:17-24.[6]

Finally, the American musical production, *1776*,[7] which opened on Broadway on 18 March 1976, provides a recent example of a tableau vivant used to enhance the significant point of a scene from a play. Depicting the events leading to the signing of the Declaration of Independence, the musical concludes with a tableau representation of John Trumbull's famous painting of that event. Trumbull's painting, which now hangs in the Capitol Building rotunda, Washington, D.C., and which may also be seen on the recently issued two-dollar bill, is, of course, familiar to every American. Interestingly, in this case, virtually the entire play was set in a physical locale similar to that depicted in the painting, so that, as in the case of *The Rent Day* in 1831, the characters had but to assume the poses of the painting to transform the play's action into a tableau vivant.

Noteworthy as these recent manifestations may be, however, tableaux really belong to a century which has ended. Tableaux vivants have joined those numerous other forms, which, though no longer central to the American stage, have become part of its rich theatrical heritage.

Figure 22. Glen Eytchison, director for the Pageant of the Masters, Laguna Beach, California, stands atop a mobile loading platform to check the positions of volunteer models in the tableau vivant representation of Leonardo da Vinci's *The Last Supper*. (Photo courtesy of Laguna Festival of Arts.)

Figure 23. A tableau vivant of *The Last Supper*, Leonardo da Vinci's masterpiece in Santa Maria delle Grazie, Milan, Italy, provides the traditional climax of the world-famous Pageant of the Masters at Laguna Beach, California, each summer. (Photo courtesy of Laguna Festival of Arts.)

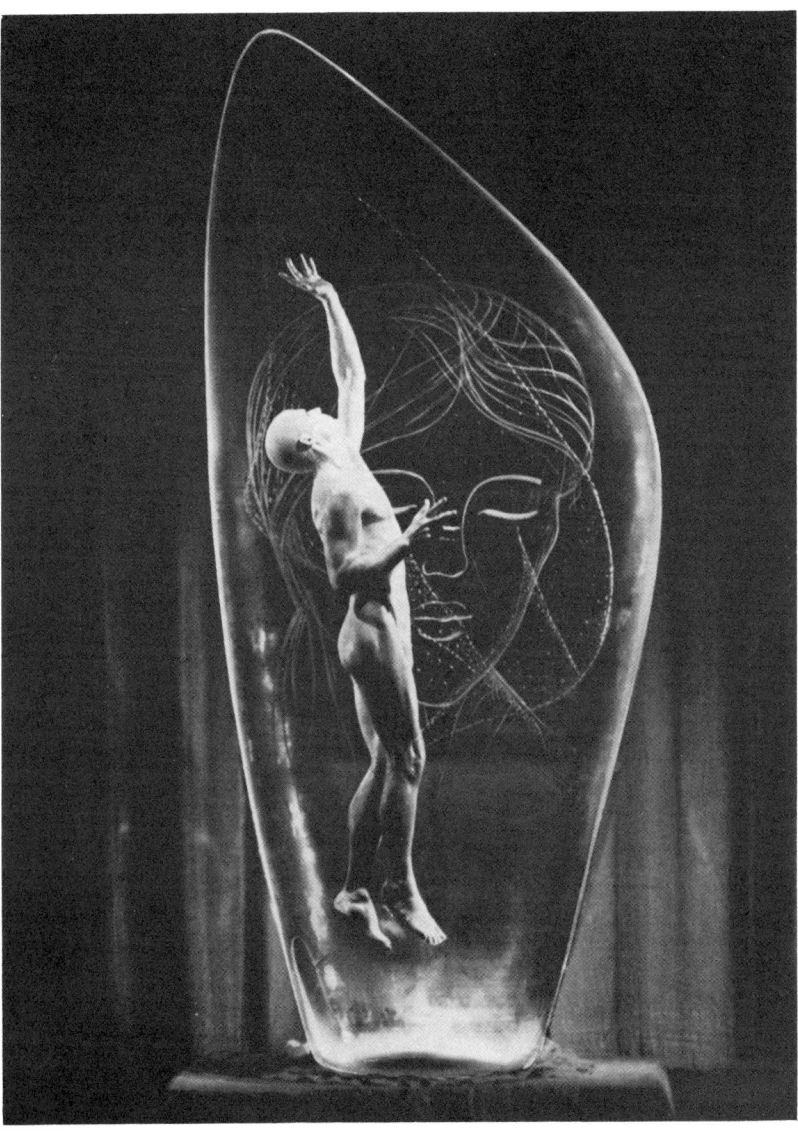

Figure 24. This modern tableau vivant, presented at the 50th anniversary 1983 Pageant of the Masters, Laguna Beach, California, represents *Orpheus,* designed by George Thompson and etched by Tom Vincent. The original free-form Steuben glass, inspired by a poem by Cecil Hemley, is in a private collection. (Photo courtesy of Laguna Festival of Arts.)

Figure 25. *At the Inn* (1886), oil on canvas, by Francis Davis Millet. (Courtesy of the Union League Club, New York.)

Figure 26. Tableau vivant of Millet's *At the Inn*, presented at the Brooklyn Museum, 20-21 October 1979. The tableau was accompanied by Edwards' song, "The Girl Who Cares for Me" (1904).

Appendix

Specifications and drawings for Edward Kilanyi's United States patents, #528,372 and #528,373, "Apparatus for Displaying Tableaux Vivant [*sic*]" (United States Patent Office, *Specifications of Patents,* 30 October 1894, pp. 2872-74; *Drawings of Patents,* 30 October 1894, pp. 695-96).

154 Appendix

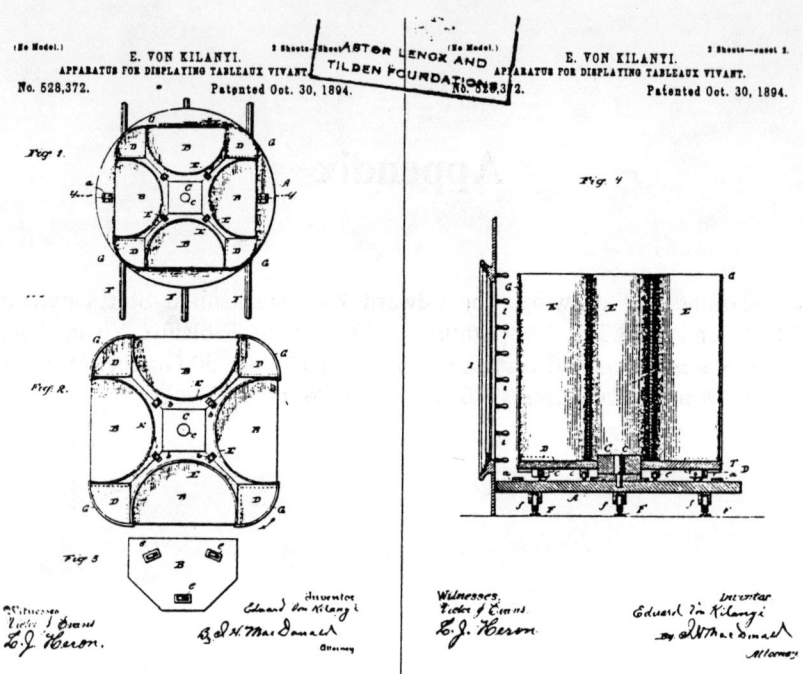

528,372. APPARATUS FOR DISPLAYING TABLEAUX VIVANT. Eduard von Kilanyi, Buda-Pesth, Austria-Hungary. Filed Mar. 29, 1894. Serial No. 505,625. (No model.) Patented in Germany Feb. 25, 1892, No. 1,909.

To all whom it may concern:

Be it known that I, EDUARD VON KILANYI, a subject of the Emperor of Austria-Hungary, residing at Buda-Pesth, Austria-Hungary, have invented certain new and useful Improvements in Apparatus for Displaying Tableaux Vivant or Living Pictures, (patented in Germany February 25, 1892, No. 1,909;) and I do hereby declare the following to be a full, clear, and exact description of the invention, such as will enable others skilled in the art to which it appertains to make and use the same.

My invention relates to mechanism for displaying living pictures.

The object of the device is to present to view rapidly and accurately pictures consisting of one or more persons properly posed with appropriate scenic effects.

It is well known that in theatrical performances an audience tires of long delay or intermissions and it is therefore essential that in displays of the nature stated the apparatus must be quickly placed in position and quickly operated and removed.

To this end the apparatus consists of the mechanism shown in the accompanying drawings, in which—

Figure 1 is a top plan view, showing the tracks and lower hinged platform; Fig. 2, a plan view of the upper platform or table; Fig. 3, a detail plan view of one of the sections showing the independent rollers therefor, and Fig. 4 a vertical section of the apparatus and the illuminated frame.

Referring more particularly to the drawings (Fig. 4) the lower table A is provided with grooved rollers f which move upon the railing F so placed that the platform may be quickly and accurately brought in front of the frame I illuminated within at sides and top by electric lights i. This lower table is hinged as indicated at a, so it may be folded, thus taking up less space in storage and transportation, and at the same time permitting it to be more easily and quickly placed in position on the track.

Upon the lower table is placed a second table T, having a central block C, and pivot c journaled in the seat in the lower table. Upon table T is placed a series of removable sections B, each provided with independent rollers e.

The scenic back grounds E are placed in position on the different sections—the sections being bolted together as indicated at b, and blocks D are inserted at the corners, and let into the sections B, the pieces G, occupying the space between the sections. The sections may however be joined to each other in any other suitable mechanical way.

In operation the tables are brought into position before the frame I (of any desired size) the persons forming the first two or three tableaux to be exhibited are posed in their respective sections and the background properly arranged. The curtain is then drawn and while picture No. 1 is being exhibited, sections 3 and 4 are being prepared, section 2 being ready for exhibition. As soon as picture No. 1 disappears from view, that section becomes No. 4 and its background and other scenic accessories are removed and new ones substituted. This is being done while picture No. 2 is being exhibited and thus the entire set can be quickly shown.

I have here shown but four sections for convenience, but it is obvious that I may place upon the platform as many sections as may be desired. It is found in practice that four, six, or eight sections are all that is desirable. It is also obvious that different means may be used for moving the tables and the different means may be used for securing the sections and backgrounds in place without departing from the spirit of my invention.

Having thus described my invention, what I claim as new, and desire to secure by Letters Patent, is—

In an apparatus of the nature described, the combination with a track and supporting table, of a sectional scene table provided with removable backgrounds, as and for the purpose set forth.

In testimony whereof I affix my signature in presence of two witnesses.

EDUARD VON KILANYI.

Witnesses:
A. L. SCANTLEBURY,
JAMES J. KENEEY.

156 Appendix

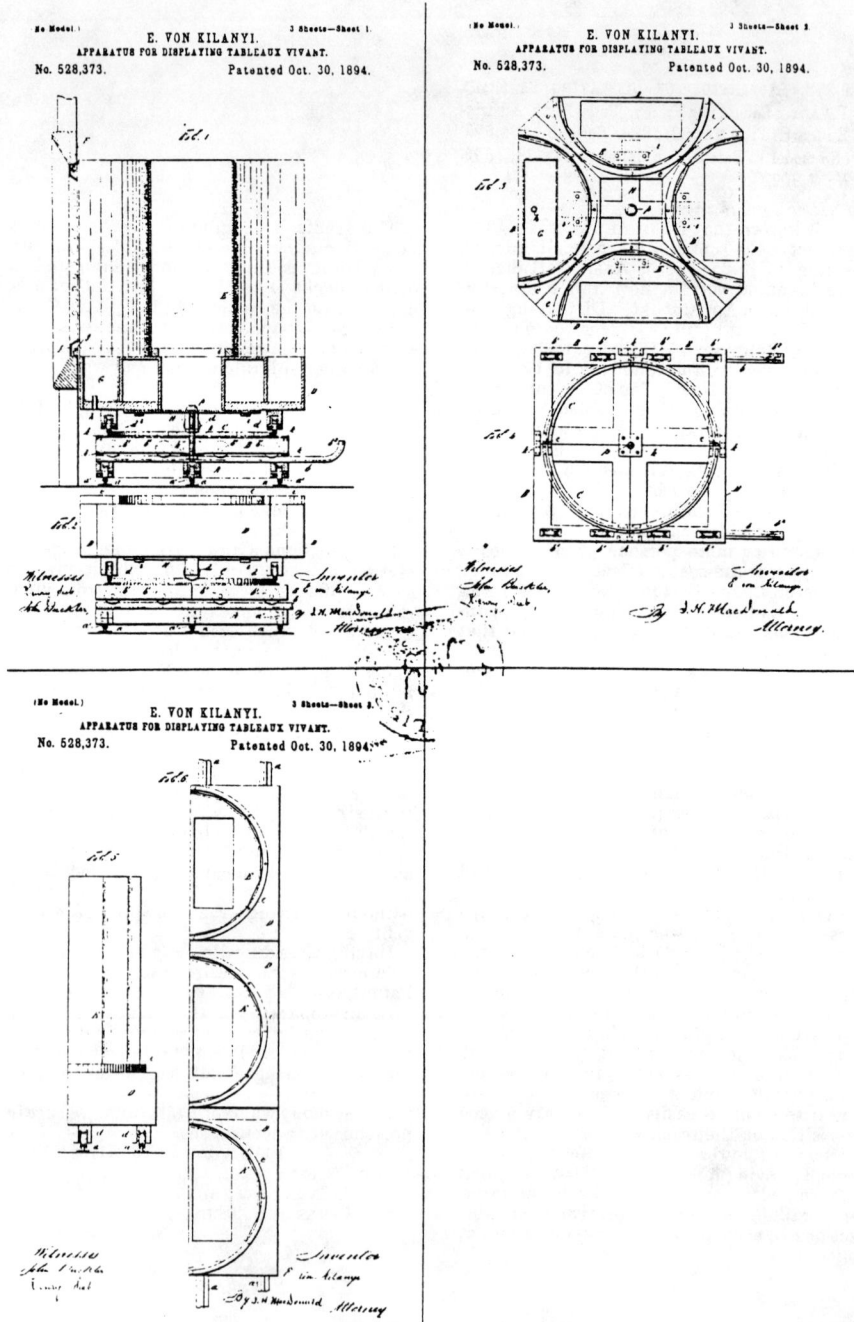

528,373. APPARATUS FOR DISPLAYING TABLEAUX VIVANT. Eduard von Kilanyi, Buda-Pesth, Austria-Hungary. Filed Apr. 19, 1894. Serial No. 508,143. (No model.)

To all whom it may concern:

Be it known that I, EDUARD VON KILANYI, a subject of the Emperor of Austria-Hungary, and a resident of Buda-Pesth, Austria-Hungary, have invented certain new and useful Improvements in Apparatus for Displaying Tableaux Vivant, of which the following is a specification.

My invention relates to apparatus for displaying living pictures and is an improvement on that filed by me March 29, 1894, Serial No. 505,625.

In the accompanying drawings which embody my invention Figure 1 is a vertical section of the device. Fig. 2 is a side view of same. Fig. 3 is a top plan view of same. Fig. 4 is a top plan view of the lower supporting frame; Fig. 5, an end view, and Fig. 6 a plan view of the upper table and scenic sections, without the central track and moved in a straight line back and forth on the stage track.

Referring more particularly to the drawings, it will be noted that I have substituted for the lower table in the application above referred to a frame A, consisting of pieces suitably bolted or joined together so as to be readily assembled or taken apart and provided with wheels or rollers a' journaled in said frame at suitable intervals apart, said rollers moving upon a detachable track a laid upon the floor of the stage.

The frame A, movable as described, has secured to it a transverse track b, upon which moves a second supporting frame or table B, provided with wheels or rollers b', moving upon said track. This table has secured to it on its top a circular track C upon which move the wheels d' of the scene supporting table D. This latter table consists of sections (preferably four or more), each independent of the other but suitably joined together, as will be hereinafter explained. The sections are of box form to give strength and in addition to provide a tank or tanks G for water effects. The four sections as here shown (Fig. 3) are joined together by a four arm cross plate H bolted to the under side of the sections as shown at i, and at the center is a central pintle p passing down through table B.

Upon the upper surface of table D upon each independent section are secured stays e, against which rest the scenic back grounds E. These stays are removably attached to the table. The scenic back grounds are hinged together so as to be readily and quickly detached and folded up. This construction enables me to place the apparatus in its desired position on the stage easily and quickly, and having arrived at the proper position at the rear and near to the frame F has a reciprocal motion and a motion of translation relative to said frame, that is to say, the front of each section must be very near the edge of the frame so as to hide the table sections and make the illusions complete. However, to do this quickly and noiselessly the table must be run back so as to clear the edges of the frame, and this is done by moving it back and forth on track b by means of a suitable lever, or in any other mechanical way. Having drawn the table back on its track until arrested by the stops b^2 at the ends of track b, these stops being placed at a distance just enough to clear the edge of the picture frame and permit the table to be revolved, hence it is shown that the table D has a combined motion of translation and rotation.

The picture frame F has an interior mat f, about which is arranged a series of lights g, which light up by reflection the back ground E with the posed figures.

The track C is preferably hinged as shown at c, so as to be readily folded for transportation, and the several parts of the table or frame B are secured together by bolt plates k.

In operation, the track a is laid upon the floor of the stage and the apparatus moved up to the frame F provided with legs let into the stage floor.

The scenic effects E for the first two, three or four pictures are placed in position against the stays e, and the figurants for the first two or three pictures are posed in their respective sections on table D. After picture No. 1 is shown, the table is moved backward, then revolved to bring into view picture No. 2. Then the back ground E of No. 1 is removed and back ground of picture 5 with its figurants substituted. This motion of translation and rotation is continued until all the pictures have been displayed and the apparatus is then moved back on its track, the track removed, and the stage is clear for any other part of the play.

In some theaters the stage may be too narrow to revolve the scene table, and in this instance the circular track may be dispensed with and the scene sections be arranged in a straight line and moved back and forth on the lower frame A or stage track a. The back grounds will be removably arranged and the operation of setting and remounting the pictures will be the same as before described.

Having thus described my invention, what I claim as new, and desire to secure by Letters Patent, is—

1. In an apparatus of the nature described, a movable platform in combination with a table supported by and movable thereon, and a scene supporting table divided into independent sections and rotatable on said table.

2. The combination with the movable frame A of the table B moved laterally thereon, and a sectional table D rotating on table B, said table D having one or more water compartments.

3. The combination with the laterally moving frame A and table B of a table D pivotally mounted and rotatable on table B, said table D having removable back grounds E and supports e.

Signed at New York, in the county of New York and State of New York, this 16th day of April, A. D. 1894.

    EDUARD VON KILANYI.

Witnesses:
 I. H. MacDonald,
 Alex. Haman.

Notes

Chapter 1

1. The tableaux vivants illustrated in Figures 2 and 4 were presented in the Auditorium Court of the Brooklyn Museum, 20-21 October 1979, as part of the "Festival of Fairs," a performance event in connection with the Museum's exhibit, "The American Renaissance, 1876-1917." The event included several entertainments typical of such fairs as the Midway Plaisance at the World's Columbian Exposition (1893), Chicago. Among these were a Vienna sidewalk cafe, performances by belly dancers, instrumental and vocal bandstand music, and demonstrations of mural painting, stained glass preparation, scrimshaw, and period costumes. Eight tableaux vivants were presented throughout the day, each accompanied by appropriate music from the bandstand. The tableaux represented the following works of art, all of which were included in the exhibit:

    1. Kenyon Cox, *Venice* (1893), oil and pencil on canvas, Bowdoin College Museum of Art.
    2. Daniel Chester French, *The Concord Minuteman of 1776* (1889), statue in bronze, United States Navy Department.
    3. Francis Davis Millet, *At the Inn* (1886), oil on canvas, The Union League Club, New York City.
    4. Charles C. Curran, *On the Heights* (1909), oil on canvas, The Brooklyn Museum.
    5. Thomas Eakins, *William Rush Carving His Allegorical Figure of the Schuylkill River* (1908), oil on canvas, The Brooklyn Museum.
    6. Edwin Austin Abbey, *Two Figures* study for *Galahad and the Siege Perilous* (1898) from "The Quest of the Holy Grail" murals, Boston Public Library, black chalk heightened with white on bluish-gray paper, Yale University Art Gallery.
    7. Thomas Wilmer Dewing, *The Days* (1887), oil on canvas, The Brooklyn Museum.
    8. Auguste Bartholdi, *Liberty Enlightening the World* (1886), statue in bronze, Bedloe's Island, New York Harbor. (The Brooklyn Museum exhibit included a plaster model of this work, by the sculptor.)

2. Bamber Gascoigne, *World Theatre: An Illustrated History* (Boston and Toronto: Little, Brown and Co., 1968), pp. 69-70.

3. Gascoigne, p. 90.

4. Gascoigne, p. 91.

5. Gascoigne, p. 95. The account if taken from Gaspar Barlaeus, *Marie de Medici entrant dans Amsteradm* (Amsterdam, 1638), p. 67ff.

6. Lucien Rimels, "Quadro Vivente," *Enciclopedia dello Spettacolo*, 9 vols. (Rome: Casa Editrice le Maschere, 1954-1964). 8 (1961):612-14. I am indebted to Laura Celino for the English translation of this entry.

7. Kirsten Gram Holmström, *Monodrama, Attitudes, Tableaux Vivants: Studies on Some Trends of Theatrical Fashion, 1770-1815* (Stockholm: Almqvist & Wiksell, 1967), p. 218.
8. Ibid.
9. Holmström, pp. 110-11.
10. Holmström, pp. 110ff., passim. Biographical information about Emma is plentiful, though varied in quality. Many impressionistic accounts make little or no pretense at documentation. Only a few biographers claim to have attempted objective studies, and even these are frequently colored by personal bias. Among the most useful accounts—and the least sensational—are: Mollie Hardwick, *Emma, Lady Hamilton* (New York: Holt, Rinehart and Winston, 1969); Walter S. Sichel, *Emma, Lady Hamilton* (London: A. Constable, 1905); Hugh Tours, *The Life and Letters of Emma Hamilton* (London: V. Gollancz, 1963); and Norah R. Lofts, *Emma Hamilton* (New York: Coward, McCann & Geoghegan, 1978). The Lofts work is especially notable for its many illustrations, though these show Emma mainly as a painter's model, not as a performer. Two editions of Emma's "memoirs" have been published, neither of which was written by Lady Hamilton herself. Sichel's edition, *Memoirs of Emma, Lady Hamilton* (New York: P.F. Collier & Sons, 1910), virtually duplicates his biography of her. The other version, edited by W.H. Long, *Memoirs of Emma, Lady Hamilton, with Anecdotes of her Friends and Contemporaries* (London: W.W. Gibbings, 1891), is really an adaptation of the priggishly slanted story by John Cordy Jeaffreson, *Lord Nelson and Lady Hamilton* (London: Hurst & Blockett, 1888).
11. Johann Wolfgang von Goethe, *Elective Affinities*, tr. James Anthony Froude and R. Dylan Boylan (New York: Frederick Ungar Publishing Co., 1963), pp. 164-67.
12. Holmström, p. 215.
13. Holmström, p. 216.
14. Holmström, p. 226.
15. Holmström, p. 216.
16. Holmström, p. 222.
17. Holmström, p. 228.
18. Holmström, p. 236.
19. Rimels, p. 613.
20. Richard D. Altick, *The Shows of London* (Cambridge, Massachusetts, and London: The Belnap Press of Harvard University Press, 1978), p. 342.
21. Altick, p. 343.
22. A.H. Saxon, *Enter Foot and Horse: A History of Hippodrama in England and France* (New Haven and London: Yale University Press, 1968), p. 35. For a more detailed study of Ducrow, see the same author's *The Life and Art of Andrew Ducrow & The Romantic Age of the English Circus* (Hamden, Conn.: Archon Books, 1978).
23. Altick, p. 343.

Chapter 2

1. George C.D. Odell, *Annals of the New York Stage*, 15 vols. (New York: Columbia University Press, 1927-49), 3:545.

Notes for Chapter 2   161

2. *New York Daily Advertiser,* 1 September 1831, p. 3.

3. An unidentified newspaper clipping (Theatre Collection, New York Public Library, MWEZ+n.c.703, p. 51) gives some biographical information about William Barrymore and his wife. Brief corroborating references may be found in Joseph N. Ireland, *Records of the New York Stage: 1750-1860,* 2 vols. (New York: T.H. Morrell, 1866-67), and in Saxon, *Enter Foot and Horse* and *Andrew Ducrow.* Incidentally, William Barrymore was not related to the famous family of Barrymores, according to *The Oxford Companion to the Theatres,* ed. Phyllis Hartnoll, 3rd ed. (London: Oxford University Press, 1967), p. 86.

4. *New York Evening Post,* 25 August 1831, p. 2; *New York Daily Advertiser,* 27 August 1831, p. 2.

5. Anonymous, in *Euterpeiad,* 1 October 1831, p. 125.

6. J.O. Bailey, *British Plays of the Nineteenth Century* (New York: The Odyssey Press, 1966), p. 259, asserts that the Wilkie paintings were Jerrold's inspiration for the play.

7. Martin Meisel, "Wilkie's Tableaux Vivants: An Amplification," *Master Drawings,* spring 1973, p. 56.

8. William W. Clapp, Jr., *A Record of the Boston Stage* (Boston: James Monroe and Co., 1853; reprint ed., New York: Greenwood Press, 1969), pp. 330, 314, 420-22.

9. Arthur Herman Wilson, *A History of the Philadelphia Theatre, 1835-1855* (Philadelphia: University of Pennsylvania Press, 1935; reprint ed., New York: Greenwood Press, 1968), p. 187.

10. A.H. Saxon, *Andrew Ducrow,* pp. 437-38, n. 98.

11. *New York Daily Advertiser,* 12 October 1831, p. 3.

12. *New York Daily Advertiser,* 1 October 1831, p. 2. Frimbly's performance was sandwiched between the main attraction, *The Tragedy of Pizarro; or, The Death of Rolla,* and a concluding farce, *Teddy the Tyler* (*New York Evening Post,* 1 October 1931, p. 2).

13. George G. Foster, *New York by Gas-Light* (New York: DeWitt and Davenport, 1850), p. 14.

14. *New York Daily Advertiser,* 13 December 1831, p. 3.

15. Alan S. Downer, ed., *The Autobiography of Joseph Jefferson* (Cambridge, Mass.: The Belnap Press of Harvard University Press, 1964), p. 9, n. 10.

16. Downer, ed., *Joseph Jefferson,* p. 9.

17. Saxon, *Andrew Ducrow,* pp. 149-51.

18. *New York Evening Post,* 15 June 1832, p. 3. Odell, 3:595, identifies "Rand and Guild" as the performers and laments that "these may have been the forerunners of the disgraceful 'living pictures' of years somewhat later."

19. *New York Standard,* 17 April 1834, p. 2; Odell, 4:35, 76.

20. Odell, 4:175-76.

21. Odell, 4:238; *New York Evening Post,* 11 September 1837, p. 3.

22. *New York Herald,* 26 June 1839, p. 3. The Ravel family "first arrived in the United States in 1832 and scheduled regular seasons before finally returning to Toulouse in 1858" (though some members of the family may have returned during the 1860's). Their act consisted of "individual skills of balancing..., tightrope..., exhibitions of military and sporting

Notes for Chapter 2

skills..., and exhibition of 'art' (tableaux and statuary)." In addition, the troupe performed ballets and pantomime. (Gretchen A. Schneider, "Gabriel Ravel and the Martinetti Family: The Popularity of Pantomime in 1855," *American Popular Entertainment: Papers and Proceedings of the Conference on the History of American Popular Entertainment*, ed. Myron Matlaw [Westport, Conn.: Greenwood Press, 1979], pp. 242-45.)

23. Odell, 4:417.
24. Odell, 4:381.
25. *New York Herald*, 16 October 1841, p. 3.
26. *New York Herald*, 3 October 1843, p. 2.
27. Oral Sumner Coad and Edwin Mims, Jr., *The American Stage*, The Pageant of America, Vol. 14 (New Haven: Yale University Press, 1929), p. 112.
28. *New York Herald*, 5 November 1845, p. 3.
29. Odell, 4:422.
30. *New York Herald*, 7 December 1840, p. 3. Similar notices appear in each issue through 10 December 1840.
31. *New York Herald*, 9 December 1840, p. 2.
32. *New York Post*, 11 January 1833, p. 3; Odell, 3:616.
33. Saxon, *Andrew Ducrow*, pp. 226-31, provides a detailed reconstruction of the work based upon a manuscript in the Lord Chamberlain's Collection and upon bills for performances.
34. *New York Herald*, 6 September 1841, p. 4.
35. Odell, 4:31.
36. *New York Herald*, 8 June 1839, p. 3.
37. Odell, 4:505. Abram C. Dayton, *Last Days of Knickerbocker Life* (New York: George W. Harlan, Publisher, 1882), p. 221, describes Mitchell's Olympic as "a tiny box," situated on Broadway between Howard and Grand streets. "This seven by nine cubby-hole he devoted to sensational burlesque.... His corps of assistants was of course very limited in number, for the stage was scarcely more spacious than an ordinary parlor, but as regarded fitness for the business required it was a rare combination."
38. Odell, 4:577.
39. Although the progress of tableaux vivants in New York is the focus of this study, it should not be inferred, of course, that such performances were unique to that city. Performers toured widely, and many of the acts which began in New York were seen in theatres, halls, and opera houses across the country.
40. *New York Herald*, 28 June 1846, p. 3.
41. *New York Herald*, 7 December 1840, p. 3.
42. *New York Post*, 11 January 1833, p. 3.
43. Edinburgh *Evening Courant*, 2 February 1828, quoted in Saxon, *Andrew Ducow*, p. 150.
44. *New York Evening Post*, 4 January 1831, p. 2.
45. *New York Herald*, 5 September 1835, p. 3.
46. *New York Herald*, 6 October 1836, p. 3.

Chapter 3

1. Dr. Collyer's origins appear to be lost to us. No biographical information seems to be available about him, and newspaper articles about his model artist exhibits provide no background about the man himself. George C.D. Odell, *Annals of New York Stage,* 15 vols. (New York: Columbia University Press, 1927-49) 4:512-13, notes that a Dr. R.H. Collyer presented lectures on "Animal Physiology and Phrenology" at the American Museum and Peale's Museum during the 1840-41 season; however, there is no assurance that this was the same Dr. Collyer.

2. George G. Foster, *New York by Gas-Light* (New York: DeWitt and Davenport, 1850), p. 15.

3. Meade Minnigerode, *The Fabulous Forties, 1840-1850, A Presentation of Private Life* (New York: G.P. Putnam's Sons, 1924), p. 142. Interestingly, the press took no notice of "The Greek Slave" among Dr. Collyer's tableaux until 20 November 1847, almost two months after the troupe opened (*New York Herald,* p. 2.).

4. Bernard Sobel, *A Pictorial History of Burlesque* (New York: G.P. Putnam's Sons, 1956), p. 109. Foster, p. 15, offers a far less attractive impression of the models: "The women... were lank-sided, flabby-breasted, in-toed concerns, whose attitudes were about as lascivious as those of a new milch cow; and who shrunk and scrambled about in such fashion as to set one's stomach, for the time being, against all womankind. And then the fleshings, being baggy and unfitted to the form, drew across the bosom, until it looked like a bag of bran, rather than an exquisitely-formed female bust." Similar observations may be found in James Rees, *Mysteries of City Life* (Philadelphia: J.W. Moore, 1849), p. 378, and in "The Police and the Model Artists," *New York Times,* 10 April 1852, p. 2.

5. *New York Herald,* 22 September 1847, p. 3.

6. *Spirit of the Times,* 25 September 1847, p. 368. The reference here to "revolve on CANOVA'S PEDESTAL" is tantalizingly obscure on two counts. First, while frequent remarks throughout the nineteenth century refer to living statues "revolving," I have found no specification of how this was accomplished. I can only guess that a turntable of some kind—a revolve—was used to make living statues visible from all sides. The technique seems reasonable enough, of course; the viewer in a museum was free to move around a sculpture to change his point of view, but the audience in a theatre was stationary. Thus, the alternative was to revolve the statue. Some precedent for the circular platform is provided by Bernard Sobel, *A Pictorial History of Burlesque,* pp. 115-16, where he describes living pictures as part of "the circus 'concert,' a brief variety entertainment," which often served as a come-on for circus side-show attractions. Sobel reports, "These models appeared on a circular platform surrounded by a circular curtain which, when drawn, showed men and women in 'plastic poses,' their hair covered with white wigs and their bodies with some sort of liquid that gave them the alabaster chastity of marble." Sobel does not, however, specify that such platforms revolved.

    The reference to "Canova's Pedestal," which is also repeated during the century, is even more puzzling. I assume the reference is to the Italian sculptor, Antonio Canova (1757-1882), whose works were often the subjects of tableaux. However, my examination of biographical and critical studies of the artist has revealed no mention of any pedestal or its significance.

7. *New York Herald,* 24 September 1847, p. 1.

8. *New York Herald,* 25 September 1847, p. 2.

9. *Spirit of the Times,* 25 September 1847, p. 368; *New York Herald,* 19 October 1847, p. 1.

10. *New York Herald,* 4 October 1847, p. 3.

Notes for Chapter 3

11. *New York Herald*, 11 October 1847, p. 3.
12. Odell, 5:378.
13. *New York Herald*, 9 November 1847, p. 3.
14. *New York Herald*, 4 December 1847, p. 2.
15. Odell, 5:325, notes that *The Bottle*, an afterpiece presented at the Park Theatre beginning 15 November 1847, was "founded on illustrations by George Cruikshank." The Ravels are listed in the *New York Herald*, 1 October 1847, p. 2.
16. *New York Herald*, 1 October 1847, p. 2.
17. *New York Herald*, 2 October 1847, p. 2.
18. Tableaux opened at Pinteux' on 13 December 1847, according to Odell, 5:396.
19. *New York Herald*, 28 December 1847, p. 2.
20. Minnigerode, pp. 142-44.
21. Odell, 5:360, 371, 398; *Spirit of the Times*, 15 January 1848, p. 560. The troupe at Pinteux', following Collyer's lead, left on 25 January for Havana to begin touring, according to the *New York Herald*, 26 January 1848, p. 3.
22. *New York Herald*, 27 December 1847, p. 3.
23. Odell, 5:380; the *New York Herald*, 23 January 1848, p. 1, provides the full list of tableaux to be presented: "Programme—Part I—1, Landing of Columbus, Thiers; 2, Dream of Washington before the Revolution, Thiers; 3, Murder of the Innocents, Adams; 4, Samson and Dallilah [sic], two positions, Rubens; 5, The Storm, Hildebrandt. Fifteen minutes intermission. Part II—1, The Young Men of the Destroyed Tribe of Benjamin Seizing their Brides in the Vineyards, Millias; 2, Venus and Cupid, Rubens; 3, Triumph of the Amazonian Queen, Haberziet; 4, Ruth and Boaz, Burveydel; 5, Diana and Endymion, Girrodet. Intermission of fifteen minutes. Part III—1, Romulus and Remus, David; 2, The Supplicant, Raphael; 3, The Listeners, Rubens; 4, Adam and Eve's Expulsion from Paradise, MacGowan; 5, Tableau Finale, in Honor of the United States, Thiers."
24. *New York Herald*, 27 January 1848, p. 2.
25. *New York Herald*, 30 January 1848, p. 2.
26. "Letter from a Gentleman, present at the Festivities at Fonthill, to a Correspondent in Town,' dated 28 December 1800, *The Gentleman's Magazine* (London), April 1801, p. 298. For a more detailed account of "attitudes" and Lady Hamilton's part in them, see Kirsten Gram Holmström, *Monodrama, Attitudes, Tableaux Vivants: Studies on Some Trends of Theatrical Fashion, 1770-1815* (Stockholm: Almquist & Wiksell, 1967).
27. *New York Herald*, 2 February 1848, p. 2.
28. *New York Herald*, 14 February 1848, p. 2. It should be noted at this point that the *Herald* was the only New York newspaper giving the model artists such full attention and offering so much editorial commentary about the issue of the propriety of the exhibitions. Other newspapers contained little more than the paid theatre and exhibition hall advertising.
29. An interesting peripheral observation about attendance at Professor Thier's exhibition is this remark in the *Herald*, 19 February 1848: "Judging from the number of ladies present, we should think these exhibitions were rapidly becoming popular with the softer sex."
30. *New York Herald*, 4 March 1848, p. 1. Note also the audience pictured in Figure 6.

31. *New York Herald*, 4 March 1848, p. 1.
32. *New York Herald*, 5 March 1848, p. 2.
33. *New York Sun*, 21 February 1848. The name appears in various spellings in other articles and advertisements.
34. *New York Herald*, 11 March 1848, p. 2.
35. *New York Herald*, 14 March 1848, p. 3.
36. *New York Herald*, 18 March 1848, p. 2.
37. *New York Herald*, 15 March 1848, p. 2.
38. Full texts of the letters containing these legal opinions were published in the *National Police Gazette*, from which they were quoted in the *Herald*, 18 March 1848, p. 2. The quotations here presented are taken from the *Herald*.
39. Ibid.
40. Ibid.
41. *New York Herald*, 20 March 1848, p. 3.
42. 5:380.
43. *New York Herald*, 23 March 1848, p. 2. Similar accounts appeared on the same date in the *Sun*, p. 2; the *Daily Tribune*, p. 4; and the *Evening Express*, p. 1.
44. *New York Herald*, 23 march 1848, p. 2. The article is quoted at length because it provides a fairly detailed picture of this performance. Two items are especially noteworthy: (1) The method of staging is similar to the "parlor door" technique used in many homes for perfectly respectable family tableau entertainments later in the century. (2) The term, "nude," in this context, may be meant literally. In legitimate public performances tights, or fleshings, would be used to suggest nudity, but in this "illigitimate" performance one might expect actual nudity. Some support for this possibility is provided by Foster, p. 16, where he describes a clandestine exhibition similar to the one in question. He claims, "In many of these establishments things were carried to the most filthy and incredible extent—dances being sometimes performed by men and women in a state of complete nudity, (without even the tights)...."
45. *New York Herald*, 23 March 1848, p. 2.
46. *New York Daily Tribune*, 24 March 1848, p. 1.
47. *New York Daily Tribune*, 24 March 1848, p. 4; *Sun*, p. 2.
48. *New York Herald*, 15 February 1848, p. 2. Burke was thus described in the article announcing his benefit as "leasee" of Palmo's Opera House, at a time when model artists' exhibitions enjoyed greater favor in the city.
49. *New York Herald*, 25 March 1848, p. 3.
50. *New York Herald*, 24 March 1848, p. 2.
51. *New York Herald*, 3 April 1848, p. 2.
52. *New York Herald*, 18 March 1848, p. 2.
53. *New York Herald*, 24 March 1848, p. 2.
54. *New York Herald*, 25 March 1848, p. 2.

166   Notes for Chapter 4

55. *New York Herald,* 1 May 1848, p. 3.
56. *New York Herald,* 2 May 1848, p. 3.
57. *New York Herald,* 4 May 1848, p. 3.
58. *New York Herald,* 21 May 1848, p. 3.
59. *New York Herald,* 16 November 1848, p. 3. The "Nixon Artists" appeared regularly for several years in New York and on tour. In 1856 they were a part of Jim Meyers' equestrian and gymnastic show playing in Brooklyn where they presented "finished and artistic delineations of classic statuary and ancient groupings." (*New York Herald,* 18 April 1856, p. 7.)
60. *New York Herald,* 28 May 1848, p. 3.
61. Odell, 5:399.
62. *New York Herald,* 4 May 1848, p. 3.
63. Quoted in Mary C. Crawford, *The Romance of the American Theatre* (New York: Halcyon House, 1940), pp. 450-51.
64. *New York Herald,* 5 February 1849, p. 2.
65. Comment from the *New York Herald,* quoted in Odell, 5:397.
66. *Transcript* (Boston), 15 February 1848, p. 2.
67. Quoted in *New York Herald,* 6 May 1848, p. 4.
68. *Transcript* (Boston), 26 June 1848, p. 2; 30 June 1848, p. 1.
69. *New York Herald,* 22 November 1848, p. 3.

Chapter 4

1. *New York Herald,* 14 December 1848, p. 3.
2. *New York Herald,* 1 February 1849, p. 3.
3. *New York Herald,* 26 January 1849, p. 4.
4. *New York Herald,* 13 February 1850, p. 5. It is possible Professor Quiriu Mutter is an erroneous rendition of the name, "Quirin-Muller," who was a "specialist in statuary groups" in mid-century France, according to Lucien Rimels, "Quadro Vivente," *Enciclopedia dello Spettacolo,* 9 vols. (Rome: Casa Editrice le Maschere, 1954-64) 8:613.
5. T. Allston Brown, *A History of the New York Stage,* 3 vols. (New York: Dodd, Mead & Co., 1903; reprint ed., Benjamin Blom, 1964), 1:261. Brown attributes the change in name to Lea's hope of inducing the "moral classes" to visit his exhibitions. While that may have been his motivation in 1848 when he operated the Franklin in imitation of Barnum's successful museum, it seems unlikely in 1850 when Lea shifted to tableau features.
6. *New York Herald,* 26 September 1849, p. 3.
7. *New York Herald,* 16 November 1849, p. 3. A programme from Mme. Warton's Wallhalla, Leicester Square, London, is reproduced in Figures 8 and 9. In addition, a playbill for the Theatre Royal, Coventry, dated Monday, 30 September [1850], lists the following tableaux by Mme. Warton "as presented by her at the Wallhalla, Leicester Square, London" (Theatre Collection, Museum of the City of New York):

PROGRAMME—PART THE FIRST.
1. The Triumph of the Greeks .... David.
2. May and the Morning Star .... H. Biefield.
3. Cleopatra arming Anthony for Battle .... H. Tresham, R.A.
4. Herman and Thusnelda .... Angelica Kauffman, R.A.
5. Venus retiring from the Bath .... Canova.
6. Euphrosyne (from the Original
   Picture) .... E.W. Frost, A.R.A.
7. Acis and Galatea (in two Moving Tableaux) .... Professor Warton.
8. Venus rising from the Sea .... Titian.
9. Venus attired by the Graces .... Antique.

PART THE SECOND
1. Education de la Reine .... [illegible]
2. The Greek Slave (from the Original Statue) .... Hiram Power
3. Nymphs and Satyrs .... S. Hart, R.A.
4. To arms, ye Greeks! .... W. Etty, R.A.
5. Judgment of Paris (in two Moving Tableaux) .... Rubens.
6. Ceres receiving from Bacchus the Restorative Cup .... Antique.
7. Woman interceding for the Vanquished .... W. Etty, R.A.
8. The Lute Player .... Hyldrabrandt.
9. Grand New Tableaux. Finale in
   honour of the United Kingdom .... Madame Warton.

8. *New York Herald*, 27 February 1850, p. 5.
9. *New York Herald*, 15 April 1852, p. 7.
10. *New York Herald*, 28 March 1852, p. 5.
11. *New York Times*, 10 April 1852, p. 2.
12. *New York Herald*, 19 September 1853, p. 7.
13. *New York Herald*, 12 August 1853, p. 7.
14. *New York Herald*, 12 February 1854, p. 7.
15. *New York Herald*, 15 August 1852, p. 4. Featuring the "Bloomer Troupe" was an obvious attempt to capitalize on a fashion fad considered scandalous in its day, though, by modern standards, the bloomer costume was far from provocative. It consisted of a skirt which extended below the knees, under which was worn a pair of Turkish pantaloons secured by bands around the ankles. The style was introduced in 1849 and publicly recommended by Amelia Jenks Bloomer as a "sensible" costume for women. In a day when women's hemlines swept the ground, such an innovation was not viewed favorably by the general public, and bloomers became a common source of either ridicule or titillation onstage and in the press.
16. George C.D. Odell, *Annals of the New York Stage,* 15 vols. (New York: Columbia University Press, 1927-49), 1:262, 362. At this same time, George Lea was also operating Vauxhall Garden as an ice cream garden, saloon, and ballroom (Odell, 1:174). One can only speculate about the reasons for Lea's move. The Chatham Square location was extremely small. "Built on a plot just 25 feet wide, the theatre seated only 550 at its opening in 1835," according to Mary C. Henderson, *The City and the Theatre* (Clifton, N.J.: James T. White & Co., 1973), p. 64. I have been unable to determine the size of White's Melodeon, but it could hardly have been smaller. Theatrical activity was moving further uptown during this period, and this, too, may have influenced Lea.

168   Notes for Chapter 4

17. *New York Herald,* 4, 5, 9, 11, 15 August 1855, p. 7.
18. *New York Herald,* 1 January 1855, p. 7. *The Enciclopedia dello Spettacolo* (8:613) mentions a Frenchman, "a professor Flor, who reproduced famous classical or modern paintings to which he added plastic representations." Possibly, the two spellings are variations of the same name.
19. *New York Herald,* 3 March 1855, p. 7.
20. *New York Herald,* 7 May 1855, p. 7.
21. There is some confusion on this point in Brown, 2:23. Brown asserts that "the first floor [of 127 Grand Street] was tenanted by a Mr. Parmelee, who kept a concert saloon. The entire upper part of the building was occupied by Geo. Lea, who leased the place at the close of his management of 53 Bowery (April 1854), and named it the Franklin Museum." Brown's date here is two years early, for the Franklin Museum address was advertised as 53 Bowery until February 1856, and the name, Grand Street Hall, was used for the 127 Grand Street address throughout 1855.
22. *New York Sun,* 22-27 August 1855.
23. *New York Herald,* 11 September 1855, p. 5; 21 November 1855, p. 3.
24. *New York Herald,* 3 December 1855, p. 7.
25. *New York Herald,* 31 December 1855, p. 7.
26. *New York Herald,* 2 February 1856, p. 7.
27. *New York Herald,* 31 March 1856, p. 7.
28. *New York Herald,* 13 April 1856, p. 7.
29. *New York Herald,* 25 April 1856, p. 7.
30. *New York Herald,* 19 September 1856, p. 7.
31. *New York Times,* 20 October 1856, p. 8.
32. Ibid. The article also includes interesting comments about several of the girls who were arrested:

    Anna Waterman, a pretty girl of 18, said she had been two months at the business; had previously been a tailloress; has a mother living in Oswego.

    Mary Livingston, of the same age, lives in Sullivan-street. Has only a stepmother of all her relatives living. Was formerly a paper-box maker; has been a model for four months....

    Catherine Crotty was born in Albany nineteen years ago, has been a living statue two months, and is paid $5 per week for her beauty. Was a model a year ago nearly opposite Bowery Theatre, at a place kept by the same Lea.... Catherine has a father and mother, a child three months old, and a husband in Nicaragua. She supports all except the husband. Her father has been sick in a hospital and lately came out.

    Helen Belle is 19 years old, lives in Mulberry-street; has been a widow two years and a model two months. Was formerly a model at "Gothic Hall," kept by Lea.

    Sarah Jane Flanegan, a native of New York, age 18 years, residing at No. 39 Mulberry-street, and Julia Finigan, a native of New York, age 18 years and residing also at No. 39 Mulberry-Street told similar stories.

33. *New York Times,* 20 October 1856, p. 4.
34. *New York Times,* 29 January 1858, p. 5.

Notes for Chapter 4   169

35. *New York Times,* 19 February, 1858, p. 5.
36. *New York Times,* 3 December 1858, p. 1.
37. *New York Herald,* 1 April 1856, p. 7; *New York Sun,* 31 March 1856, p. 3.
38. *New York Sun,* 1 April 1856, p. 4.
39. The claim may well be true. An unidentified clipping in the Harvard Theatre Collection provides a biography of Keller relating his successful performances in Prussia, Germany, England, France, Italy, Spain, and Russia.
40. *New York Times,* 1 April 1856, p. 4.
41. *New York Herald,* 1 April 1856, p. 4.
42. *New York Herald,* 6 and 7 April 1856, p. 1.
43. *New York Herald,* 8 April 1856, p. 1; *New York Times* 7 April 1856, p. 1. I have been unable to locate the actual denunciation of the Rubens picture, and the references to it in other papers do not cite the source by name. In a reply to the attack, Keller observed, "The journal which has so grossly misrepresented the motives and the character of my representations, has, I find, an established reputation obtained by availing itself of every opportunity to make personal and political capital for its editors, by attacking the religion and the clergy of the church of Rome, and by assuming an exclusive and aggressive 'American' position." (*New York Herald,* 12 April 1856, p. 5.)
44. *New York Times,* 11 April 1856, p. 5.
45. *New York Herald,* 5 May 1856, p. 8. Unfortunately, the particular stage improvements are not specified.
46. *New York Herald,* 4 May 1856, p. 7. Omissions of artists' and composers' names occur in the original as shown.
47. *New York Herald,* 4 May 1856, p. 1.
48. *New York Herald,* 5 May 1856, p. 8.
49. *New York Times,* 6 May 1856, p. 1.
50. *Spirit of the Times,* 31 May 1856, p. 152.
51. The painting was first completed in Dusseldorf in 1850 but was destroyed almost immediately when the artist's studio burned down on 5 November 1850. A letter from Emanuel Leutze to George Washington Parke Custis, dated 10 November 1850, and published in the *National Intelligencer* (Washington), 5 December 1850, p. 3, indicated that the painter was already securing new canvas and expected to complete a new painting "by next year." This he accomplished, and the picture was purchased by Messrs. Goupil and Company "at a high price, for the purpose of exhibition" (*New York Organ,* 13 September 1851, p. 85). The work was then displayed at Stuyvesant Institute, 659 Broadway (*The Home Journal* [New York], 27 September 1851, p. 3). So great was the popularity of the painting, that, the following year, a proposal was made to Congress for Leutze to prepare a copy for display in the Capitol Building (*Daily National Intelligencer* [Washington], 9 April 1852, p. 3). A full story of the Leutze painting and the events which inspired it is the subject of Ann Hawkes Hutton, *Portrait of Patriotism* (Radnor, Pennsylvania: Chilton Book Company, 1959). Incidentally, on 2 December 1982 a recently "rediscovered" painting of "Washington Crossing the Delaware," by artist-historian William Everitte Pedrick, was unveiled at the Trenton (New Jersey) Free Public Library. Pedrick claimed that his 1893 painting, while smaller than the

170   Notes for Chapter 4

Leutze work, was historically more accurate. He felt that Leutze had depicted an early morning crossing rather than a dark nighttime trip; that the river should have been choked with more ice; and that Washington appears to be sailing toward Pennsylvania, not New Jersey. Needless to say, however, Pedrick's work did not inspire the public adoration accorded that of Leutze. (Steve Marsh, "Truth in Art," *The Trenton Times* [New Jersey], 3 December 1982, p. B1; Ann Rinaldi, "The Other 'Washington's Crossing' Painting...," *The Trentonian* [Trenton, New Jersey], 3 December 1982, p. 3.)

52. Peter C. Marzio, *The Democratic Art: Pictures for a 19th-Century America: Chromolithography, 1840-1900* (Boston: David R. Godine in association with the Amon Carter Museum of Western Art, Fort Worth, 1969), pp. 8, 23, 127.

53. *New York Clipper,* 14 June 1856, p. 62.

54. *New York Herald,* 29 July 1856, p. 8. One can only speculate about what this "thrilling event" might have been. During the previous several years, several expeditions involving Americans had attempted to wrest control of Cuba from Spain, mainly to protect Southern interests in maintaining the island as a base for slave trade. In August 1851, a General Narciso Lopez enlisted followers in New Orleans and launched such an expedition. He was quickly defeated, however, and publicly garrotted in Havana. Similar abortive attempts continued from time to time, any one of which might have been viewed as heroic by sympathetic observers. In America, public sentiment generally favored annexation of Cuba, though the justifications for this and the proposed methods for accomplishing it differed widely. For a description of the events of the period, see Hugh Thomas, *Cuba: The Pursuit of Freedom* (New York: Harper & Row, 1971), chaps. 17 and 18.

55. *New York Post,* 20 June 1859, p. 1.

56. *New York Tribune,* 20 June 1859, p. 5.

57. *New York Herald,* 28 April 1858, p. 8. The reference occurs in an advertisement addressed "TO MANAGERS, PROPRIETORS OF ROOMS, EXHIBITIONS, &c.," in which Madame Warton sought bookings for a projected tour. The substitution of "J" for "L" as Keller's first initial is probably a typesetter's error.

58. Brown, 1:432-33.

59. Brown, 1:433. Programmes in the Theatre Collection, Museum of the City of New York, document productions at Laura Keene's Varieties, 10 June 1856, and at the Holliday Street Theatre, 6 October 1856. They also note that Act I of the piece was set in an sculptor's studio in ancient Athens and represents a dream in which the sculpture comes to life.

60. *New York Herald,* 20 March 1857, p. 4.

61. *Porter's Spirit of the Times,* 16 May 1857, p. 176.

62. *Spirit of the Times,* 1 May 1858, p. 144.

63. Alan S. Downer, ed., *The Autobiography of Joseph Jefferson* (Cambridge, Mass.: The Belnap Press of Harvard University Press, 1964), p. 143.

64. Jefferson, *Autobiography,* pp. 144-46.

65. *Spirit of the Times,* 1 May 1858, p. 144.

66. *New York Herald,* 13 January 1860, p. 7.

67. *New York Herald,* 26 April 1861, p. 7.

68. *New York Times,* 27 November 1860, p. 1.

69. *New York Herald*, 21 November 1861, p. 7.
70. *New York Clipper*, 25 December 1858, p. 286.

Chapter 5

1. Programme, New Chestnut Street Theatre, Philadelphia, n.d., Theatre Collection, New York Public Library.
2. George L. Aiken, *Uncle Tom's Cabin*, in *Dramas of the American Theatre, 1762-1909*, ed. Richard Moody, (Boston: Houghton Mifflin Co., 1966), pp. 360-96.
3. *Spirit of the Times*, 3 September 1870, p. 48.
4. George D. Lyman, *The Saga of the Comstock Lode: Boom Days in Virginia City* (New York and London, 1934), p. 281, quoted in A.H. Saxon, *Enter Foot and Horse: A History of Hippodrama in England and France* (New Haven and London: Yale University Press, 1968), p. 193.
5. *New York Tribune*, 17 September 1866, quoted in Bernard Hewitt, *Theatre U.S.A.* (New York: McGraw Hill Book Company, 1959), p. 196.
6. *Wilkes' Spirit of the Times*, 12 October 1861, p. 96.
7. *New York Herald*, 22 January 1862, reports a "Ravel Pantomime" at the Canterbury and lists Mlle. Marietta Ravel on the bill. The Canterbury advertisement on 26 January 1862 states that the management has, "at an outlay of ten thousand dollars, purchased all the wardrobe, properties, machinery, &c., of the Ravels, and has also secured the services of Monsieur E. Lehman, for over ten years scenic artist of the Ravels."
8. *New York Herald*, 13 October 1961, p. 7.
9. *New York Herald*, 29 June, 1863, p. 7.
10. *New York Herald*, 31 December 1861, p. 12.
11. *Wilkes' Spirit of the Times*, 17 May 1862, p. 176.
12. *New York Herald*, 2 January 1860, p. 2.
13. *Spirit of the Times*, 4 May 1861, p. 144; 11 May 1861, p. 160.
14. *New York Herald*, 2 March 1863, p. 7.
15. *Wilkes' Spirit of the Times*, 1 March 1862, p. 16. George Washington Morrison Nutt was a New Hampshire midget whom Barnum added to his stable of attractions in 1862. For a time, "Commodore" Nutt appeared with the already-popular Tom Thumb and even became Tom Thumb's unsuccessful rival for the hand of Mercy Lavinia Warren Bumpus. (Neil Harris, *Humbug: The Art of P.T. Barnum* [Boston: Little, Brown & Co., 1973], pp. 162-63; Irving Wallace, *The Fabulous Showman: The Life and Times of P.T. Barnum* [New York: Alfred A. Knopf, 1959], pp. 89-91.) After the marriage of Tom Thumb and Lavinia Warren, Nutt's name was sometimes linked romantically with that of Minnie Warren, Lavinia's younger sister, since Barnum often exhibited the two couples together. However, the "Commodore" was still a bachelor when he died in 1881 at thirty-three years of age. (M.R. Werner, *Barnum* [New York: Harcourt, Brace & Co., 1923], pp. 270-71.)
16. *New York Herald*, 31 March 1863, p. 7. The wedding of Tom Thumb to Lavinia Warren, "one of the great social events of 1863," had taken place less than six weeks earlier, on 10 February. (A.H. Saxon, ed., *Selected Letters of P.T. Barnum* [New York: Columbia University Press, 1983], p. 121.)

17. *New York Herald*, 11 November 1866, p. 7. The production ran 11-16 November.
18. *New York Herald*, 30 January 1869, p. 12.
19. The marble statues were part of the variety bill accompanying Fox's famous *Humpty Dumpty*. The *Spirit of the Times* reviewer (25 May 1872, p. 240), not usually given to praise of tableaux vivants, puns about these as "specimens of high art, Living-stone found at last" and calls them "unusually good and artistic."
20. *New York Herald*, 6 January 1870, p. 2.
21. *New York Herald*, 15 October 1861, p. 5.
22. *New York Standard*, 29 August 1870, p. 3. The production closed 22 September 1870.
23. *New York Herald*, 19 August 1863, p. 7.
24. *New York Herald*, 14 September 1863, p. 7.
25. Douglas Gilbert, *American Vaudeville* (New York and London: McGraw Hill Book Company, 1940), p. 57.
26. *Wilkes' Spirit of the Times*, 3 June 1865, p. 224. *The Seven Daughters of Satan* was the title of the original German piece from which Laura Keene's *The Seven Sisters* had been adapted, according to Glenn Hughes,*A History of the American Theatre, 1700-1950* (New York: Samuel French, 1951), p. 191.
27. *New York Herald*, 28 May 1865, p. 7.
28. *Wilkes' Spirit of the Times*, 28 April 1866, p. 144; 12 May 1866, p. 176.
29. T. Allston Brown, *A History of the New York Stage*, 3 vols. (New York: Dodd, Mead & Co., 1903; reprint ed., New York: Benjamin Blom, 1964), 3:84.
30. *Wilkes' Spirit of the Times*, 26 December 1869, p. 304.
31. *Wilkes' Spirit of the Times*, 18 September 1869, p. 80.
32. *New York Herald*, 20 September 1869, p. 3. It is interesting that descriptions of Mace's performances bear a noteworthy resemblance to the "artful" posing of today's champion body builders.
33. *New York Times*, 22 Spetember 1869, p. 5.
34. *New York Herald*, 9 October 1869, p. 12; 11 October 1869, p. 12.
35. *New York Herald*, 27 February, 1870, p. 6. Brown (3:87) reports that thereafter the Tammany opened only briefly before it ceased operation as a place of amusement on 18 June 1870.

Chapter 6

1. *New York Herald*, 25 April 1875, p. 3.
2. *New York Herald*, 15 September 1875, p. 9.
3. *New York Dramatic News*, 2 October 1875, p. 2.
4. *Spirit of the Times*, 2 October 1875, p. 192.
5. *New York Herald*, 3 October 1875, p. 3.
6. *New York Dramatic News*, 9 October 1875, p. 2.

Notes for Chapter 6   173

7. *New York Times*, 14 November 1875, p. 6. See also the *New York Herald*, 24 November 1875, p. 2.
8. *New York Herald*, 3 January 1876, p. 1.
9. *New York Herald*, 18 January 1876, p. 3.
10. *New York Dramatic News*, 18 March 1876, p. 2; *New York Times*, 19 March 1876, p. 7.
11. *New York Times*, 19 March 1876, p. 7.
12. *New York Sun*, 9 April 1876, p. 7.
13. *New York Dramatic News*, 15 April 1876, p. 2.
14. *New York Times*, 30 April 1876, p. 11.
15. Brown, 2:122.
16. *New York Herald*, 25 September 1875, p. 2. George C.D. Odell, *Annals of the New York Stage*, 15 vols. (New York: Columbia University Press, 1927-49), 10:84-85 indicates that the run extended from 2 August through 25 September, however the act was not listed consistently during that period.
17. *New York Herald*, 26 September 1875, p. 3.
18. Programme, Theatre Comique, 15 November 1875, Theatre Collection, Museum of the City of New York. Similar announcements appeared in the *New York Herald*, 21 November 1875, p. 3, and in the *New York Daily Graphic*, 15-20 November 1875.
19. *New York Daily Graphic*, 23 November 1875, p. 182.
20. *New York Dramatic News*, 27 November 1875, p. 2. Interestingly, the *Spirit of the Times* raises no question of propriety—a departure from its customary stance. Its reviewer simply states, "The tableaux are exceedingly beautiful, clever, and artistic, and, in power of pleasing, excell any thing of the kind ever before offered to the New York public" (4 December 1875, p. 406).
21. *New York Daily Graphic*, 30 November 1875, p. 231; 6 December 1875, p. 278; *New York Herald*, 6 December 1875, p. 2; *Spirit of the Times*, 11 December 1875, p. 431; Odell, 10:83.
22. *New York Clipper*, 11 December 1875, p. 294.
23. *New York Dramatic News*, 11 December 1875, p. 4.
24. *New York Dramatic News*, 11 December 1875, p. 4.
25. Anthony Comstock, *Frauds Exposed; or, How the People are Deceived and Robbed, and Youth Corrupted* (n.p., 1880; reprint ed., Montclair, New Jersey: Patterson Smith, 1969), p. 6. Comstock describes and defends his activities in this publication and in its sequal, *Traps for the Young* (n.p., 1884; reprint ed., edited by Robert Bremner, Cambridge, Mass.: The Belnap Press of Harvard University Press, 1967). Comstock's life and career are described in detail in his "authorized" biography by Charles Gallaudet Trumbull, *Anthony Comstock, Fighter: Some Impressions of a Lifetime of Adventure in Conflict with the Powers of Evil* (New York, 1913), and in a somewhat more objective study by Heywood Broun and Margaret Leech, *Anthony Comstock: Roundsman of the Lord* (New York: Albert & Charles Boni, 1927).
26. Comstock, *Frauds Exposed*, p. 435.
27. *New York Times*, 23 March 1880, cited by Robert Bremner in his "Editor's Introduction" to Comstock, *Traps for the Young*, p. xvi.

28. *Spirit of the Times*, 18 December 1875, p. 454.

29. Quoted in Joe Laurie, Jr., *Vaudeville: From the Honky-Tonks to the Palace* (New York: Henry Holt and Company, 1953), p. 37.

30. *New York Dramatic News*, 18 December 1875, p. 1.

31. *New York Dramatic News*, 25 December 1875, p. 4.

32. *Spirit of the Times*, 25 December 1875, p. 494.

33. *New York Dramatic News*, 1 January 1876, p. 2. Nowhere did the reviewers see fit to describe Mr. Doyle's "Steam effect," but one might speculate that steam jets in the stage floor contributed considerable realism to the volcanic eruption for this tableau. Such scenic techniques were well-known and, apparently, widely used at the time. Olive Logan described the method briefly in a fascinatingly detailed article entitled "The Secret Regions of the Stage," *Harper's New Monthly Magazine*, March 1874, p. 642:
    In the conflagrations represented on the New York stage the scene is filled with smoke—imitation smoke, that is—by means of long narrow traps stretching quite across the stage, through which volumes of steam are sent up from below. The effect is quite surprising, and is very easily managed.

34. *New York Dramatic News*, 29 January 1876, p. 2.

35. *Spirit of the Times*, 5 February 1876, p. 639.

36. *New York Dramatic News*, 26 February 1876, p. 1.

37. *New York Times*, 11 March 1876, p. 9; Brown, 2:469.

38. *New York Herald*, 27 February 1876, p. 13.

39. *New York Dramatic News*, 4 March 1876, p. 8; *New York Herald*, 26 September 1875, p. 3.

40. George C.D. Odell, *Annals of the New York Stage*, 15 vols. (New York: Columbia University Press, 1927-49), 12:513, 516; 13:165, 316, 317, 320, 332, 511, 520, 522, 528.

41. *New York Sun*, 9 April 1876, p. 7; programme, Chateau Mabille Varieties, n.d., Theatre Collection, New York Public Library (Classmark: MWEZ+n.c. 4547).

42. *New York Sun*, 9 April 1876, p. 7; *New York Clipper*, 15 April 1876, p. 22.

43. *New York Clipper*, 21 October 1876, p. 238; *New York Sun*, 16 October 1876, p. 1; *New York Times*, 15 October 1876, p. 12; 16 October 1876, p. 8; *New York Dramatic News*, 21 October 1876, p. 5.

44. *New York Sun*, 16 October 1876, p. 1.

45. *Spirit of the Times*, 21 October 1876, p. 292.

46. *New York Sun*, 16 October 1876, p. 1.

47. *New York Clipper*, 28 October 1876, p. 243.

48. *New York Daily Graphic*, 22 January 1877, p. 563. The same announcement continued through 3 February 1877. The theatre changed management several times during the remainder of the 1876-77 season and then became the Apprentice's Library in July 1877.

49. *Spirit of the Times*, 21 October 1876, p. 292.

50. Brown, 2:595.

51. *New York Herald*, 24 September 1876, p. 13. Odell (10:288) sets the beginning of the season at 2 September 1876.

52. *New York Herald*, 1 April 1877, p. 4.
53. *New York Herald*, 31 December 1876, p. 2.
54. *New York Times*, 19 March 1877, p. 8.
55. Ibid.
56. *New York Times*, 31 March 1877, p. 8.
57. *New York Sun*, 27 March 1877, p. 1; 28 March, p. 3; *New York Times*, 27 March 1877, p. 3; *New York Dramatic News*, 31 March 1877, p. 3; *New York Clipper*, 27 April 1877, p. 14.
58. *New York Sun*, 1 July 1877, p. 8.
59. *New York Sun*, 3 July 1877, p. 1. Similar accounts appeared in most New York dailies. Apparently this particular troupe included minstrel performers, and it is possible that some of these also posed in tableaux. Robert C. Toll, *Blacking Up: The Mistrel Show in Nineteenth Century America* (New York: Oxford University Press, 1974), pp. 136-37, notes that in the post-Civil War period, minstrel companies often assimilated successful features from other entertainment forms. He cites freak exhibits, animal acts, and living statues as examples. When tableaux were included under such circumstances, they seem to have been only a part of the minstrel show itself, however, and did not form the main attraction.
60. *New York Times*, 4 July 1877, p. 3.
61. Odell, 10:281-82.
62. Odell, 10:476-77. The act was sometimes replaced by "Prof. McClane's Grand Revolving and Statuary Troupe."
63. *New York Daily Graphic*, 18 June 1877, p. 761. The only descriptive press comment about the act seems to be the observation that "Beauty unadorned reigns at Tony Pastor's" (*New York Daily Graphic*, 9 July 1877, p. 43). It should be noted that Tony Pastor's move uptown and his landmark inauguration of "clean" vaudeville bills did not take place until October 1881. Furthermore (and there is no intention here of maligning Pastor's character), it is probable that, as Douglas Gilbert puts the matter, "Pastor's move was mainly (and frankly) for profit, a definite and canny bid to double the audience by attracting respectable women...." (*American Vaudeville: Its Life and Times* [New York: McGraw-Hill Book Co., 1940], pp. 113-14). Pastor's earlier theatres were far less savory affairs than one might expect from such a person. His first, "444" Broadway, was "a honky-tonk, offering beer, wine, liquor, and a few hostesses," according to Joe Laurie, Jr. (*Vaudeville: from the Honky-Tonks to the Palace* [New York: Henry Holt & co., 1953], p. 334). Bernard Sobel observes that, before 1881, "Pastor had booked variety acts that were the ultimate in vulgarity when they were not actually obscene." (*A Pictorial History of Burlesque* [New York: G.P. Putnam's Sons, 1956], p. 30).
64. *New York Daily Graphic*, 17 July 1877, p. 107.
65. *New York Herald*, 29 July 1877, p. 16, *et passim;* Odell, 10:297.
66. *New York Herald*, 25 August 1877, p. 1; 26 August 1877, p. 14.
67. *New York Clipper*, 18 August 1877, p. 166; *New York Sun*, 19 August 1877, p. 8.
68. *New York Herald*, 25 February 1878, p. 1; Odell, 10:482.
69. *New York Times*, 26 February 1878, p. 3. Similar accounts of the arrests appeared in virtually all New York newspapers on this date, with follow-up stories on succeeding days.
70. *New York Evening Post*, 26 February 1878, p. 4; *New York Times*, 27 February 1878, p. 3.

Notes for Chapter 6

71. *New York Herald*, 27 February 1878, p. 5.
72. *New York Daily Tribune*, 27 February 1878, p. 3.
73. *New York Times*, 8 March 1878, p. 2
74. *New York Times*, 15 March 1878, p. 3; *New York Daily Tribune*, 15 March 1878, p. 3.
75. *New York Times*, 26 March 1878, p. 3.
76. *New York Times*, 30 April 1878, p. 2; *New York Daily Tribune*, 30 April 1878, p. 3.
77. *New York Times*, 30 April 1878, p. 2.
78. *New York Times*, 1 May 1878, p. 2; *New York Daily Tribune*, 1 May 1878, p. 8.
79. *New York Herald*, 5 March 1878, p. 7.
80. *New York Herald*, 5 March 1878, p. 16.
81. *New York Herald*, 3 June 1878, p. 1.
82. *New York Sun*, 16 June 1878, p. 1.
83. *New York Times*, 16 June 1878, p. 7.
84. *New York Times*, 16 June 1878, p. 7.
85. *New York Sun*, 17 June 1878, p. 1.
86. *New York Times*, 17 June 1878, p. 8.
87. *New York Herald*, 8 November 1878, p. 1.
88. *New York Times*, 2 February 1879, p. 7; 3 February 1879, p. 8; 6 February 1879, p. 8.
89. Odell, 10:478. The entire National Varieties bill for 15, 16, and 17 July 1878 is reproduced in William Mouton Marston and John Henry Feller, *F.F. Proctor: Vaudeville Pioneer* (New York: Richard R. Smith, 1943), foll. p. 64.
90. *New York Herald*, 7 July 1878, p. 16.
91. *New York Herald*, 4 August 1878, p. 14.
92. Irving Zeidman, *The American Burlesque Show* (New York: Hawthorn Books, 1967), p. 39. Zeidman, however, also described the troupe as "a few girls in tights... huddled together in tableau settings and 'living pictures'."

    The reference to the Miner Theatres indicates that the Siddons Company played one of the first "chains" of vaudeville theates, inaugurated by Henry Miner and Thomas Canary in the early 1880's. Their numerous theatres were scattered from New York to New Orleans, and they employed many top vaudeville acts of the day. Their advertising announcements guaranteed "ten to sixteen weeks' playing time for 'first class talent'." (Douglas Gilbert, *American Vaudeville: Its Life and Times* [New York and London: Whittlesley House, McGraw-Hill Book Co., 1940], p. 14.)
93. In 1880, newspaper advertisements for Buckingham Palace, Cremorne Gardens, and the Haymarket appeared regularly, all advertising "pretty barmaids" and "pretty waiter girls."
94. *New York Times*, 4 October 1882, p. 5.
95. *Spirit of the Times*, 7 October 1882, p. 228.
96. *New York Times*, 5 October 1882, p. 8.
97. Quoted in *The Theatre: A Weekly Record of the Stage*, 17 May 1886, p. 267.

Notes for Chapter 6   177

98. *New York Times,* 17 February 1887, p. 1.
99. *New York Times,* 14 March 1893, p. 10.
100. *New York Times,* 10 January 1888, p. 8; 11 January 1888, p. 1; *New York Sun,* 10 January 1888, p. 1. In a follow-up story, the *New York Times* (12 January 1888, p. 5) reported that the Medico-Legal Society passed a resolution objecting to attempts to close or censor these museums, on the grounds that the exhibits served educational purposes.
101. *New York Times,* 7 December 1884, p. 3.
102. Quoted in the *New York Clipper,* 14 March 1891, p. 3.
103. *New York Times,* 8 March 1891, p. 13.
104. *New York Clipper,* 14 March 1891, p. 3.
105. *New York Times,* 7 October 1890, p. 5.
106. *New York Times,* 1 October 1893, p. 19.
107. *New York Clipper,* 9 December 1893, p. 611.
108. *New York Sun,* 3 December 1893, p. 2; 5 December 1893, p. 7; 7 December 1893, p. 5; *New York Times,* 3 December 1893, p. 2; 5 December 1893, p. 8; 6 December 1893, p. 3; 7 December 1893, p. 3.
109. *New York Daily Graphic,* 26 October 1880, p. 883; *New York Herald,* 26 October 1880, p. 5.
110. *New York Daily Graphic,* 26 October 1880, p. 883. Rice's reputation had been established by his production, with J.C. Goodwin, of the opera bouffe, *Evangeline,* at Niblo's Garden in July 1874. The production enjoyed frequent revivals over several years.
111. Mary Anderson made her stage debut as Juliet during November 1875 at Macauley's Theatre in Louisville, Kentucky, her hometown. Two years later, she appeared in New York, beginning a bright, though brief, stardom, lasting only until 1889 when she retired at less than thirty years of age. She gained immense popularity, though she played only eighteen different roles during her short career. "Galatea," in Gilbert's *Pygmalion and Galatea* was one with which she became closely associated in the public mind (Garff B. Wilson, *Three Hundred Years of American Drama and Theatre* [Englewood Cliffs, New Jersey: Prentice-Hall, 1975], pp. 263-65).
112. *New York Herald,* 9 October 1887, p. 21.
113. Programme, Bijou Opera House, 28 August 1885, Theatre Collection, Museum of the City of New York.
114. *New York Herald,* 3 May 1891, p. 8.
115. *New York Times,* 1 September 1891, p. 4. The plot summary of *Niobe* gives a good indication of the nature of many of these plays: "A statue of the Theban queen is taken home by Peter Amos Moss, in whose company it is insured for a fabulous sum, and who is afraid something will happen to it. Something does. A careless lineman leaves a wire about the statue's feet, the current is turned on, and Niobe comes to life. She falls upon the neck of Peter Amos Moss, and then his wife and sisters come in. That is the idea of the play."
116. *New York Herald,* 3 December 1881, p. 2.
117. Odell, 13:511. The troupe also played the National Theatre in 1888 (Odell, 13:516).
118. Odell, 12:99.

Notes for Chapter 7

119. Odell, 13:516, 524, 569.
120. Odell, 12:513, 516; 13:165, 315, 317, 320, 332, 511, 520, 522, 528.
121. *New York Herald*, 30 April-1 July 1882, passim.
122. *New York Herald*, 22 January 1882, p. 17. Topicality was apparently an important part of Atherton's act, for in the same issue of the *Herald* Kate Claxton is listed in *The Two Orphans* at the Windsor Theatre, and Mary Anderson is listed as *Galatea* at the Booth. Both Emmett and Jefferson had also appeared in New York during the preceding few weeks.
123. *New York Times*, 12 June 1893, p. 5.
124. Odell, 11:108, 114, 554.
125. Odell, 12:526ff.
126. The earliest tableau vivant listed for the Tissots appears to be in the Koster and Bial's advetisement in the *New York Herald*, 1 February 1885, p. 18. They helped to round out a bill which featured Marie Vanoni in *Nanon*.
127. Programme, Comedy Theatre, n.d., Theatre Collection, Museum of the City of New York. Although the programme is undated, it bears the heading, "Inauguration of the season by Kellar." (Note that this Kell*ar* is not the Louis Kell*er* who presented tableaux at Empire Hall earlier.)
128. *New York Times*, 22 September 1885, p. 5.
129. *New York Times*, 27 August 1893, p. 16.
130. *New York Herald*, 7 November 1885, p. 1.
131. Odell, 13:276.
132. *New York Daily Graphic*, 12 June 1880, p. 866.
133. *New York Herald*, 15 February 1891, p. 16, gives the purpose of the Kit-Kat Club as: "To assist and promote art study, art practice and artistic recreation and to cultivate social relations between and among artists and those interested in art."
134. *New York Times*, 17 February 1891, p. 5.

Chapter 7

1. *1492* had already proved its worth outside of New York. An article in *The Illustrated American*, 30 September 1893, p. 410-11, traced the show's production history:
    It was originally produced, by the Independent Corps of Cadets, at the Tremont Theatre, Boston, on February 8, 1892, enjoying there a run of seven performances. It was afterwards brought out, by Mr. R.A. Barnet,... at the Globe Theatre, where it was played twenty-five times. Then Mr. Edward E. Rice... presented it afresh at the Park Theatre on September 3, 1892, with his 'Surprise Party.' After Ninety-eight consecutive performances, Boston was left for a time and a short tour of New England was undertaken. Seventeen more performances were given in Boston, in December, at the Hollis Street Theatre; then came another New England tour of Twenty-seven performances, prior to a season of four weeks' duration, commencing on February 6, at the Columbia Theatre, Boston. A third New England tour preceded an engagement of three weeks at the Walnut Street Theatre, Philadelphia; then came seven more New England performances, prior to a farewell engagement, consisting of eight performances, at the Globe Theatre, commencing on May

Notes for Chapter 7 179

1 last.... The New York season commenced at Palmer's Theatre on May 15.... The hundredth representation in New York will take place on the 16th of next month.

2. The biographical material here presented about Kilanyi's early life is drawn from two obituary notices, both of which contain essentially the same information: *New York Dramatic Mirror*, 14 December 1895, p. 15; and *New York Clipper*, 14 December 1895, p. 653.

3. *The Stage* (London), 26 October 1893, p. 13.

4. *The Stage* (London), 2 November 1893, p. 16.

5. *The Stage* (London), 2 February 1894, p. 8.

6. *The Stage* (London), 1 March 1894, p. 15. A Palace playbill for 17 June 1894 (Theatre Collection, New York Public Library) lists fifteen tableaux by Dando. Two of these titles, "Adriadne" and "Will o'the Wisp," also appear in the earlier Kilanyi production.

7. *The Stage* (London), 22 February 1894, p. 15; 1 March 1894, p. 15. The Brighton run apparently lasted about two weeks, for there are no notices of Kilanyi in issues of 15 February or 8 March.

8. *New York Herald*, 11 march 1894, p. 5; 18 March 1894, p. 10.

9. *New York Herald*, 18 March 1894, p. 3.

10. *New York Times*, 22 March 1894, p. 5. Similar sentiments were expressed in the *New York Herald*, 22 March 1894, p. 16, and in the *New York Dispatch*, 25 March 1894, p. 4.

11. *New York Clipper*, 31 March 1894, p. 31.

12. *New York Dramatic Mirror*, 31 March 1894, p. 14.

13. *New York Herald*, 18 March 1894, p. 3.

14. United States Patent Number 528,372. German Patent Number 1909, 25 February 1892. (See Appendix.)

15. *New York Herald*, 1 April 1894, p. 2.

16. *New York Herald*, 22 March 1894, p. 16.

17. *New York Times*, 22 March 1894, p. 5. The *Herald* reviewer, on the same date, was less impressed, remarking only that Venus "appeared very stumpy" (p. 16).

18. *Spirit of the Times*, 7 April 1894, p. 424.

19. *New York Clipper*, 7 April 1894, p. 70.

20. Programme, Columbia Theatre, Chicago, Illinois, 24 April 1894, (Theatre Collection, New York Public Library).

21. *New York Times*, 3 June 1894, p. 12.

22. *New York Dramatic Mirror*, 7 July 1894, p. 5. Quite possibly, this Kilanyi booking represents early, "unofficial" activity by the Theatrical Syndicate. The Syndicate was formally organized on 31 August 1896 and included Marc Klaw, Abraham Erlanger, Al Hayman, and Charles Frohman, in New York; and Samuel F. Nirdlinger (Nixon) and J. Frederick Zimmerman, in Philadelphia. Most of the control mechanisms of the Syndicate were probably in place by 1894, according to Alfred L. Bernheim, *The Business of the Theatre: An Economic History of the American Theatre, 1750-1932* (New York, 1932; reprint ed., New York: Benjmain Blom, 1964), p. 44:

180 Notes for Chapter 7

During the fifteen years from about 1880 to 1895, booking offices experienced a very rapid growth of size and power, and by the end of the period, booking control had very largely passed from the circuits to the booking exchanges.

The two outstanding booking exchanges at the dawn of the Syndicate were Klaw & Erlanger's and Charles Frohman's. The former of these controlled nearly two hundred theatres, mainly in the South.

23. *New York Times,* 7 October 1894, p. 10.
24. *New York Herald,* 14 October 1895, p. 4.
25. *New York Times,* 16 October 1894, p. 5.
26. *New York Dramatic Mirror,* 3 November 1894, p. 3.
27. *New York Times,* 11 November 1894, p. 10; 18 November 1894, p. 10.
28. *New York Herald,* 14 October 1895, p. 4.
29. *New York Times,* 16 October 1894, p. 5.
30. *New York Dramatic Mirror,* 3 November 1894, p. 3.
31. *New York Dramatic Chronicle,* 3 June 1895, p. 162.
32. *New York Herald,* 5 August 1894, p. 8; *New York Clipper,* 1 September 1894, p. 405. The impact of the new series, however, was still overshadowed by the "full stage picture of 'The Dancing Hour in the Temple of Dionysus,' acclaimed for its "skillful light effects."
33. *New York Dramatic Chronicle,* 8 July 1895, p. 203. Kilanyi's patent, Number 528,373, had actually been filed on 19 April 1894 and was an improvement over his earlier version of the same device. Patents for both versions were granted 30 October 1894. (See Appendix.)
34. *New York Dramatic Mirror,* 23 November 1895, p. 19. A similar, but briefer announcement appeared the same day in the *Spirit of the Times,* p. 629. The *New York Dramatic Chronicle,* 8 July 1895, p. 203, had described the Glyptorama without naming it and had announced that "a prominent American theatrical firm have made Herr Kilanyi a very flattering offer for the presentation of the newly invented spectacular pictures."
35. *New York Times,* 25 November 1895, p. 9. A similar description appeared in the *New York Dramatic Chronicle,* 2 December 1895, p. 422.
36. *New York Dramatic Mirror,* 7 December 1895, p. 19.
37. *New York Times,* 3 December 1895, p. 6. The reviewer also provides the following list of the pictures which appeared:

Michael Angelo and Pope Julius Second.............................. Julius Pabst
Roman Bath .... L. Hierle
Joyous Band .... Emile Bayard
Moses in the Bullrushes .... Chadouin
Caravan .... Adaptation
Slave Market .... Victor Giraud
Football .... Overend
Garden of Love .... Schweninger
Siege of Vicksburg .... De Thulstrup
Female Attraction .... Hans Dahl
The Tourists.. Operti
Bay of Naples .... Adaption [*sic*]

Blue Cave of Capri .... Adaptation
The Deluge .... Kilanyi
Other, less detailed reviews appeared on 7 December 1895 in the *Spirit of the Times*, p. 684; the *New York Clipper*, p. 632; and the *New York Dramatic Mirror*, p. 19.

38. *New York Dramatic Mirror*, 30 November 1895, p. 20; 21 December 1895, p. 20.

39. *New York Dramatic Mirror*, 14 December 1895, p. 19; *Spirit of the Times*, 14 December 1895, p. 712.

40. M. St. Clare Byrne, "Stage Lighting," *The Oxford Companion to the Theatre*, ed. Phyllis Hartnoll, Third Ed. (London: Oxford University Press, 1967), pp. 566-67.

41. *New York Times*, 11 May 1894, p. 4.

42. *New York Dramatic Mirror*, 7 December 1895, p. 19.

43. *New York Herald*, 1 December 1895, p. 4.

44. *New York Times*, 3 December 1895, p. 6.

45. *New York Dramatic Chronicle*, 2 December 1895, p. 422; *New York Dramatic Mirror*, 7 December 1895, p. 19.

46. *New York Dramatic Mirror*, 7 December 1895, p. 20.

47. *New York Dramatic Mirror*, 4 January 1896, p. 17.

48. *New York Dramatic Mirror*, 21 December 1895, p. 20.

49. *New York Clipper*, 7 December 1895, p. 632.

50. *New York Dramatic Mirror*, 7 December 1895, p. 19.

51. *New York Times*, 8 December 1895, p. 20.

52. *New York Dramatic Mirror*, 11 January 1896, p. 17; *New York Clipper*, 14 December 1895, p. 648.

53. *New York Dramatic Mirror*, 14 December 1895, p. 19.

54. *New York Times*, 16 December 1895, p. 3.

55. A Koster and Bial programme (Theatre Collection, Museum of the City of New York), dated 17 February 1896, lists the following "New Series of Living Pictures," most of which repeat earlier offerings at that theatre: 1. Football, Overend; 2. Female Attraction, Hans Dahl; 3. Bay of Naples, Operti; 4. Roman Bath, L. Hierle; 5. Joyous Band, Emile Bayard; 6. Moses in the Bullrushes, Chandouin; 7. Caravan (adaptation); 8. Blue Cave of Capri (adaptation); 9. Slave Market, Victor Giraud; 10. Custer's Last Rally, John Mulvany; 11. Garden of Love, Schweninger; 12. The Deluge, Operti.

56. *New York Sun*, 2 February 1896, p. 3.

57. *New York Herald*, 14 April 1896, p. 12. (Italics added.)

Chapter 8.

1. Koster and Bial's 34th Street Theatre was originally built by Oscar Hammerstein as the Manhattan Theatre. Even after the name of the theatre was changed, Hammerstein continued active management, though in partnership with John Koster and Adam Bial. It is interesting that, at the time Kilanyi opened at the Garden, Hammerstein was building his

182 Notes for Chapter 8

fourth New York theatre, the fabulous Olympia which was to open in 1895. At the same time, he was managing the Columbus Theatre and the Harlem Opera House, a total of four major ventures at one time. For a biography of Hammerstein, see Vincent Sheean, *Oscar Hammerstein I: The Life and Exploits of an Impresario* (New York: Simon and Shuster, 1956).

2. *New York Times,* 31 March 1894, p. 8. The "announcement" referred to in the article did not appear in the preceding day's *Times.*

3. *New York Herald,* 8 May 1894, p. 14.

4. *New York Tribune,* 11 May 1894, p. 7.

5. *New York Times,* 11 May 1894, p. 4.

6. *New York Herald,* 11 May 1894, p. 6. The following is the full inventory of pictures as shown in a Koster and Bial programme, 14 May [1894] (Theatre Collection, New York Public Library): 1. Montana Silver Statue, Park; 2. The Helping Hand, Renouf; 3. The Last Message (adaptation); 4. Arabian Pastime, Gernier; 5. Romeo and Julet, Moulon; 6. L'orchestra d'Amour, Gill; 7. Nymph of the Wave, Sanders; 8. Homage to Edison (statue presented to him by the French nation); 9. Queen of Flowers, Vineo; 10. General Grant at the Battle of the Wilderness, (production); 11. Tannhauser and Venus, Knille; 12. Between Two Fires, Estes; 13. The Three Muses, Tojetti; 14. Give Me a Kiss, Lupini; 15. Battle for the Dead (production); 16. The Angelus, Millet; 17. Truth, Fedro; 18. Diana, Perry; and 19. Aurora, Perry. The concluding three pictures were presented simultaneously.

7. *New York Dramatic Mirror,* 28 July 1894, p. 12.

8. *New York Times, 11 May 1894, p. 4.*

9. *New York Tribune,* 11 May 1894, p. 7.

10. *New York Dramatic Mirror,* 28 July 1894, p. 21; *New York Herald,* 16 August 1894, p. 7.

11. *New York Herald,* 29 July 1894, p. 6; 1 August 1894, p. 12.

12. *New York Times,* 10 June 1894, p. 10.

13. *Leslie's Weekly,* 30 August 1894, p. 137.

14. *New York Dramatic Chronicle,* 17 December 1894, p. 183. A Koster and Bial programme (Theatre Collection, Museum of the City of New York) for the week of 31 December 1894 lists the following "Third Series Living Pictures:" 1. Blind Man's Buff, Mackart; 2. Christmas Eve, Operti; 3. La Source, Mazerolli; 4. Dot Leetle German Band, Wuest; 5. A Japanese Toilet, Girard; 6. The Wounded Drummer Boy, Eastman Johnson; 7. Sally in our Alley, Abbey; 8. Birth of a Naiad, Coomans; 9. Evening Prayer, Birket Foster; 10. Salambo, Gabriel Ferrier; 11. Love is Lighter Than A Butterfly, Picou; 12. An Old Sinner, Felli; 13. Paul and Francesca, Dore; 14. Home Sweet Home, Operti; 15. In Vino Veritas, Landelle; 16. Rock of Ages, Gertel; 17. Morning, Markart; 18. Noon, Makart; 19. Evening, Makart; 20. The Last Stand, Fred'k Remington.

15. On 10 September 1894 Mlle. Marietta di Dio, an Austrian singer, made her debut at Koster and Bial's and became the catalyst for an explosion which left the partnership of that house in ruins. According to Vincent Sheean, Mlle. di Dio had "aroused the devotion of a champagne salesman named George Kessler" who was one of Koster and Bial's main suppliers. Kessler proposed that the singer be put on the bill at the music hall, but Hammerstein adamantly refused. Kessler appealed to the other partners, and finally, over Hammerstein's continued objections, Mlle. di Dio was given a booking.

> On the night of her first appearance Hammerstein took a box next to Kessler's. Kessler had, in fact, taken a large number of boxes and filled them with persons who could be depended upon to applaud Mlle. de Dio. The moment the young lady came out and began to sing, Hammerstein stood up and hissed. He hissed loud and long; the whole audience turned to him rather than toward the performer. His mighty silk hat, pointed imperial beard, and Prince Albert coat were a uniform known to all in the audience. No doubt the cigar waved in the air as he hissed. Everybody knew that he was Oscar Hammerstein and that he was the general director of this theatre. Laughter broke out. [Sheean, p. 80]

Years afterward, Oscar's friend, George Blumenthal, remembered the after effects of that incident:

> Di Dio and George Kessler had questioned him about it, there was a fight between Oscar Hammerstein and Kessler and they were taken to the police station.
>
> John Koster and Rudolph [sic] Bial followed. They bailed out Mr. Kessler, who had been a patron of their theatre and was entitled to some courtesy. They left their partner, Mr. Hammerstein, in the cell overnight.
>
> The fiery little man was not mollified by this treatment. When he got out in the morning he demanded an accounting. This resulted in Koster and Bial giving him $370,000 for his share of the theatre. ["The Hidden Folio in the Life of Oscar Hammerstein," *Liberty*, 21 May 1927, p. 9]

The cash settlement Blumenthal mentions was reached out of court, but not before Hammerstein had engaged in several legal maneuvers against Koster and Bial.

16. *New York Herald*, 14 April 1895, p. 3.
17. *New York Herald*, 10 September 1895, p. 6.
18. *New York Times*, 10 September 1895, p. 2.
19. *New York Sun*, 17 May 1896, p. 11.
20. *New York Sun*, 8 August 1897, p. 3; 21 August 1897, p. 3; *New York Clipper*, 14 August 1897, p. 384; *New York Herald* 5 September 1897, p. 12.
21. *New York Herald*, 10 October 1897, p. 8.
22. *New York Dramatic Mirror*, 13 November 1897, p. 15.
23. *New York Herald*, 22 April 1894, p. 11.
24. *New York Herald*, 5 June 1894, p. 11. Operti later painted the backgrounds for Kilanyi's Glyptorama.
25. *New York Herald*, 10 June 1894, p. 6.
26. *New York Dramatic Mirror*, 16 June 1894, p. 5.
27. *New York Herald*, 19 June 1894, p. 6.
28. *New York Dramatic Chronicle*, 1 October 1894, p. 40.
29. *New York Herald*, 7 October 1894, p. 2; *New York Dramatic Chronicle*, 8 October 1894, p. 51.
30. *New York Herald*, 11 December 1894, p. 7.
31. *New York Times*, 3 June 1894, p. 12.
32. *New York Herald*, 3 June 1894, p. 2.

184 Notes for Chapter 8

33. *New York Herald,* 17 June 1894, p. 2. The titles were, "A Famous Jockey," "A Lawyer of Great Renoun," "Female Bettors at the Races," and "Dead Broke."

34. *New York Herald,* 21 June 1894, p. 11. The *New York Times,* 21 June 1894, p. 8, lists the following tableaux in addition to those mentioned in the *Herald:* "Before, During, and After the Ballet," "Female Emigrants on Ellis Island," "On the Grand Stand at Morris Park," "The Jockeys," "The Female Bettors," "A.B.—A Prominent Lawyer," "The Jay," "The Duel," "The Reconciliation," "The Tramps," "The Egyptian," and "Gettysburg." The last named was, reportedly, the only non-burlesque tableau. The *New York Dispatch,* 24 June 1894, p. 4, provides the following titles, which are probably variations of those already cited: "The Ballet in Bad Head Row," "Gould and Wales—the Vigilant and Britannia," and "Grand Stand Habitues at the Races."

35. *New York Dispatch,* 26 August 1894, p. 4; *New York Herald,* 30 October 1894, p. 12.

36. Rudolph Aronson had already had a long and somewhat stormy association with the Casino. He had managed the house when it had opened in October 1882. Only a year later, the stage carpenter had attempted to set fire to the theatre as revenge against Aronson who had discharged him. In 1891, Aronson had engaged in a bitter court battle with Oscar Hammerstein over production rights for the opera, *Cavalleria Rusticana.* In June 1893, the Casino was placed in receivership, and Canary and Lederer took over the property at a cost of $38,000 a year. Aronson stayed on as manager of the roof garden, at a salary of $125 a week. In November 1894, the Casino again went into receivership and was then closed for about three months until the Aronson brothers took over on 19 February 1895, at which time Rudolph Aronson again exercised managerial control. (T.A. Brown, *A History of the New York Stage,* 3 vols. [New York: Dodd, Mead & Co., 1903; reprint ed., New York: Benjamin Blom, 1964], 3:485-501.)

37. *New York Times,* 2 March 1895, p. 6.

38. *New York Herald,* 10 march 1895, p. 4; 12 March 1895, p. 7; *New York Times,* 12 March 1895, p. 5.

39. Programme, Casino, 18 March 1895, Theatre Collection, New York Public Library. The Nahl-Bradley Living Bronze Statues were item 16 on the bill.

40. *New York Herald,* 19 March 1895, p. 13.

41. *New York Dramatic Chronicle,* 25 March 1895, p. 38.

42. *New York Herald,* 26 March 1895, p. 10.

43. *New York Dramatic Chronicle,* 1 April 1895, p. 51.

44. *New York Times,* 27 March 1895, p. 8.

45. *New York Tribune,* 9 April 1895, p. 10.

46. *New York Dramatic Chronicle,* 15 April 1895, p. 75.

47. *New York Times,* 18 April 1895, p. 14; *New York Clipper,* 27 April 1895, p. 118.

48. *New York Clipper,* 11 May 1895, pp. 149, 150; 18 may 1895, p. 165. The troupe was scheduled to play in Paterson, New Jersey, the week of 13 May. Bradley anticipated a European tour during the following fall and winter.

49. *New York Herald,* 12 May 1895, p. 4; 17 May, p. 7; *New York Dramatic Chronicle,* 13 May 1895, p. 123.

50. *New York Herald,* 14 May 1895, p. 6.

51. *New York Dramatic Chronicle,* 20 May 1895, p. 136; *New York Clipper,* 25 May 1895, p. 181.
52. William Moulton Marston and John Henry Feller, *F.F. Proctor: Vaudevile Pioneer* (New York: Richard R. Smith, 1943), pp. 46-47.
53. Brown, 3:514.
54. *New York Sun,* 20 May 1894, p. 12.
55. *New York Herald,* 20 May 1894, p. 8; *New York Tribune,* p. 21.
56. *New York Tribune,* 17 June 1894, p. 10.
57. *New York Herald,* 1 July 1894, pp. 2, 10. The *New York Times,* 1 July 1894, p. 12, lists the tableaux as follows: "Rebecca at the Well," "Grace Darling," "The Birth of Venus," "Diana," "Cupid and Psyche," "The Flower Girl," "Two Frogs," "Night and Morning," "Mary Magdalen," "The North Star," "Sappho," "The Moon Fairy," "Nymph of the Wave," "The Kiss," "The Storm," "Silence," "The Angelus," "Uncle Sam," "Zephyr," "Nature's Mirror," "Soap Bubbles," "The Spring," "Little Puck," "The Diver," and "Comrades Up to Date."
58. *New York Herald,* 29 July 1895, pp. 6, 8.
59. *New York Sun,* 15 August 1894, p. 5.
60. *New York Tribune,* 19 August 1894, p. 21; 9 September 1894, p. 24; 16 September 1894, p. 22; *New York Herald,* 26 August, 1894, p. 6; 2 September 1894, p. 6; 9 September 1894, p. 6.
61. Advertisement reproduced in Marston and Feller, foll. p. 96.
62. Marston and Feller, foll. p. 96.
63. *New York Herald,* 23 September 1894, p. 2; 30 October 1894, p. 12.
64. *New York Herald,* 4 November 1894, p. 2. Virtually every Sunday issue of the *Herald* throughout 1895 continued to list additions to the living pictures at Proctor's.
65. *New York Herald,* 27 January 1895, p. 4. "Trilby" tableaux were to be seen at this time in most theatres exhibiting living pictures.
66. *New York Herald,* 4 December 1895, p. 13; *New York Dramatic Chronicle,* 9 December 1895, p. 434.
67. *New York Dramatic Mirror,* 4 January 1896, p. 17.
68. *New York Dramatic Chronicle,* 23 December 1895, p. 458.
69. *New York Dramatic Chronicle,* 2 March 1896, p. 9; *New York Sun,* 1 March 1896, p. 3.
70. *New York Dramatic Mirror,* 14 March 1896, p. 19. I assume the writer means that the woman was on the horse's back.
71. *New York Herald,* 21 February 1897, p. 8; *New York Sun,* 21 February 1897, p. 3.
72. *New York Herald,* 23 February 1897, p. 7.
73. *New York Dramatic Mirror,* 6 March 1897, p. 17. The *New York Herald,* 28 February 1897, p. 9, refers to these as "their original tableaux" and observes, facetiously perhaps, that "the Cherrys are well worth seeing as a product of Western Civilization." In fairness, it should be noted that the Cherry Sisters apparently took themselves quite seriously as song, dance, and sketch artists. In 1930 they attempted a come-back appearance in New York, at which time one retrospective article summed up reaction to them with the headline, "They were so bad they were good." (Undated clipping, Theatre Collection, Museum of the City of New York).

186   Notes for Chapter 9

74. *New York Herald*, 3 October 1897, p. 5; *New York sun*, 3 October 1897, p. 11.
75. *New York Herald*, 3 October, 1897, p. 4.
76. *New York Herald*, 17 June 1894, p. 3.
77. *New York Herald*, 26 August 1894, p. 10; 2 September 1894, p. 4.
78. *New York Herald*, 9 September 1896, p. 6; 16 September 1896, p. 8.
79. *New York Herald*, 16 September pp. 5, 8.
80. *Evening Transcript* (Boston), 3 July 1894, p. 5.
81. *Evening Transcript* (Boston), 2 June 1894, p. 8; 5 June 1894, p. 5; 15 June 1894, p. 5.
82. *Evening Transcript* (Boston), 31 July 1894, p. 5.
83. *Evening Transcript* (Boston), 4 September 1894, p. 5.
84. *Evening Transcript* (Boston), 22 September 1894, p. 8.
85. *New York Dispatch*, 15 July 1894, p. 4.
86. *New York Dispatch*, 29 July 1894, p. 4.
87. *New York Times*, 31 July 1894, p. 8.
88. *New York Times*, 26 August 1894, p. 10; *New York Tribune*, 25 November 1894, p. 11.
89. *New York Herald*, 10 May 1896, p. 6.
90. *New York Dramatic Mirror*, 30 May 1896, p. 17. See also *New York Times*, 19 May 1896, p. 5.
91. *New York Herald*, 3 December 1899, p. 15.
92. *New York Dramatic Mirror*, 16 December 1899, p. 18.
93. *New York Herald*, 26 August 1894, p. 10.
94. *New York Times*, 26 August 1894, p. 10.
95. *New York Herald*, 2 September 1894, p. 6.
96. *New York Herald*, 14 October 1894, p. 8; *New York Tribune*, 14 October, 1894, p. 24.
97. *New York Herald*, 18 November 1894, p. 3.
98. *New York Herald*, 28 July 1895, p. 1; *New York Dramatic Chronicle*, 29 July 1894, p. 227.
99. *New York Times*, 19 November 1895, p. 4.
100. *New York Dramatic Mirror*, 23 April 1898, p. 18; 21 May 1898, p. 16. "New living pictures" were announced 7 May 1898, p. 19.

Chapter 9

1. *The Illustrated American*, 7 July 1894, p. 25.
2. Ibid.
3. *New York Herald*, 22 March 1894, p. 16.
4. *New York Clipper*, 31 March 1894, p. 31.

5. *New York Dramatic Mirror*, 31 March 1894, p. 14.
6. *New York Times* 11 May 1894, p. 4.
7. *New York Dramatic Mirror*, 19 May 1894, p. 6.
8. *New York Tribune*, 25 March 1894, p. 7.
9. *Illustrated American*, 7 April 1894, p. 397. The writer also remarks earlier in the same review, "It is a pleasure to find that, although many nude pictures are realized, there is not a suspicion of indelicacy about the entire show...." Dr. Charles Henry Parkhurst, mentioned by the writer, was a prominent Presbyterian cleric whose pulpit attacks on political corruption and organized vice in New York prompted federal investigations of city government and eventually led to the defeat of Tammany Hall. Although he denounced the theatre generally, and living pictures in particular, his main campaign was aimed at political targets.
10. *New York Clipper*, 31 March 1894, p. 8.
11. *New York Dramatic Mirror*, 31 March 1894, p. 4.
12. *Spirit of the Times*, 19 May 1894, p. 685.
13. Robert Bremner, "Editor's Introduction" to *Traps for the Young* by Anthony Comstock (Cambridge, Mass.: The Belnap Press of Harvard University Press, 1967), p. xxvi.
14. *New York Dispatch*, 13 may 1894, p. 4, for example, published a vitriolic editorial on "Comstock the Critic," attacking him as a demagogue.
15. Bemner, pp. xxvi-xxvii.
16. "Living Pictures by Flashlight," *The Standard* (London), 22 December 1894, p. 3. Page 10 of the same issue carries an unsympathetic account of Lady Henry Somerset's efforts. It concludes that the attention she has focused on tableaux had made them more popular rather than less so.
17. *New York Herald*, 19 August 1894, p. 7.
18. *New York Times*, 2 October 1894, p. 5.
19. *New York Times*, 3 October 1894, p. 3.
20. *New York Herald*, 28 November 1894, p. 12; *New York Tribune*, 28 November 1894, p. 3.
21. *New York Herald*, 28 November 1894, p. 12.
22. *New York Tribune*, 29 November 1894, p. 1; *New York Times*, 29 November 1894, p. 15.
23. *New York Tribune*, 30 November 1894, p. 7; 1 December 1894, p. 7.
24. For a sampling of such letters and editorials, see *New York Tribune*, 2 December 1894, p. 8; *New York Times*, 28 March 1895, p. 4; 29 March 1895, p. 4; *Leslie's Weekly*, 11 February 1897, pp. 82, 88-89.
25. *New York Tribune*, 9 April 1895, p. 10.
26. *New York Times*, 2 September 1894, p. 10.
27. *New York Dispatch*, 29 April 1894, p. 1; 6 May 1894, p. 1.
28. *New York Herald*, 28 October 1894, p. 2.
29. *New York Herald*, 23 September 1894, p. 8.

Notes for Chapter 10

30. *New York Herald,* 5 April 1896, p. 7; *New York Sun,* 5 April 1896, p. 11.
31. *New York Sun,* 7 April 1896, p. 5.
32. *New York Sun,* 12 April 1896, p. 3.
33. *New York Dramatic Mirror,* 25 April 1896, p. 15.
34. *New York Herald,* 3 May 1896, p. 6.
35. *New York Sun,* 19 May 1896, p. 2; 26 May 1896, p. 9. Doris carried the case to the Appellate Divisions of the Supreme Court of New York which upheld the decision and imposed a fine of $250 (*New York Sun,* 6 October 1897, p. 5).
36. *The New York Dramatic Mirror,* 10 November 1894, p. 9, reported a comment in *The Era* that Hope Booth was "arousing much ire" in London. *The Dramatic Chronicle,* 1 April 1895, p. 52, observed, "Our fair Hope Booth, so the cable informs us, has made another disastrous failure abroad in 'The Terrible Girl,' at the Royalty. She was hooted and jeered at by one and all."
37. *New York Sun,* 23 July 1896, p. 7.
38. *New York Herald,* 9 August 1896, p. 6.
39. *New York Sun,* 20 and 27 September 1896, p. 3; *New York Herald,* 29 September 1896, p. 11.
40. *New York Herald,* 11 October 1896, p. 4.
41. *New York Herald,* 10 January 1897, p. 5.
42. *New York Herald,* 12 January 1897, p. 12.
43. *New York Dramatic Mirror,* 23 January 1897, p. 17.
44. *New York Dramatic Mirror,* 30 January 1897, p. 19.
45. *New York Dramatic Mirror,* 15 March 1897, p. 19.
46. *New York Herald,* 6 June 1897, p. 6.
47. New York Society for the Suppression of Vice, *23rd Annual Report,* 19 January 1897, pp. 12-13.
48. *New York Herald,* 3 April 1898, p. 11.
49. *New York Dramatic Mirror,* 16 April 1898, p. 16.

Chapter 10

1. Useful studies of revue include: Robert Baral, *Revue: The Great Broadway Period* (New York: Fleet Press, 1962); Raymond Mander and Joe Mitchenson, *Revue: A Story in Pictures* (New York: Taplinger, 1971); and Marjorie Farnsworth, *The Ziegfeld Follies* (New York: G.P. Putnam's Sons, 1956).
2. A recent example is to be found in an illustration of "Living Statuary" pictured in the bulletin, *Springfield College in Exhibition,* an announcement of a gymnastic exhibition (Springfield, Mass.: Springfield College, 1977).
3. John and Alice Durant, *Pictorial History of the American Circus* (New York: Castle Books, 1957), p. 184.

Notes for Chapter 10 189

4. Official programs and other publications about the tableaux are available from "Festival of Arts and Pageant of the Masters," 650 Laguna Canyon Road, Laguna Beach, CA 92651. For a brief descriptive history of the Pageant, see Stephen J. Sansweet, "Laguna Beach Show Brings Old Masters to Life, So to Speak," *Wall Street Journal*, 10 July 1980, pp. 1, 11. Photos of several tableaux in the 1980 Pageant may be found in "Living Pictures," *Lighting Dimensions*, September/October 1980, pp. 16-20.

5. See Chapter 1, note 1. This production, directed by the author, was attended by some four thousand persons and was reported by CBS Television News, 21 October 1979.

6. *Passion Oberammergau*, Official Illustrated Catalogue, published by the community of Oberammergau, 1980.

7. Music, lyrics, and conception by Sherman Edwards; book by Peter Stone: directed by Peter Hunt; scenery and lighting by Jo Mielziner; costumes by Patricia Zipprodt; choreography by Onna White; *1776* opened 18 March 1976 at the Forty-sixth Street Theatre, New York City.

Bibliography of Works Cited

Books and Articles

Aiken, George L. *Uncle Tom's Cabin*. in *Dramas from the American Theatre, 1762-1909,* edited by Richard Moody, pp. 349-96. Boston: Houghton Mifflin Co., 1966.
Altick, Richard D. *The Shows of London*. Cambridge, Massachusetts, and London: The Belnap Press of Harvard University Press, 1978.
Bailey, J.O. *British Plays of the Nineteenth Century*. New York: The Odyssey Press, 1966.
Baral, Robert. *Revue: The Great Broadway Period*. New York: Fleet Press, 1962.
Bassham, Ben L. *The Theatrical Photographs of Napoleon Sarony*. Kent, Ohio: Kent State University Press, 1978.
Bernheim, Alfred L. *The Business of the Theatre: An Economic History of the American Theatre, 1750-1932*. New York: 1932; reprint ed., New York: Benjamin Blom, 1964.
Blumenthal, George, "The Hidden Folio in the Life of Oscar Hammerstein." *Liberty,* 21 May 1927, p.9.
Broun, Heywood, and Leech, Margaret. *Anthony Comstock, Roundsman of the Lord*. New York: Albert and Charles Boni, 1927.
Brown, T. Allston. *A History of the New York Stage*. 3 vols. New York: Dodd Mead and Co., 1903; reprint ed., New York: Benjamin Blom, 1964.
Clapp, William W., Jr. *A Record of the Boston Stage*. Boston: James Monroe & Co., 1853; reprint ed., New York: Greenwood Press, 1969.
Coad, Oral Sumner, and Mims, Edwin, Jr. *The American Stage*. The Pageant of America, vol. 14. New Haven: Yale University Press, 1929.
Comstock, Anthony, *Frauds Exposed; or, How the People are Deceived and Robbed, and Youth Corrupted*. N.p.; 1880; reprint ed., Montclair, New Jersey: Patterson Smith, 1969.
_____. *Traps for the Young*. N.p., 1884; reprint ed., edited by Robert Bremner, Cambridge, Massachusetts: The Belnap Press of Harvard University Press, 1967.
Crawford, Mary C. *The Romance of the American Theatre*. Boston: Little, Brown, & Co., 1925; reprint ed., New York: Halcyon House, 1940.
Dayton, Abram C. *Last Days of Knickerbocker Life*. New York: George W. Harlan, 1882.
Durant, John and Alice, *Pictorial History of the American Circus,* New York: Castle Books, 1957.
Enciclopedia dello Spettacolo. Roma: Casa Editrice le Maschere, 1954-64. S.v. "Quadro vivente," by Lucien Rimels.
Farnsworth, Marjorie. *The Ziegfeld Follies*. New York: G.P. Putnam's Sons, 1956.
Foster, George G. *New York by Gas-Light*. New York: DeWitt and Davenport, 1850.
Gascoigne, Bamber. *World Theatre: An Illustrated History*. Boston and Toronto: Little, Brown & Co., 1968.
Gilbert, Douglas. *American Vaudeville: Its Life and Times*. New York: Dover Publications, 1940.

Bibliography

Goethe, Johann Wolfgang von. *Elective Affinities.* Translated by James Anthony Froude and R. Dylan Boylan. New York: Frederick Ungar Publishing Co., 1963.

Hardwick, Mollie. *Emma, Lady Hamilton.* New York: Holt, Rinehart and Winston, 1969.

Harris, Neil. *Humbug: The Art of P.T. Barnum.* Boston: Little, Brown & Co., 1973.

Henderson, Mary C. *The City and the Theatre.* Clifton, New Jersey: James T. White & Co., 1973.

Hewitt, Bernard Wolcott. *Theatre U.S.A., 1668 to 1957.* New York: McGraw-Hill, 1959.

Holmström, Kirsten Gram. *Monodrama, Attitudes, Tableaux Vivants: Studies on Some Trends of Theatrical Fashion, 1770-1815.* Stockholm: Almqvist & Wiksell, 1967.

Hughes, Glenn. *A History of the American Theatre, 1700-1950.* New York: Samuel French, 1951.

Hutton, Ann Hawkes. *Portrait of Patriotism.* Radnor, Pennsylvania: Chilton Book Co., 1959.

Ireland, Joseph N. *Records of the New York Stage: 1750-1860.* 2 vols. New York: T.H. Morrell, 1866-67.

Jeaffreson, John Cordy. *Lord Nelson and Lady Hamilton.* London: Hurst and Blockett, 1888.

Jefferson, Joseph. *The Autobiography of Joseph Jefferson.* Edited by Alan S. Downer. Cambridge, Massachusetts: The Belnap Press of Harvard University Press, 1964.

Kilanyi, Eduard [Edward] von. Patent #528,372 and #528,373, "Apparatus for Displaying Tableaux Vivant [sic];" United States Patent Office: *Specifications of Patents,* pp. 2872-74; *Drawings of Patents,* pp. 695-96. Patented 30 October 1894.

Laurie, Joe, Jr. *Vaudeville: From the Honky-Tonks to the Palace.* New York: Henry Holt & Co., 1953.

"Letter from a Gentleman, present at the Festivities at Fonthill, to a Correspondent in Town." Fonthill, 28 December 1800, *The Gentleman's Magazine;* March 1801, pp. 206-208; April 1801, pp. 297-98.

"Living Pictures." *Lighting Dimensions,* September/October 1980, pp. 16-20.

"Living Pictures by Flashlight." *The Standard* (London), 22 December 1894, pp. 3-10.

Lofts, Norah R. *Emma Hamilton.* New York: Coward, McCann & Geoghegan, 1978.

Logan, Olive, "The Secret Regions of the Stage." *Harper's New Monthly Magazine,* March 1874, pp. 628-42.

Long, W.H., ed. *Memoirs of Emma, Lady Hamilton, with Anecdotes of her Friends and Contemporaries.* New Edition. London: W.W. Gibbings, 1891.

Lyman, George D. *The Saga of the Comstock Lode: Boom Day in Virginia City.* New York and London, 1934.

Mander, Raymond and Mitchenson, Joe. *Revue: A Story in Pictures.* New York: Taplinger, 1971.

Marsh, Steve, "Truth in Art." *The Trenton Times* (New Jersey), 3 December 1982, p. B1.

Marston, William Moulton, and Feller, John Henry. *F.F. Proctor: Vaudeville Pioneer.* New York: Richard R. Smith, 1943.

Marzio, Peter C. *The Democratic Art: Pictures for a 19th Century America. Chromolithography 1840-1900.* Boston: David R. Godine in association with the Amon Carter Museum of Western Art, Forth Worth; 1979.

Meisel, Martin, "Wilkie's Tableaux Vivants: An Amplification" (letter to the editor). *Master Drawings,* spring 1973, pp. 55-58.

Minnigerode, Meade. *The Fabulous Forties: 1840-1850: A Presentation of Private Life.* New York: G.P. Putnam's Sons, 1924.

New York Society for the Suppression of Vice. *23rd Annual Report.* New York: n.p., 19 January 1897.

Odell, George C.D. *Annals of the New York Stage.* 15 vols. New York: Columbia University Press, 1927-49.

The Oxford Campanion to the Theatre. 3d ed. Edited by Phyllis Hartnoll. London: Oxford University Press, 1967.

Rees, James. *Mysteries of City Life.* Philadelphia: J.W. Moore, 1849.

Rinaldi, Ann, "the Other 'Washington's Crossing' Painting..." *The Trentonian* (Trenton, New Jersey), 3 December 1982, p. 3.

Russell, Francis, "An Album of Tableaux Vivants; Sketches by Wilkie." *Master Drawings,* spring 1972, pp. 35-40.
Sansweet, Stephen J., "Laguna Beach Show Brings Old Masters to Life, So to Speak." *Wall Street Journal,* 10 July 1980, pp. 1, 11.
Sarony, Napoleon. *Sarony's Living Pictures, photographed from Life by Napoleon Sarony.* New York: A.E. Chasmar & Co., [1894].
Saxon, A.H. *The Life and Art of Andrew Ducrow & The Romantic Age of the English Circus.* Hamden, Conn.: Archon Books, 1978.
_____. *Enter Foot and Horse: A History of Hippodrama in England and France.* New Haven and London: Yale University Press, 1968.
_____, ed. *Selected Letters of P.T. Barnum.* New York: Columbia University Press, 1983.
Schneider, Gretchen A. "Gabriel Ravel and the Martinetti Family: The Popularity of Pantomime in 1855." In *American Popular Entertainment: Papers and Proceedings of the Conference on the History of American Popular Entertainment,* edited by Myron Matlaw, pp. 241-58. Westport, Conn.: Greenwood Press, 1979.
Sheean, Vincent. *Oscar HammersteinI: the life and exploits of an impresario.* New York: Simon & Shuster, 1956.
Sichel, Walter Sidney. *Emma Lady Hamilton.* 2d ed., revised. New York: Dodd, Mead & Co., 1906.
_____. *Memoirs of Emma, Lady Hamilton.* New York: P.F. Collier & Sons, 1910.
Sizer, Theodore. *The Works of Colonel John Trumbull, Artist of the American Revolution.* Revised ed. New Haven and London: Yale Unviersity Press, 1967.
Sobel, Bernard, *A Pictorial History of Burlesque.* New York: G.P. Putnam's Sons, 1956.
Thomas, Hugh. *Cuba: The Pursuit of Freedom.* New York: Harper & Row, 1971.
Toll, Robert C. *Blacking Up: The Misntrel Show in Nineteenth-Century America.* New York: Oxford University Press, 1974.
Tours, Hugh. *The Life and Letters of Emma Hamilton.* London: V. Gollancz, 1963.
Trumbull, Charles Gallaudet. *Anthony Comstock, Fighter: Some Impressions of a Lifetime of Adventure in Conflict with the Powers of Evil.* New York: Fleming H. Revell Co., 1913.
United States Patent Office. *Drawings of Patents.* 30 October 1894, pp. 695-96.
_____. *Specifications of Patents.* 30 October 1894, pp. 2872-74.
Wallace, Irving. *The Fabulous Showman: The Life and Times of P.T. Barnum.* New York: Alfred A. Knopf, 1959.
Werner, M.R. *Barnum.* New York: Harcourt, Brace & Co., 1923.
Wilson, Arthur Herman. *A History of the Philadelphia Theatre.* Philadelphia: University of Pennsylvania Press, 1935; reprint ed., New York: Greenwood Press, 1968.
Wilson, Garff B. *Three Hundred Years of American Drama and Theatre, From "Ye Bare and Ye Cubb" to "Hair".* Englewood Cliffs, New Jersey: Prentice-Hall, 1973.
Winter, Marian Hannah. *The Pre-Romantic Ballet.* New York: Pitman Publishing Corp., 1974.
Zeidman, Irving. *The American Burlesque Show.* New York: Hawthorn books, 1967.

Ephemera

Anderson, Mary, as "Galatea." Photograph by Mora, n.d.; two photographs by Napoleon Sarony, 1883; photograph by H. Rocher, 1881. The Billy Rose Theatre Collection. The New York Public Library at Lincoln Center. Astor, Lenox and Tilden Foundations.
[Barrymore, William, and Barrymore, Ada Adams]. Unidentified newspaper clipping of biographical information. Theatre Collection, New York Public Library.
Bijou Opera House, New York. Programme, 28 August 1885. Theatre Collection, Museum of the City of New York.
Brooklyn Museum. *The American Renaissance, 1876-1917.* Announcement of exhibition, October 1979.

Casino Theatre, New York. Programme, 18 March 1895. Theatre Collection, New York Public Library.
Chateau Mabille Varieties, New York. Programme, n.d. Theatre Collection, New York Public Library.
Coal Hole Tavern, Strand, London. Handbill advertising Madame Pauline's tableaux, n.d. Harvard Theatre Collection, Harvard College Library.
Columbia Theatre, Chicago. Programme, 24 April 1894. Theatre Collection, New York Public Library.
Comedy Theatre, New York. Programme, n.d. [1885?]. Theatre Collection, Museum of the City of New York.
Festival of Arts and Pageant of the Masters. *Official Souvenir Program.* Laguna Beach, California: Laguna News-Post, 1973, 1975, 1980.
Franklin Museum, New York. Playbill, [18 August 1858]. Harvard Theatre Collection, Harvard College Library.
Hiesinger, Ulrich. Sculpture Division, Philadelphia Museum of Art. Telephone interview, 15 June 1979.
Holliday Street Theatre, New York. Programme, 6 October 1856. Theatre Collection, Museum of the City of New York.
Koster & Bial's Music Hall, New York. Programme, week of 31 December 1894. Theatre Collection, Museum of the City of New York.
Koster & Bial's Music Hall, New York. Programme, 17 February 1896. Theatre Collection, Museum of the City of New York.
Laura Keene's Varieties, New York. Programme, 10 June 1856. Theatre Collection, Museum of the City of New York.
Palace Theatre, London. Programme, 17 June 1894. Theatre Collection, New York Public Library.
Passion Oberammergau. Official illustrated catalogue published by the community of Oberammergau, 1980.
Springfield College in Exhibition. Announcement of gymnastic exhibition. Springfield, Mass.: Springfield College, 1977.
Theatre Comique, New York. Programme, 15 November 1875. Theatre Collection, Museum of the City of New York.
Theatre Royal, Coventry. Programme, 30 September [1850]. Theatre Collection, Museum of the City of New York.
"They Were So Bad They Were Good." Unidentified newspaper clipping about the Cherry Sisters, [1930?]. Theatre Collection, Museum of the City of New York.
Walhalla, Leichester Square, London. Programme [1840's?], listing Mme Wharton's tableaux vivants and poses plastiques. Harvard Theatre Collection, Harvard College Library.
Washington Crossing Foundation. Programme, Fifth Washington Crossing Assembly, Pennsylvania Tricentennial. The Union League of Philadelphia, 29 October 1982.

Newspapers

Boston Evening Transcript, February-June 1848, June-September 1894.
The Euterpeiad (New York), 1 October 1831.
Evening Courant (Edinburgh), 2 February 1828.
Leslie's Weekly (New York), August 1894-February 1897.
National Police Gazette (New York), March 1848.
New York Clipper, June 1856-May 1895.
New York Daily Advertiser, August-December 1831.
New York Daily Graphic, November 1875-June 1880.

New York Dispatch, March-August 1894.
New York Dramatic Chronicle, July 1894-March 1896.
New York Dramatic Mirror, December 1895-December 1899.
New York Dramatic News, October 1875-March 1877.
New York Evening Express, January-March 1848.
New York Evening Post, January 1831-January 1833.
New York Herald, June 1839-April 1898.
New York Home Journal, 27 September 1851.
New York Illustrated American, September 1893-July 1894.
New York Organ, 13 September 1851.
New York Post, June 1859-February 1878.
New York Standard, April 1834-August 1870.
New York Sun, February 1848-October 1897.
New York Times, October 1856-May 1896.
New York Tribune, March 1848-April 1895.
Porter's Spirit of the Times (New York), May 1857.
Spirit of the Times (New York), September 1847-May 1894.
The Stage (London), October 1893-March 1894.
The Standard (London), 22 December 1894.
The Theatre: A Weekly Record of the Stage (New York), May 1886.
Washington National Intelligencer, 5 December 1850, 9 April 1852.
Wilkes' Spirit of the Times (New York), October 1861-September 1869.

Index

Aberle's New Theatre, 93
Abt, Professor (stereoptican), 126
Academy of Music, 66
Advertising: "Free Love" exploitation, 42; Human interest stories, 111; Language style, 23, 34-35, 37, 60-61, 71-72, 80, 130; Lawsuit exploitation, 115; Playbills, 51-52, 162-63n.7, Figs. 7-10; Posters, 91-92, 141; "Public" rehearsal, 49; Sensationalism, 42, 72-74, 80, 82, 119; Typography, 23; Verses in, 72, 80; Warnings in, 40, 104. See also Hoax
Aesthetics. See Criticism, aesthetic
Alhambra (Brighton, England), 103
Alhambra Saloon, 34
American Alhambra. See Columbia Opera House
American Roof Garden, 131, 140
Anderson, Mary (actress), 93, 96, 173n.11, 174n.122, Figs. 14-17
Apollo Rooms, 20, 22
Aronson, Rudolph (mgr., Casino), 121-24, 131, 180n.36
Arrests: of Matt Morgan (1875), 75-78; re *Orange Blossoms* (1896), 140. See also Court proceedings; Police; Raids
Atherton, Alice (tableaux), 93, 174n.122
"Attitudes," 7, 25, 69. See also Hamilton, Emma
Au Bain (operetta), 142
Austin, William and Ida (tableaux), 124

Barnum, Phineas Taylor, 66
Barnum's Museum, 67
Barrymore, Ada Adams (poseur), 11-12
Barrymore, William (stage mgr.), 12
Bartholdi, Frederic Auguste (sculptor), 98, 155n.1
Bashful Venus (afterpiece), 90
Belasco, David (mgr.), 140

Belle, Helen (poseur), 164n.32
Bennie, Mr. (poseur), 15
Berry, Miss Belle (tableaux), 84
Berry, Jake (mgr., Columbia Opera House), 82-87
Black Crook, The (extravaganza), 64, 96
Blakely. See Sheffer and Blakely Company
Blanchard (poseur), 13
Blanche, Mme. (poseur), 71
Blandowski, M. (tableaux), 72
Bloomer, Amelia Jenks (reformer), 163n.15
Bloomer Troupe, 163n.15
Bolton, Frank (tableaux), 84
Booth, Edwin (actor, mgr.), 70
Booth, Hope (poseur), 140-41, 184n.36
Boucicault, Dionysius Lardner (playwright), 63
Bourjeaux, Violetta (poseur), 73
Boyle, Rev. A. (reformer), 91
Bradley, Giles (poseur), 122-24
British Blondes, 64-65, 80
Broadway Odeon, 23-24
Broadway Varieties, 65
Brooklyn Museum, 145, 155n.1, Fig. 1-4, 25-26
Burke, Michael K. (mgr., Palmo's), 32-35
Byrne, Charles (critic), 140
Byrnes (Supt. of Police), 134-38

Campbell, Henry J., or Harry J. (tableaux), 80, 83, 93
Canary, Thomas (mgr., Casino), 120, 124, 172n.92
Canova's Pedestal, 20. See also Revolving statues
Canterbury Music Hall, 65, 167n.7
Carrero, Senor (poseur), 14
Carroll, Earl (producer), 144
Casino Roof Garden, 96-121
Casino Theatre, 96, 120-24, 180n.36
Castel-Bert, M. Eugene (scenic artist), 128

Castel-Bert, Mme. (costumer), 128
Cazinet, Mlle. (poseur), 38
Central Park Garden, 84
Censorship: of advertising posters, 91-92, 141; of concert saloons, 65-66; opposition to, 78, Fig. 13; petitions for, 26-27, 141. *See also* Advertising, sensationalism; Comstock, Anthony; Laws; Police; Raids; Society for the Prevention of Vice; Women's Christian Temperance Union
Chase, William B. (painter), 122-23
Chateau Mabille Varieties. 80-82. *See also* Egyptian Hall
Chatham Square Theatre, 38, 40-41, 163n.16
Cherry Sisters (poseurs), 126, 181n.73
Circus tableaux, 144-45
Clark, John (mgr., Egyptian Hall), 88
Classic Museum, 36
Claxton, Kate (actress), 96, 174n.122
Clifford, Miss (poseur), 40
Cline, C.B. (bus. mgr.), 138
Coles, Miss Fannie (poseur), 41
Collyer, Dr. (tableaux), 19-24, 35-36, 38, Fig. 6
Columbia Opera House, 82-87, 98
Columbia Theatre (Chicago), 106
Columbian Exposition (1893), Chicago, 92, 145, 155n.1
Columbus Theatre, 131
Comedy Theatre, 96
Comstock, Anthony (reformer), 76-78, 80, 91, 131, 135, 137, 141. *See also* Society for the Suppression of Vice
Comstock's Minstrels, 130
Concert Room, 28, 32
Concert saloons, 63, 65-66. *See also* individual saloons
Connelly, Marie (tableaux), 84
Continuous performance, 89
Cony, Barkham (poseur), 13
Corelli, Mme. (tableaux), 84
Cosmoramas, 16-17
Costume: changes onstage, 67, 139-40; "fleshings" or tights, 45-46, 64, 88, 91, 123, 130, 139-41, 143; similarity to ballet, 48, 58, 121; special effects, 53, 88, 104, 122, 130. *See also* Nudity
Coulin (Chief of Police), 141
Court proceedings: *re* Jake Berry, 85-87; *re* Nahl-Bradley Troupe, 122-24. *See also* Police; Raids
Cremorne Vaudeville Theatre, 89
Criticism, aesthetic: *re* Mrs. Barrymore, 11; *re* Frimbly, 13; *re* Hammerstein and Kilanyi, 138-39; *re* "leg art," 70; *re* Matt Morgan, 74-75
Crotty, Catherine (poseur), 164n.32

Daly's Theatre, 93, 131
Dando, W.P. (tableaux), 102-3
"Danse du Ventre," 92
Davis, J. Charles (mgr., Egyptian Hall), 82, 84-85
Davis, Myra (singing comedienne), 125
Dawson, John J. (mgr., Egyptian Hall), 88
DeCours, Mlle. (tableaux), 88
Descent from the Cross (painting by Rubens), 50
D'Est, Mlle. Marie (tableaux), 84
Devulti, Madame (poseur), 40
Dickens, Charles (novelist, lecturer), 14
di Dio, Mlle. Marietta (singer), 178-79n.15
"Dime" museums, 91
Dioramas, 16-17
Dixey, Henry E. (actor), 93
Dockstader, Lew (minstrel), 124, 130
Doris' Gaiety Theatre, 139-40
Doris' Museum, 130
Dowling, Joseph J. (tableaux), 125
Doyle, Mr. (scenic machinist), 170n.33
Drayton's Parlor Opera Hall, 66-67
Drummond light, 20, 53
Duclos, Mlle. Ninon (tableaux), 72-73, 84
Ducrow, Andrew (equestrian), 8, 11-13, 15-16. *See also Raphael's Dream*
Duvernois, Mlle. Suzanne (poseur), 129-30

Edison, Thomas A. (inventor), 112. *See also* Vitascope
Eggert, Miss Alma (poseur), 107
Egyptian Hall, 82-84, 87-89, 98
Eldorado Theatre, 129
Emmett, J.K. (actor), 96, 174n.122
Empire Theatre (London), 102
Equestrian tableaux, 31, 60, 162n.59. *See also* Ducrow, Andrew; Menken, Adah Issacs
Erlanger, Abraham (agent), 106, 175n.22
Eytchison, Glen (director), Fig. 22

"Festival of Arts and Pageant of the Masters," 145, Figs. 22-24
"Festival of Fairs," 155n.1
Finigan, Julia (poseur), 164n.32
Fisk, May (tableaux), 89, 93
Flanegan, Sarah Jane (poseur), 164n.32
Flea, The (afterpiece), 140
Fletcher, John (poseur), 13, 23
Fleur, Professor (tableaux), 41
Flor, Professor (tableaux), 8
444 Broadway (Tony Pastor's), 171n.63
1492 (burlesque), 101, 103-4, 106, 115, 131, 133-34, 174-5n.1
Fourteenth Street Theatre, 93
Fox, G.L. (actor, pantomimist), 67

Frame, for tableaux, 8, 117, 118, 124, 129, 130
Franklin Museum, 164n.21; 53 Bowery, 41-42, 163n.116; 127 Grand Street, 42, 45-46, Fig. 10; 175 Chatham Square, 38-40, 163n.16
Freeman, Max (tableaux), 121
Frimbly, Mr. (actor, poseur), 12
Frohman, Charles (agent), 175-76n.22

Gaieties Concert Room, 65
"Galatea:" Mary Anderson as, 93, 173n.111, Figs. 14-17; Laura Keen as, 57
Gar, Senor (tableaux), 41-42
Garden Theatre, 101, 103, 106, 138
Gerry, "Commodore" Elbridge Thomas (reformer), 133
Gerry Society, 133, 139
Ghost shows, 67, 88
Gilroy (mayor of New York City), 133
"Glyptorama," 108, 110-12, 131, 175n.22, Fig. 20, Appendix
Goethe, Johann Wolfgang von (novelist), 6-8
Gossin, Mrs. (poseur), 15
Gothic Museum. *See* Temple of the Muses
Grand Opera House, 67
Grand Street Hall, 42, 164n.21. *See also* Franklin Museum, 127 Grand Street
Greek Slave, The (statue of Hiram Powers), 19-20, 37
Grotius, Hugo (tableaux), 38

Hamilton, Emma (poseur), 6-7, 25, 156n.10, Fig. 5. *See also* "Attitudes"
Hamilton, William (art collector), 6-7
Hammerstein, Oscar, I (mgr., Koster & Bial's), 110, 115-19, 131, 134-35, 138, 178-79n.1, 178-79n.15
Hannele (play by Hauptmann), 120, 139
Hart, Emma. *See* Hamilton, Emma
Hauptmann, Gerhart (playwright), 120, 139
Haverly's Fourteenth Street Theatre, 93
Hayman, Al (agent), 175n.22
Hearings. *See* Court proceedings
Henderson, G.A. (mgr., Parisian Varieties), 71
Herrmann (magician), 131
Hirt, Aloys Ludwig (art historian), 8, Fig. 5
Hoax, ticket swindle, 28-29
Holliday Street Theatre, 57
Hooker, Prof. (tableaux), 129
Hope Chapel, 66-67
Huber's New Palace Museum, 129

Imperial Music Hall, 119-20, 138
International Museum, 41
Irving Hall, 66
Italian Brigands. See Ravel Family

Jack, Sam T. (mgr.), 131
Jackits-Chy Japanese Troupe, 84
Jarrett, Henry C. (mgr.), 68
Jefferson, C.B. (agent), 106
Jefferson, Joseph (actor), 13, 58-59, 96, 114n.122
Jeffries, James J. (boxer), 130
Johnson, Louisa (poseur), 13-14

Keene, Laura (mgr.), 57-60, 61, 67-68, 168n.26
Keith, B.F. (mgr), 128-29
Keith's New Theatre (Boston), 128-29
Kellar (magician), 96
Keller, Louis (mgr.), 38, 49-53, 56-57, 60-61, Fig. 11
Kilanyi, Edward A. (tableaux), 101-4, 106-8, 110-12, 115, 128, 131, 133-34, 137-38, Figs. 19, 20, Appendix
Kirwin, Suzie (poseur), 124-25; reply to Lady Somerset, 136
Kit Kat Club, 98, 174n.133
Klaw, Marc (agent), 106, 175-76n.22
Kohler, William (poseur),, 122
Koster and Bial's Music Hall, 93, 98, 108, 110-12, 135, 138, 142-43
Koster and Bial's Roof Garden, 118
Kraus, George K. (mgr., Imperial), 119, 131

Lacy, Thomas (proprietor, Egyptian Hall), 88
La Fleur Sisters (poseur), 126
La Franck, Mlle. Papeta (poseur), 73
Laguna Beach, 145, Fig. 22-24
Lanner, Kathi (tableaux), 67
La Remyas, Mme. (tableaux), 84
Laura Keene's New Theatre, 57
Laura Keene's Varieties, 57
Laws: banning prostitution in concert saloons, 66; banning tights onstage, 91; failure to amend, 141-42; inability to ban tableaux, 82, 83-84, 135, 137-38; opinions regarding prosecutions, 30-31; to prohibit indecent modeling, 135, 137. *See also* Comstock, Anthony; Court proceedings; Police; Raids; Society for the Suppression of Vice
Lawrence, Prof. (tableaux), 73, 80, 93
Lea, Adolphe (poseur), 41
Lea, George (mgr., Franklin Museum), 38, 40-42, 45-46, 48, 61, 163n.16, Fig. 10
Lea, Henry (mgr., Melodeon), 66
Laderer, George W. (mgr.), 120-24
"Leg art," 63-70, 90. *See also* British Blondes; Tammany Hall
Lehman, Monsieur E. (scenic artist), 167n.7
Leslie, Julia (poseur), 41
Leutze, Emanuel (painter), 165n.51

Liberty Enlightening the World ("The Statue of Liberty" by Bartholdi), 98, 155n.1
Lina Edwin's Theatre, 67
Lineff, Mme. Eugenie (poseur), 130
Lingard, Horace (sketch artist), 67
Little Christopher Columbus (burlesque), 106-7, 131
Little Egypt, 92
Livingston, Mary (poseur), 164n.32
London Pavillion, 102

McClane, F.A. (tableaux), 89, 171n.62
McClure, Mrs. (poseur), 15
Mace, "Jem" (boxer, poseur), 68-70
Machinery, stage. *See* Scenery
Martin, Mrs. Emilie D. (reformer), 135-37
May, Jane (actress), 131
Mazeppa (burlesque extravaganza), 64
Medico-Legal Society, 173n.6/100
Melodrama, 63-64, 70
Menken, Adah Isaacs (actress), 64
Metropolitan Opera House, 98
Metropolitan Theatre, 73
Meyers, Jim (equestrian), 162n.59
Miner, Henry (mgr.), 172n.92
Miner Theatres, 80, 89, 93, 96, 140, 172n.92
Mitchell, William (mgr., Olympic), 15
Model Artists, use of term, 23, 60
Modern tableaux, 1, 144-45, 155n.1/1, Fig. 2, 4, 12, 22-24, 26
Moffit, James S. (tableaux), 93
Monier, Eliza (poseur), 13
Monticelli, Signor (tableaux), 28, 34
Moore, Mary (poseur), 41
Morgan, Matt (tableaux),74-78, 80, Fig. 13
"Mose, the Fireboy," 34
Murdock, James (actor), 90
Mutter, Quiriu (tableaux), 38, 162n.4

Nahl, Oscar (poseur), 122-24
National Theatre, 84, 93
National Varieties, 89
New Bowery Theatre, 66
Niblo's Garden, 56, 64, 96, 125
Nicholas Music Hall, 141
Nirdlinger (Nixon), Samuel F. (agent), 175-76n.22
Nixon, James (tableaux), 34
Nixon Artists (poseur), 162n.59
Novels: tableaux described in Goethe's *Elective Affinities,* 7; tableaux of scenes from Sir Walter Scott's 98
Novissimo, Senor (tableaux), 73
Nudity: actual rather than suggested, 32, 144, 161n.44; attributed to Collyer, 20, 22; in Jake Berry's tableaux, 82-83; in Glyptorama, 111; in Hammerstein's tableaux, 117; in Matt Morgan's tableaux, 72-77; by Nahl-Bradley Troupe, 122-23; objections to, 133-34 in Thier's tableaux, 25-28. *See also* Censorship; Costume; Laws; Leg shows; Raids
Nutt, "Commodore" George Washington Morrison (midget, poseur), 66, 167n.15

Oberammergau Passion Play, 145
Olympic Theatre, 66-67, 158n.37
Operti, Albert (scenic artist), 108, 111, 179n.24
Orange Blossoms (afterpiece), 139-40
Oriental Free Concert Hall, 65-66
Osten, Professor Charles (tableaux), 130

Pageant of the Masters, 145, Fig. 22-24
Palace Theatre (London), 102-3
Palm, von Prittwitz (tableaux), 124, 129
Palmer, A.M. (mgr.; Garden, Palmer's), 106-7, 115, 131
Palmer, Harry (mgr., Tammany), 68
Palmer's Theatre, 107
Palmo's Opera House, 22, 25-28
Panoramas, 16, 50
Parisian Varieties, 71-73, 80-82, 84
Park Theatre (Boston), 128
Parker's American Theatre, 90
Parkhurst, Dr. Charles Henry (reformer), 134, 183n.9
Parmelee, Mr. (concert saloon mgr.), 164n.21
Passing Show, The (burlesque), 120-21
Pastor, Tony (mgr.; "144," Tony Pastor's), 96, 163n.63. *See also* Theatre names
Patents, 104, 125, Appendix.
Patriotic tableaux, 22, 52, 59-60, 66, 124-25
Paul, William N. (poseur), 85
Pauline, Madame (tableaux), 38, Fig. 7
Pedrick, William Everitte (painter), 165-66n.51
Performances described: at Antwerp (1582), 1, 6; by Frimbly (1831), 12-13; at Palmo's (1848), 27-28; of clandestine tableaux (1848), 31-32; at Franklin Museum (1856), 48; of *Washington Crossing the Delaware* (1856), 52-53, 56; of Laure Keene's *Variety* (1857), 57-59; of *Blanche of Brandywine* (1857), 58-59; by "Jem" Mace (1869), 69; in *The Passing Show* (1894), 121; at the Casino (1895), 122; at the Columbus Theatre (1985), 131; of *Orange Blossoms* (1896), 139-40; by Sandow (1896), 126. *See also* Costume; Scenery
Phillips, Lillie (poseur), 88
Physioc, Joseph (scenic artist), 125
Pilar-Morin, Mlle. (pantomimist), 139-40

Pinteux' Saloon, 23-24
Plaisted, T.D. (scene painter), 98
Pleasure Palace. *See* Proctor's Pleasure Palace
Police: abuse of prisoners, 45, 81; neglect of duty charges, 82-83; surveillance in theatres, 29-34, 83, 138, 141. *See also* Arrests; Court proceedings; Raids
Powers, Hiram (sculptor). See *Greek Slave, The*
Price, Mr. (mgr.), 137
Proctor, F.F. (mgr.), 124-26, 128, 131
Proctor's Pleasure Palace, 125, 141
Proctor's Twenty-third Street Theatre, 124-25
Pygmalion and Galatea. See "Galatea"

Queen Isabella's Art Gallery (tableaux in *1492*), 103-4
Quirin-Muller (tableaux), 162n.4
Quitsch, Mme. (tableaux), 93

Raids: at the Anatomical Museum, 32-33; on *Bashful Venus,* 90; at Columbia, 82-85; at Concert Room, 32; at "dime" museums, 91; at Egyptian Hall, 84, 87, 88; at Francisco Hotel, 46; at Franklin Museum, 45-46; on Little Egypt, 92; at Metropolitan Theatre, 73; at Novelty Hall, 32; objections to 46; at Palmo's 31-34; at Pinteux', 24, 31-32; at Temple of the Graces, 38, 40; at Temple of the Muses, 32-35; at Thirty-fourth Street Opera House, 81. *See also* Arrests; Court proceedings; Police
Rand and Guild (poseurs), 157n.18
Raphael's Dream (tableau act), 8, 15, 16
Ravel Family, 14, 16, 157-58n.22, 167n.7
Rea, Mr. (poseur), 13
Reeves, Charlie (treasurer, Columbia), 83
Reichshaller Theatre (Berlin), 102
Reilly, John J. (mgr., Egyptian Hall), 88
Religious tableaux: by Collyer, 22; by Keller, 50, 165n.43; at Laguna Beach, Fig. 22-23; at Oberammergau, 145; at Pinteux', 23-24
Revels (comic opera), 93, 101
Revolving statues, 14, 20, 73, 84, 93, 159n.3/6, 171n.62, Fig. 6. *See also* Canova's pedestal
Rice, Edward E. (producer), 92-93, 101-6, 174n.1
Richie, Adele (poseur), 142
Richings (poseur), 15
Riot in audience, 27-28
Riviera, Matilde (poseur), 37
Roberts, Professor (tableaux), 69
Robinson, Julius K. (proprietor, Parisian Varieties), 81
Robinson Hall, 71, 74. *See also* Parisian Varieties
Roote, James (locomotive engineer), 120

St. James Hall, 130
St. Luke, John (mgr.), 38, 40-41
Sandiland and Ruthden (poseurs), 93
Sandow, Eugene (strong man), 96, 126, Fig. 18, 21
Sangali, Mlle. (tableaux), 66
Sarony, Napoleon (photographer), Fig. 16, 17, 18
Scenery: early use, 14; electric motors, 111-12; in "ghost" shows, 67, 88; lighting effects, 104, 108, 124, 129, 141; in melodrama, 63; methods used, 53, 56; pictorial, 15, 116; for Sandow, 96; scene-changing machinery, 104, 108, 110-11, Appendix; steam effect, 170n.33 for "Venus de Milo," 104; waterfall effect, 107, 111. *See also* Drummond light; Revolving statues
Schomberger, Jacob. *See* Berry, Jake.
Scott, Sir Walter (novelist), 98
Seavey, Lafayette W. (scenic artist), 125
Sharkey, Thomas (boxer, poseur), 130
Sheffer and Blakely Company, 93
Shubert Brothers (producers), 144
Siddons, Ida (tableaux), 89, 172n.92
Singing pictures, 118
Smith, G.W. (poseur), 34
Smith, Richard S. (scene painter), 63
Society for the Prevention of Cruelty to Children. *See* Gerry Society
Society for the Suppression of Vice, 85, 91, 135-39, 141. *See also* Censorship; Comstock, Anthony; Laws; Police; Raids
Somerset, Lady Henry (reformer), 135-38
Staging. *See* Performances described; Scenery
Spigalin, Herr von (poseur), 41
Standard Theatre, 96
Stanton, Miss (poseur), 123
Statue of Liberty. See *Liberty Enlightening the World*
Stedle, Edward (tableaux), 128
Stephenson, Mabel (child actresss), 120-21
Stratton, Charles S. ("General Tom Thumb"), 66, 167n.15, 167n.16
Stratton, Mrs. Charles ("Mrs. Tom Thumb"), 167n.15, 157n.15
Swindle. *See* Hoax
Swiss Brothers (poseur), 14, 16

Tableaux in other productions: *Brunhilda* (play), 67; *Dedalus und seine Statuen* ("gala divertissement"), 8, Fig. 5; *Donnybrook Fair* (play), 60; *The Elves* (burlesque), 57-58, 68; *The Forgery* (play), 12; *Ghost of Altenberg* (play), 67; *Jeanie Deans* (play), 59; *Jessie Brown* (play), 60, 63; *The Marble Heart* (afterpiece), 57;

Napoleon the Great (play), 67; *The Nena Sahib* (equestrian drama), 60; *Les Noces d'Arlequin* (play), 6; *Novelty* (extravaganza), 57; *The Painter's Dream* (ballet), 60; *The Peasant Boy* (play), 8; *Pygmalion and Galatea* (*See* "Galatea"); *Raphael's Dream*, q.v.; *The Rent Day* (play), 12, 16, 144, 196; *Seven Sisters* (burlesque), 59, 67; *1776* (musical), 1, 145; *Soldier's Wife and Soldier's Widow* (interlude?), 11-12; *Uncle Tom's Cabin* (play), 63-64, 80; *Variety* (burlesque), 57-58; *The War in Italy* (play), 56
Tammany Theatre, 68-70
Temple of the Graces, 38, 40-41
Temple of the Muses, 28, 32-35, 42, 45
Thalia Theatre, 98
Theatre Comique, 67, 74-80
Theatrical Syndicate, 175-76n.22
Thier, Professor (tableaux), 25-33
Thirty-fourth Street Opera House, 81
Thompson, Henrietta (poseur), 41
Thompson, Lydia, 64, 90
Thumb, Mrs. Tom. *See* Stratton, Mrs. Charles
Thumb, Tom. *See* Stratton, Charles S.
Tissot, Jules and Amanda (poseur), 96, 98, 174n.126
Tony Pastor's Theatre, 66, 84, 89, 93, 96, 130, 141
Trials. *See* Court proceedings
Trilby (Play), 125
Trocadero, 141
Trumbull, John (painter), 145-46
Twenty-third Street Theatre (Proctor's), 124-25

Union Square Theatre, 101, 128-29

Vauxhall Garden, 163n.16
Vigée-Lebrun, Mme. (painter), 7
Vinette Sisters (poseur), 118
Vitascope, 112, 129, 131
Voegtlin, Augustus (scenic artist), 125

Volatti, Signore (poseur), 73
von Palm, Professor. *See* Palm, von Prittwitz

"Waiter Girls," 65, 68, 172n.93
Wallack's Theatre, 101
Wallhalla (London), 162-63n.7
Wallhalla (New York), 38
Warren, George (mgr., Egyptian Hall), 84-85
Warren, Lavinia. *See* Stratton, Mrs. Charles
Warren, Minnie (midget), 167n.5/15
Warton, Madame (tableaux), 38, 42, 45, 57, 162-63n.7, Fig. 8, 9
Washburn Sister's Company (tableaux), 140
Washington Crossing the Delaware (painting by Leutze), 52-53, 56, 165-66n.51, Fig. 11-12
Waterman, Anna (poseur), 164n.32
Watts, George Frederick (painter), 139
Wax museums, 17
Wharton. *See* Warton
White's Melodeon. *See* Franklin Museum, 53 Bowery
Wieland, George (mime), 12
Wilbur Opera Company, 124
Wilkie, David (painter), 12, 16
Williams, George (mgr., Egyptian Hall), 84-85
Wilson, Carrie (poseur), 73
Wintergarden Theatre, 67
Women's Christian Temperance Union (WCTU), 135-39, 141
Wood, George (mgr.), 67-68
Wood, W. (poseur), 15
Woodley, W.M. (mgr., Parisian Varieties), 81
World's Fair, 1893. *See* Columbian Exposition
Worrell Sisters (poseurs), 68

Young, Miss (poseur), 41
Young Men's Christian Association (YMCA), 75-78. *See also* Society for the Suppression of Vice; Comstock, Anthony

Ziegfeld, Florenz (producer), 144
Zimmerman, J. Frederick (agent), 175-76n.22
Zulilia, Mlle. (tableaux), 80-81